LINCOLN, THE RISE OF THE REPUBLICANS, AND THE COMING OF THE CIVIL WAR

LINCOLN, THE RISE OF THE REPUBLICANS, AND THE COMING OF THE CIVIL WAR

A REFERENCE GUIDE

Kerry Walters

Guides to Historic Events in America
Randall M. Miller, Series Editor

 ABC-CLIO

Santa Barbara, California • Denver, Colorado • Oxford, England

Copyright 2013 by ABC-CLIO, LLC

All rights reserved. No part of this publication may be reproduced, stored
in a retrieval system, or transmitted, in any form or by any means, electronic,
mechanical, photocopying, recording, or otherwise, except for the inclusion
of brief quotations in a review, without prior permission in writing
from the publisher.

Library of Congress Cataloging-in-Publication Data

Walters, Kerry S.
  Lincoln, the rise of the Republicans, and the coming of the Civil War : a reference
guide / Kerry Walters.
      pages cm. — (Guides to historic events in America)
    Includes bibliographical references and index.
    ISBN 978–1–61069–204–5 (hardcopy : alk. paper) — ISBN 978–1–61069–205–2
(ebook) 1. United States—History—Civil War, 1861-1865—Causes. 2. Lincoln,
Abraham, 1809–1865—Political and social views. 3. Slavery—Political aspects—United
States—History—19th century. 4. Republican Party (U.S. : 1854–)—History—19th
century. 5. United States—Politics and government—1845–1861. 6. United States—
Politics and government—1861–1865. 7. United States—Politics and government—
1865–1883. I. Title.
  E459.W245   2013
  973.7092—dc23   2013013147

ISBN: 978–1–61069–204–5
EISBN: 978–1–61069–205–2

17 16 15 14 13   1 2 3 4 5

This book is also available on the World Wide Web as an eBook.
Visit www.abc-clio.com for details.

ABC-CLIO, LLC
130 Cremona Drive, P.O. Box 1911
Santa Barbara, California 93116-1911

This book is printed on acid-free paper ∞

Manufactured in the United States of America

CONTENTS

SERIES FOREWORD

Perhaps no people have been more difficult to comprehend than the Americans. As J. Hector St. Jean de Crèvecoeur asked during the American Revolution, countless others have echoed ever after—"What then is this American, this new man?" What, indeed? Americans then and after have been, and remain, a people in the process of becoming. They have been, and are, a people in motion, whether coming from a distant shore, crossing the mighty Mississippi, or packing off to the suburbs, and all the while following the promise of an American dream of realizing life, liberty, and happiness. The directions of such movement have changed, and sometimes the trajectory has taken a downward arc in terms of civil war and economic depression, but always the process has continued.

Making sense of that American experience demands attention to critical moments—events—that reflected and affected American ideas and identities. Although Americans have constructed an almost linear narrative of progress from the days of George Washington to today in relating their common history, they also have marked that history by recognizing particular events as pivotal in explaining who and why they believed and acted as they did at particular times and over time. Such events have forced Americans to consider closely their true interests. They also have challenged their commitment to professed beliefs of freedom and liberty, equality and opportunity, tolerance and generosity. Whether fighting for independence or empire, drafting and implementing a frame of government, reconstructing a nation divided by civil war, struggling for basic rights and the franchise, creating a mass-mediated culture, standing up for capitalism and democracy and against communism, to name several critical developments, Americans have understood that historic events are more than just moments. They are processes of change made clear through particular events but not bound to a single moment or instance. Such thinking about the character and consequence of American history informs this new series of *Guides to Historic Events in America*.

Drawing on the latest and best literature, and bringing together narrative overviews and critical chapters of important historic events, the books in the series function as both reference guides and informed analyses to critical events that have shaped American life, culture, society, economy, and politics and fixed America's place in the world. The books do not promise a comprehensive reading and rendering of American history. Such is not yet, if ever, possible for any single work or series. Nor do they chart a single interpretive line, though they share common concerns and methods of inquiry. Each book stands alone, resting on the expertise of the author and the strength of the evidence. At the same time, taken together the books in this new series will provide a dynamic portrait of that on-going work-in-progress, America itself.

Each book follows a common format, with a chronology, historical overview, topical chapters on aspects of the historical event under examination, a set of biographies of key figures, selected essential primary documents, and an annotated bibliography. As such, each book holds many uses for students, teachers, and the general public wanting and needing to know the principal issues and the pertinent arguments and evidence on significant events in American history. The combination of historical description and analysis, biographies, and primary documents also moves readers to approach each historic event from multiple perspectives and with a critical eye. Each book in its structure and content invites students and teachers, in and out of the classroom, to consider and debate the character and consequence(s) of the historic event in question. Such debate invariably will bring readers back to that most critical and never-ending question of what was/is "the American" and what does, and must, "America" mean.

Randall M. Miller
Saint Joseph's University, Philadelphia

CHRONOLOGY OF EVENTS

July 1787	Northwest Ordinance enacted by Continental Congress. Bans slavery in territories north of the Ohio River and east of the Mississippi River.
September 1787	Three-Fifths Compromise enacted by Constitutional Convention, counting three-fifths of a state's slave population in deciding congressional representation.
February 1793	Fugitive Slave Law enacted by Congress.
February 1809	Abraham Lincoln born in Kentucky.
December 1816	Lincoln's family relocates to Indiana wilderness.
March 1820	Missouri Compromise approved by Congress.
1828	Tariff of Abominations enacted by Congress. Andrew Jackson elected president.
January 1831	William Lloyd Garrison founds *The Liberator*, a weekly abolitionist newspaper.
July 1831	Lincoln settles in New Salem, Illinois.
1832	Nullification Crisis.
August 1832	Lincoln's first unsuccessful bid for public office.
December 1832	Andrew Jackson reelected president.
1833	Henry Clay founds Whig Party.

August 1834	Lincoln elected to the Illinois General Assembly's House as a Whig. Reelected three times, eventually becoming Whig floor leader.
February 1836	Congresses passes gag rule automatically tabling antislavery petitions.
1840	The first antislavery political party, the Liberty Party, is founded.
December 1840	William Henry Harrison, first Whig president, is elected. Dies one month after his inauguration in March 1841 and is succeeded by Vice President John Tyler.
1843	Lincoln unsuccessfully tries for Whig nomination to U.S. House.
November 1844	Democrat James Polk elected to presidency.
January 1845	Annexation of Texas.
May 1846– March 1848	Mexican-American War. Treaty of Guadalupe Hidalgo settlement cedes land to the United States that increases its size by one-third.
August 1846	Wilmot Proviso, proposing to ban slavery in Mexican cessions, is introduced in Congress.
	Lincoln elected to U.S. House. He serves a single undistinguished term, but challenges Polk on the causes of the Mexican War in 1848.
November 1848	Whig Zachary Taylor elected to presidency. The newly formed antislavery Free Soil Party runs former president Martin Van Buren as its candidate.
1849–54	Lincoln devotes himself to his law practice in Springfield, Illinois, while campaigning for local, state, and national Whig candidates.
July 1850	Taylor dies in office and is succeeded by Millard Fillmore.
September 1850	Congress passes a version of Henry Clay's compromise resolutions to deal with Mexican cessions.

November 1852	Democrat Franklin Pierce elected to presidency.
February 1854	Pierce privately endorses Stephen Douglas's Kansas-Nebraska bill.
May 30, 1854	Kansas-Nebraska bill, which focuses on popular sovereignty, becomes law.
Summer 1854	Lincoln reenters politics in opposition to Kansas-Nebraska Act.
October 1854	Ostend Manifesto outlines scheme to wrest Cuba from Spain.
	Lincoln delivers his anti-Kansas speech in Peoria.
November 1854	Lincoln elected to Illinois General Assembly but resigns to run as candidate for U.S. Senate.
1855	The American "Know-Nothing" Party, a nativist coalition, is formed. Former president Millard Fillmore becomes its presidential candidate in the 1856 election.
February 1855	Lincoln throws his votes to anti-Kansas Democrat Lyman Trumbull in the U.S. Senate race in Illinois.
March 1855	Fraudulent election of proslavery Kansas territorial legislature.
January 1856	Rival free soil elections held in Kansas. Violence in "Bleeding Kansas" soon erupts between opponents and proponents of slavery.
1856	Lincoln becomes a state leader in the newly organized Republican Party and campaigns for John C. Frémont during the presidential campaign.
May 1856	In the space of a week, Lawrence, Kansas, is burned by proslavery guerillas, John Brown massacres proslavers at Pottawatomie, and Massachusetts senator Charles Sumner is beaten in Senate chamber by South Carolina congressman Preston Brooks.

November 1856	Democrat James Buchanan elected to presidency, defeating Republican candidate Frémont. For all practical purposes, the Whig Party disappears.
March 1857	*Dred Scott* Supreme Court decision nullifies Missouri Compromise and the Kansas-Nebraska Act's defense of popular sovereignty.
August–October 1858	Lincoln is Republican nominee for U.S. Senate. He delivers "House Divided" speech. He and incumbent Stephen Douglas campaign throughout Illinois in a series of seven debates. Lincoln loses to Douglas in November but begins to acquire a national reputation.
October 1859	John Brown's raid on federal arsenal at Harpers Ferry.
1859–1860	Made famous by the Senate race, Lincoln gives speeches in Midwest and New England. He delivers his Cooper Union Address in February 1860. Nominated for presidency by Republican Party, May 18.
1860	Democrats split after two troubled conventions. Northerners nominate Stephen Douglas and southerners nominate John C. Breckinridge.

Constitutional Union Party formed; nominates John Bell. |
November 1860	Lincoln wins the national election in a four-way race, becoming the first Republican president.
December 1860	South Carolina secedes, followed in January and February by Mississippi, Florida, Alabama, Georgia, Louisiana, and Texas.
December 1860– March 1861	Various proposals to reconcile North and South and avert war are proposed in Congress. A peace conference, chaired by former president John Tyler, convenes in Washington, D.C.

February 1861	Seceded states form the Confederate States of America.
March 1861	Lincoln delivers his First Inaugural Address.
	Confederacy calls for 75,000 volunteer troops.
April 1861	Bombardment of Fort Sumter, April 12. Lincoln calls for volunteers.
	Virginia, Arkansas, Tennessee, and North Carolina secede.
	Lincoln calls for states to muster 75,000 militiamen. Invoking executive authority, he suspends habeas corpus, authorizes funding for military, and orders blockade of southern coastline.
1861–1865	United States fights Civil War.

PREFACE

T
he subject of this book is vast—far too vast for a single volume—
and this necessarily means that one of several possible approaches
must be decided upon at the cost of others. In examining the
career of Lincoln and the rise of the anti-Nebraska and pro–free labor
Republican fusion of the 1850s, I have chosen a "top-down" rather than
"bottom-up" approach.

Both are valuable and offer essential insights into the period. The latter
examines economic, cultural, social, religious, and literary factors that
were fueled by and in turn influenced congressional debates about slavery.
The former focuses on presidential policy, judicial decisions, and
congressional legislation concerning slavery that responded to and exacerbated the growing sectional crisis of the 1840s and 1850s. Neither
approach wholly excludes the other, but they do have different emphases.
Accordingly, although I necessarily touch on social and cultural factors
contributing to the rise of the Republicans, my concentration in this book
is on Capitol Hill more than Main Street USA. For readers interested in
exploring the period's social history, several excellent sources are provided
in the Annotated Bibliography.

Still, the distinction between top-down and bottom-up approaches
ought not to be overplayed. In the three decades leading up to the Civil
War, the political arena in many ways was a microcosm of the social and
cultural ones. Rancor in Congress over the issue of slavery's expansion into
the western territories—rancor that included angry shouting matches
between adversaries, drawn weapons on the floors of the U.S. House and
Senate, and even the savage beating of one northern Senator by a

southern Congressman—reflected the mutual distrust and animosity between the slave states and free states. By the time civil war finally came, the United States in many ways was already a nation divided into two opposing cultures. Congressional debates, sometimes solemnly eloquent, at other times resembling street fights more than dignified statecraft, reflected that division. In studying the legislative struggles of men such as Henry Clay, John C. Calhoun, Stephen Douglas, William Henry Seward, James Henry Hammond, James Polk, James Buchanan, and Charles Sumner—not to mention Abraham Lincoln—much light is shed upon the issue that increasingly consumed both Capitol Hill and Main Street: slavery.

This volume contains two appendices. The first offers brief biographies of 26 leading figures in the years prior to the Civil War. Abraham Lincoln is an obvious omission from the list, but only because the details of his life up to the eruption of sectional hostilities in 1861 is covered in the book's six chapters. References to a few excellent biographies of him that cover the war years may be found in the Annotated Bibliography. The second appendix offers excerpts from a number of important congressional debates, political speeches, and party platforms in the 1840s and 1850s that speak to the national debate over slavery. They provide readers with a good feel for the details and timbre of the escalating crisis that eventually led to war.

ACKNOWLEDGMENTS

I owe several debts of gratitude. Michael Millman of ABC-CLIO was good enough to commission the book. It is my good fortune that the noted historian Professor Randall M. Miller of St. Joseph's University is the editor of the series in which this book is a volume. His meticulous and thoughtful comments on my manuscript were invaluable. I'm very grateful to Sharon Tripp, whose expert copyediting rescued me from more than one embarrassing gaffe. It would be remiss of me not to express my deep gratitude to the Civil War Institute at Gettysburg College and the historians who have been associated with it over the years: Gabor S. Boritt, Matthew J. Gallman, Allen C. Guelzo, and Peter S. Carmichael. For nearly three decades now, I've learned much from their stimulating lectures and books on the Civil War era. Finally, special thanks go to Kim and Jonah, who sustained me in this as in my earlier books.

"THE SHEET ANCHOR OF AMERICAN REPUBLICANISM": LINCOLN IN PEORIA

No man is good enough to govern another man, *without that other's consent*. I say this is the leading principle—the sheet anchor of American republicanism.

—*Abraham Lincoln*

If the negro is a man, why then my ancient faith teaches me that "all men are created equal"; and that there can be no moral right in one man's making a slave of another.

—*Abraham Lincoln*

Abraham Lincoln's journey to the presidency and to greatness began in mid-October 1854. The place was the Illinois town of Peoria. The occasion was a duel of words and values with Stephen Douglas, the state's Democrat senator. The issue was one that would consume the nation for the next decade before culminating in civil war: slavery.

Douglas was barnstorming the state to drum up public support for a bill that Congress had approved and President Franklin Pierce had signed into law only four months earlier. The Kansas-Nebraska Act, as it was called, was Douglas's creation. He had written the bill and worked hard to push it through the Senate. It was arguably the most contentious piece of legislation to be debated in the corridors of power up to that time. When he proposed it, Douglas predicted that it would blow in "a hell of a storm." He was right.

What made the Kansas-Nebraska Act so tempestuous was its proposal to extend slavery into the vast territory west of Missouri and Iowa that was the northernmost remnant of the old Louisiana Purchase of 1803. The justification for doing so was a policy known as "popular sovereignty," which left the decision of whether to allow or prohibit slavery up to local and regional residents rather than federal legislators in the District of Columbia. The policy seemed reasonable enough on the surface, especially after Douglas touted it as a perfect expression of the spirit of democracy.

The problem was that the Kansas-Nebraska Act explicitly repealed a law that had been enacted a generation earlier, the Missouri Compromise of 1820, which closed the area above the 36-30 parallel to slavery. That piece of legislation, itself the cause of ferocious congressional debate, had been settled on in hopes of maintaining the senatorial balance of power between slave and free states that kept either from having an undue legislative advantage over the other. In sweeping aside the 1820 agreement, many northern statesmen and citizens were aghast. Not only had an agreement been thrown aside which many of them considered sacred and perpetually binding; it also, in their judgment, privileged the South at the expense of the North. If the new northern territories of Kansas and Nebraska were opened to slavery, opportunities for white homesteaders there would proportionately diminish. Available land would be snapped up for slave-worked plantations, squeezing out smaller homesteaders who worked their own claims.

LINCOLN COMES OUT SWINGING

Midterm congressional elections were slated for the fall of 1854 in Illinois and other states, and Douglas knew that his championing of the Kansas-Nebraska Act could cause trouble for Democrat candidates in his state. Although Whigs, the nation's other mainstream political party, had always been in the minority in Illinois, enough of them were infuriated by the act to mobilize popular discontent at the expense of Democrats. So Douglas returned home to do some damage control. His plan was to travel to several of the state's cities and towns, deliver a few speeches, shake a few hands, and make a few reassurances. What he didn't anticipate was having to contend with a lanky Springfield lawyer so enraged by the Kansas-Nebraska Act that he dogged Douglas wherever he went to publicly challenge him.

The lawyer, Abraham Lincoln, was no political neophyte. Although he hadn't held public office for six years—his last elected position had been a single congressional term that ended in 1849—he had lived and breathed politics his entire adult life. He first ran for office in 1832, the same year he cast his first vote in a presidential election, and was unsuccessful in both. He was thwarted in his bid to defeat Democrat Edmund Dick Taylor for a seat in the Illinois General Assembly, and his presidential candidate of choice, Henry Clay of Kentucky, was defeated by Democrat Andrew Jackson.

Disappointed supporters of Clay founded the Whig Party the very next year to challenge the policies of Jacksonian Democrats. Lincoln, who admired Clay all his life, immediately threw in his lot with the new party, a political loyalty he would maintain for the next 20 years. The so-called American System promulgated by Clay called for a program that encouraged domestic industry by imposing tariffs on imported goods, supported federal assistance for internal improvements such as canals, and advocated a national bank to stabilize currency and regulate markets. Lincoln enthusiastically embraced this program and remained loyal to it even after he became a Republican in the mid-1850s and slavery began to edge out all other political concerns. The only aspect of Whiggery he was tepid about was the zealous reformism displayed by many of his fellow party members when it came to issues such as temperance and Sabbath laws. A teetotaler himself, Lincoln was wary of legislation on drinking. Moreover, he had little use for organized religion. The gloomy, sin-obsessed, revivalist-style Baptist church in which he was raised had soured him on it.

Although Whigs were often accused (with some merit) of a class snobbishness that looked down upon laborers and self-made tradesmen, Lincoln was a great proponent of self-improvement and upward mobility. He himself was an exemplary example of someone who through sheer hard work and innate talent had risen above his humble origins. Born to barely literate parents and sweating until he was 21 on his restless father's succession of hardscrabble farms, by the time he spoke at Peoria Lincoln had gone on, after his first unsuccessful political campaign, to win election to four terms in the Illinois General Assembly and one in the U.S. Congress.

He was a Whig leader in Illinois, actively campaigning in local and state elections as well as presidential campaigns in which Whig candidates—William Henry Harrison (1836 and 1840), Zachary Taylor (1848), and Winfield Scott (1852)—ran.

Prior to the Kansas-Nebraska Act, Lincoln's political interests centered primarily on economic development and internal improvements. He had never approved of slavery, and had recoiled in disgust as a young man when, on two different trips down the Mississippi River, he encountered chained and weary slaves. His dislike of the southern states' practice of human bondage, a custom often euphemistically referred to at the time as the "peculiar institution," wasn't born from a sense of racial equality between blacks and whites—he was very much a man of his time when it came to that issue—but from a deep-seated conviction that slavery was immoral. As he said later in life, he knew from as far back as he could remember that slavery was wrong if anything was wrong. But he believed that the Constitution authorized the legal right of whites to own slaves if they wished. Until the Compromise of 1820 was annulled by the Kansas-Nebraska Act, he had been able to tolerate slavery because he was confident it could be contained within the southern states. Moral qualms to one side, slavery had always been a "minor question" from a political perspective with him because he "always believed that everybody was against it, and that it was in course of ultimate extinction."[1] But Douglas's bill changed all that. So, beginning in the summer following its passage, Lincoln's personal and political energies were increasingly devoted to the debate about slavery's extension that embroiled the nation, broke apart the Whig Party to which he belonged, severely damaged the Democrats, and gave rise to the Republican Party that he joined and ultimately led.

That's why Lincoln interrupted his busy law practice to do battle when he heard that Douglas would be crisscrossing Illinois. He spent days in the state library at Springfield taking notes on the founding fathers' views on slavery, Douglas's speeches, and past congressional debates on slavery. By mid-August, he had put together a tightly argued speech—more of a lecture, really—that spelled out his opposition to Kansas-Nebraska. It was the first time that Lincoln had thought beyond his intuitive moral repugnance of slavery to build a cogent case against extending it into the territories. He admitted that slavery couldn't be touched in states where it already existed—his hands were tied by the Constitution in that regard—but he insisted that Douglas's bill violated both the original intent of the founders and universal standards of justice accepted by all civilized nations.

Lincoln gave versions of his speech a few times in the late summer of 1854, no doubt honing it each time. On October 4, in Springfield, he clashed directly with Douglas for the first time. The senator had defended Kansas-Nebraska there the preceding day; Lincoln replied the next. Two weeks later, the two men met again at Peoria. Lincoln almost certainly said nothing there that he hadn't already said at Springfield and elsewhere. But the difference this time was that the *Illinois State Journal* published the complete transcript of his 17,000-word speech, the longest Lincoln ever gave, in seven installments. It was the first time, not excepting his two years in Congress, that Lincoln's words reached a large audience. The Peoria address was the first among his truly important speeches (others include his "House Divided" speech in 1858, his 1860 Cooper Union Address, his First Inaugural Address in 1861, his Gettysburg Address two years later, and his Second Inaugural Address in 1865). It signaled a fundamental shift of emphasis in his political thinking from economic issues to slavery. The principles he defended in it, especially its claim that the Declaration of Independence was the best argument against slavery, served as templates for the new anti-Kansas movement that even then was birthing and whose members would eventually call themselves Republicans.

RESTORING THE REPUBLICAN ROBE

When Douglas heard that Lincoln had followed him to Peoria, he was displeased. He had come to town to talk up the Kansas-Nebraska Act, not to debate a relatively obscure lawyer, and he went to Lincoln's hotel room to chide him into backing down. But it turned out that Peorians were eager for the two men to debate one another, so Douglas had no choice but to agree. But he insisted on having the final word. The deal was that after Lincoln finished his remarks, Douglas would follow up with a short rebuttal.

The two men spoke from the steps of the town's columned courthouse to a packed courtyard of people. As was fitting, given his eminence, Douglas had first billing. He spoke for most of the afternoon, describing himself as a victim of abolitionist smears and insisting that opponents of his bill were nothing more than political opportunists who changed their criticisms to fit whatever audience they happened to be addressing. The crowd received his remarks favorably, breaking into "six hearty cheers," according to an *Illinois State Journal* reporter, when he finished.[2]

Then it was Lincoln's turn. Shrewdly, he told the crowd that he realized many of them were hungry and tired after standing three hours to listen to Senator Douglas. So he proposed a short break to allow everyone a chance to grab something to eat and take a rest, and before the crowd gratefully dispersed, he promised he'd give Senator Douglas an opportunity to respond to his remarks. His suggestion of a break was designed to ensure an attentive and good-humored audience. His announcement that Douglas would have the last word guaranteed that the senator's supporters, who might otherwise have boycotted Lincoln's speech, would hang around to hear it.

Lincoln's speech, delivered that night by torchlight, was described by one observer as "highly didactic." Lincoln "stood up straight . . ., his hands hanging by his sides. . . . His articulation was good and his voice loud. . . . His speech was full of facts and argument. . . . He was not the humorous story telling Lincoln sometimes pictured in the newspapers."[3]

Lincoln carefully reviewed the "facts and argument" of Douglas's popular sovereignty before delivering his central punch: the senator's position contradicted the "ancient faith" of the nation's founders, according to which

> the just powers of governments are derived from the consent of the governed. Now the relation of masters and slaves is, PRO TANTO, a total violation of this principle. The master not only governs the slave without his consent; but he governs him by a set of rules altogether different from those which he prescribes for himself. Allow ALL the governed an equal voice in the government, and that, and that only is self government.[4]

The Declaration of Independence, the founders' primary affirmation of the principle that rule is legitimized only by consent of the ruled, was one of the ancient faith's sacred texts. The Constitution was the other, and, according to Lincoln and some antislavery advocates, it likewise spoke against slavery. The Constitution never actually mentioned the word slavery, instead using the euphemistic expression "persons held to service." But this very reticence suggested that the framers of the document were shamed by the peculiar institution and hoped for its geographical containment and eventual disappearance. In writing the Constitution, they "hid away" the blemish of human bondage, "just as an afflicted man hides away a wen or a cancer, which he dares not cut out at once, lest he bleed to death; with the promise, nevertheless, that the cutting may begin at the end of a given time."[5] Subsequent congressional acts—banning slavery in the Northwest Territory in 1787, the 1807 prohibition of the African slave trade, the Missouri Compromise of 1820—all testified, in Lincoln's opinion, to the founders' discomfort with an institution that so ran against the nation's democratic grain.

Yet Douglas, Lincoln told the crowd, ignored all this. The framer of the Kansas-Nebraska Act was fond of claiming that opponents of slavery's expansion believed that whites weren't "good enough to govern a few miserable negroes!!"[6] This was a shrewd move on Douglas's part to direct racist anger against his rivals. But Lincoln's response to it was just as shrewd. He had no doubt, he said, about the ability of whites to govern blacks. But "what I do say, is that no man is good enough to govern another man, without that other's consent." This, he asserted, was "the leading principle—the sheet anchor of American republicanism."[7] By "republicanism," Lincoln meant the principles of a republican form of government. But as events over the next few years demonstrated, his repudiation of governing another without that person's consent also reflected the Republican Party's attitude to slavery.

Lincoln went on to tell his audience that the mistake Douglas and other proponents of the Kansas-Nebraska Act made was to assume that because opponents condemned the bill's popular sovereignty justification of expanding slavery, they condemned all local self-determination. Lincoln heartily embraced the founders' vision of democracy. His objection to slavery, in fact, was that it didn't. "The doctrine of self-government is right—absolutely and eternally right." Consequently, it is a right that should be granted to all men. "If the negro is a man, is it not to that extent, a total destruction of self-government, to say that he too shall not govern himself? . . . If the negro is a man, why then my ancient faith teaches me that 'all men are created equal'; and that there can be no moral right in one man's making a slave of another."[8] "Let no one be deceived," Lincoln warned. "The spirit of seventy-six and the spirit of Nebraska are utter antagonisms; and the former is being rapidly displaced by the latter."[9]

Lincoln was especially disturbed by what he saw as Douglas's utter moral indifference to "the monstrous injustice of slavery"[10] and the Kansas Act's codification of the claim "that there can be moral right in the enslaving of one man by another."[11] The immorality of slavery was so palpably obvious to Lincoln that he could only conclude anyone who thought otherwise was animated by "covert real zeal for the spread of slavery."[12] But disregarding what was ethically right in this case was also practically perilous, because slavery "deprives our republican example of its just influence in the world—enables the enemies of free institutions, with plausibility, to taunt us as hypocrites—causes the real friends of freedom to doubt our sincerity." It leads observers around the world to conclude that the only principle of action taken seriously by American statesmen is "self-interest."[13] And at least in the case of defenders of Kansas-Nebraska, that assessment seemed more than accurate.

If truth be told, however, the moral indifference to slavery expediently embraced by Douglas and other proponents of slavery extension was easily exposed as a sham because of their inconsistent insistence that slave owners had a moral right to own human beings. The founders had reluctantly tolerated slavery because they feared at the time that abolishing it would inflict economic havoc on the South. Their "plain" and "unmistakable" attitude to slavery "was hostility to the PRINCIPLE, and toleration, ONLY BY NECESSITY."[14] But now, Lincoln worried, a troublesome reversal was taking place. Now ownership of slaves "is transformed into a 'sacred right,' " to which the Kansas-Nebraska Act says: " 'Go, and God speed you.' Henceforth it is to be the chief jewel of the nation." And what this meant, Lincoln sadly concluded, is that the "ancient faith" of the founders was giving way to an apostate one that denied all men are created equal and maintained instead "that for SOME men to enslave OTHERS is a 'sacred right of self-government.' "[15]

As a practical man of the world, Lincoln knew that not all injustices allowed for easy solutions, and he freely admitted that he didn't know what to do with slavery. "If all earthly power were given me, I should not know what to do, as to the existing institution."[16] He certainly didn't want to condemn the South univocally. If slavery existed in the North, he admitted, "We should not instantly give it up." How, then, could he chastise southerners for not doing so? Even plans for gradual emancipation were fraught with difficulties. Should freed slaves be colonized to Liberia?

Should they be kept in the United States as free but subordinate "underlings"? Should they be made "politically and socially our equals"?[17] None of these options, especially the last, seemed practical. But what was certain, to Lincoln's mind, was that the extension of slavery into the territories only compounded the moral offense of slavery, unnecessarily broke the Missouri Compromise, hallowed by time and success, and stirred up distrust and anger between North and South.

In an image that surely struck his audience as forcefully as it does us today, Lincoln cautioned that the extension of slavery threatened the ideal of liberty that served as the very foundation of the nation. "Our republican robe is soiled," he lamented, "and trailed in the dust. Let us re-purify it. Let us turn and wash it white, in the spirit, if not the blood, of the Revolution. Let us turn slavery from its claims of 'moral right,' back upon its existing legal rights . . . Let us return it to the position our fathers gave it." If that were done, Lincoln promised, "we shall not only have saved the Union; but we shall have so saved it, as to make, and to keep it, forever worthy of the saving."[18]

When Lincoln concluded his speech, the audience broke into uproarious applause, a couple of cannon were triumphantly fired, and empty tar barrels that had been piled 20 feet high were set ablaze, illuminating the cheering crowd which filled the courtyard. Senator Douglas stood up to have the final word he'd insisted on, but whatever he said was anticlimactic and scarcely heeded. Afterwards, no one even remembered how long he actually spoke. What *was* recalled, at least by one observer, was that Douglas "manifested strong symptoms of anger" and "seemed to be much worried."[19] The *Peoria Republican* gloated that for all his efforts, the senator was unable to capture the crowd's attention and "soon became conscious that the rout was complete."[20] Douglas would endure similar receptions throughout his entire northern tour. At one point, while speaking in Chicago, he was so mercilessly heckled that he stormed off the podium, telling his anti-Nebraska audience to go to hell. After it was over, Douglas ruefully cracked that his tour could have been continuously illuminated by the burning of his effigy.

"STAND WITH ANYBODY THAT STANDS RIGHT"

At Peoria and for several months thereafter, Lincoln still thought of himself as a good Whig, despite the fact that the party in which he cut his political teeth was disintegrating over the slavery issue. But even before

he abandoned the Whig ship, he advised his audience at Peoria to fuse
with any group willing to oppose Kansas-Nebraska. "Stand with anybody
that stands right," he urged them.[21] Taking his own counsel, he eventually
cast his lot with the new Republican Party, just in time to campaign in
1856 for John C. Frémont, its first presidential candidate. Lincoln made
the move because the Republicans, a fusion group comprised of anti-
Kansans from a variety of political parties and perspectives, shared the
same beliefs he'd championed on the steps of Peoria's courthouse: that
slavery was immoral even though constitutionally (and regrettably) protected in states where it already existed; that black men, just like white
ones, were endowed with certain rights that couldn't be justly denied; that
the "ancient faith" of the founders, a faith which served as the heartbeat of
American democracy, never intended slavery as a permanent institution;
and that extending slavery into the territories by a perverse application
of local self-determination was a moral scandal as well as a recipe for
national disunity and international scorn.

In both his Peoria speech and subsequent ones, Lincoln affirmed that he
had no intention of interfering with slavery in the states where it existed,
but only opposed extending it into Kansas. But he so clearly thought the
institution a moral abomination that it's not surprising his political opponents, then and later, labeled him a dangerous abolitionist. In the next five
years, especially while running for the U.S. Senate in 1858 and for the
presidency in 1860—both times, by the way, against his old nemesis Stephen Douglas—Lincoln labored to reassure his audiences that his moral
aversion to slavery didn't mean he believed the federal government could
interfere with it in the southern states. In defending this position, he *was*
genuinely more moderate than abolitionists who advocated an immediate
and if need be violent end to slavery. But there was always a somewhat suspicious edge to his public moderation. Lincoln truly believed that slavery
was constitutionally protected. But given his conviction that slavery went
against everything the "ancient faith" exemplified in the Declaration of
Independence stood for, his insistence that his only interest was in its
non-extension struck many people, and reasonably so, as something of a
dodge. His objection to the peculiar institution was morally principled
rather than politically pragmatic, which meant that he wouldn't compromise it away, even though he would sometimes rhetorically soften it. Just
a year after his showdown with Douglas, he remarked in a letter to an old

friend that he believed "the great body of the northern people do crucify their feelings [about slavery], in order to maintain their loyalty to the constitution and the Union."[22] This was as much self-description as appraisal of public sentiment, and it was his deep moral repugnance to the constitutional mandate to tolerate slavery that alarmed the South when, six years after Peoria, Lincoln won the presidency.

The political and social struggle over slavery into which Lincoln threw himself in 1854 had been brewing for at least a generation, with a steady deterioration of trust and amity between North and South the inevitable result. By the time the Civil War erupted in 1861, the two geographical sections were separate cultures in so many ways that the Confederate states' declaration of independence from the United States was but a formalization of what had been unfolding for 30-odd years. The chapters that follow will explore the lineaments of the nation's extraordinary sectional divide over human bondage that led to the birth of a brand-new political party, the tragedy of civil war, the abolition of slavery—a dramatic affirmation of American democracy's sheet anchor—and the emergence of one of the greatest men who ever occupied the White House.

NOTES

Both chapter epigraphs are from Lincoln's speech at Peoria, October 16, 1854, in Roy P. Basler (ed.), *The Collected Works of Abraham Lincoln* (New Brunswick, NY: Rutgers University Press, 1953), 2: 266. Hereafter cited as CW volume: page.

1. CW 2:492.
2. CW 2:247.
3. Lewis E. Lehrman, *Lincoln at Peoria: The Turning Point* (Mechanicsburg, PA: Stackpole Books, 2008), 57.
4. CW 2:266.
5. CW 2:274.
6. CW 2:266.
7. Ibid.
8. Ibid.
9. CW 2:275.
10. CW 2:255.
11. CW 2:274.
12. CW 2:255.

13. Ibid.

14. CW 2:275.

15. Ibid.

16. CW 2:255.

17. CW 2:255–56.

18. CW 2:276.

19. Lehrman, *Lincoln at Peoria*, 58.

20. Ernest E. East, "The 'Peoria Truce': Did Douglas Ask for Quarter?" *Journal of the Illinois State Historical Association* 29 (April 1936): 71.

21. CW 2:273.

22. CW 2:320.

SLAVE POWER, FREE SOIL, AND MR. POLK'S WAR

Indeed I tremble for my country when I reflect that God is just: that his justice cannot sleep for ever: that considering numbers, nature and natural means only, a revolution of the wheel of fortune, an exchange of situation, is among possible events: that it may become probable by supernatural interference!

—*Thomas Jefferson*

As if by magic, [the Wilmot Proviso] brought to a head the great question that is about to divide the American people.

—*Boston Whig*, August 15, 1846

Thomas Jefferson, third president of the Republic, author of the Declaration of Independence and the Virginia Statute of Religious Freedom, and lifelong slave owner, was in many ways a living embodiment of the great inconsistency that haunted the United States until 1865, when the Thirteenth Amendment abolished slavery once and for all. On the one hand, the nation was founded on the principle, so eloquently expressed by Jefferson himself, that "all men are created equal." On the other hand, by the time of the Constitutional Convention in 1787, the bondage of black persons was an established legal institution in seven of the thirteen states. In a country whose entire population was just under 4 million, slaves made up 18 percent, or 700,000 people. They were especially numerous in the agricultural South. Nearly half of them were in Virginia, representing 39 percent of the state's population. In South Carolina, slaves accounted for an astounding 43 percent of the residents.

Thomas Jefferson, third president of the United States (1801–1809), feared that northern resistance to admitting Missouri as a slave state was a "fire bell in the night." Although a lifelong slave owner, Jefferson was never comfortable with the "peculiar institution." (Library of Congress)

In the early days of the nation, most of the founders, southern as well as northern, were troubled by slavery. But the prevailing view, as Lincoln noted in his Peoria speech, was that it was a necessary evil, first because the southern economy was so dependent on slave labor, second because no one quite knew what to do with nearly 1 million ex-slaves if emancipation were to come suddenly. Because slavery was a necessary even if regrettable fact, it naturally had political repercussions. When the Constitution was framed, for example, its enumeration clause, which apportioned representation from the various confederating states, was settled on only after a sometimes fiery debate between northern and southern delegates. Southerners wanted the huge enslaved population in their region counted when determining the number of congressional representatives. Northerners objected, fearing that the South would gain an undue voting advantage. The compromise, the first of many to come in following years, was that a slave would count as three-fifths of a free white person for the purpose of calculating population and congressional representation. The solution, later critics charged, insinuated that slaves were less than fully human, and therefore that the "all men are created equal" principle didn't really apply to them.

Future generations of slave owners would gradually come to defend slavery on moral grounds, arguing that blacks were happier and healthier as slaves than they would be if they had remained "wild savages" in Africa or were freed in America. Some, such as South Carolina's James Hammond, even went so far as to claim that slaves were better off than free white laborers in the North, who had no benevolent masters to look after them but instead were at the mercy of employers indifferent to whether they lived or died. Few of the early Republic's leaders, including Thomas Jefferson, saw things this way. For them, slavery remained, at best, a national embarrassment and at worst a moral blemish on a nation founded on the principle of liberty and equality. But many of them, like Jefferson, continued to own slaves.

In his only book, the 1785 *Notes on Virginia,* Jefferson voiced this dissonance when he worried that the institution of slavery, although necessary for the moment, risked depraving everyone involved. "The whole commerce between master and slave," he warned, "is a perpetual exercise of the most boisterous passions, the most unremitting despotism on the one part, and degrading submissions on the other."[1] It makes masters lazy and self-indulgent, and it breeds anger and a spirit of dissimulation in slaves. Moreover, the toxic relationship is reproduced again and again in future generations because "our children see this, and learn to imitate it."[2] If one looks at the suffering and moral corruption caused by slavery, Jefferson continued in a brutally honest passage, future prospects were bleak.

> Can the liberties of a nation be thought secure when we have removed their only firm basis, a conviction in the minds of the people that these liberties are of the gift of God? That they are not to be violated but with his wrath? Indeed I tremble for my country when I reflect that God is just: that his justice cannot sleep for ever: that considering numbers, nature and natural means only, a revolution of the wheel of fortune, an exchange of situation, is among possible events: that it may become probable by supernatural interference! The Almighty has no attribute which can take side with us in such a contest.[3]

In his discussion of slavery in *Notes on Virginia,* Jefferson expressed the hope that the institution would gradually die out, and that "total emancipation," with the acquiescence rather than the "extirpation" of masters, lay in the near future. But three decades later, during a congressional debate about regulating slavery in the very territory that had been added to the Union under his administration, an aged Jefferson was less optimistic. "We have the wolf by the ear," he wrote, "and we can neither hold him, nor safely let him go. Justice is in one scale, and self-preservation in the other."[4]

THE MISSOURI COMPROMISE OF 1820

The crisis which prompted Jefferson's "wolf by the ear" metaphor began in late 1818, when the territory of Missouri, a region in which it was both legal and customary to own slaves (there were over 10,000 of them there by 1820), petitioned Congress to join the Union as a slave state. The request was routinely handed over to committee, where it sat until the following February when New York congressman James Tallmadge moved to amend the petition. As preconditions for admitting Missouri into the Union, the Tallmadge amendment forbade the importation of additional slaves into Missouri and stipulated that children born to slaves after statehood was granted had to be emancipated when they reached the age of 25. In effect, then, the amendment allowed Missouri to enter the Union as a slave state, but mandated that she would become a free one within a generation.

Tallmadge was a longtime foe of slavery who two years earlier had helped push through legislation to end slavery in his own state. But there was more to his amendment than his personal distaste for slavery. Nothing less than the balance of political power was at stake, and it all revolved around the extension of slavery into federal territories.

In 1784, Congress considered but rejected a proposal by Thomas Jefferson, the "Plan of Government for the Western Territory," which would have banned slavery in all the western territories (later the states of Kentucky, Tennessee, Illinois, and Indiana) after the year 1800. The trouble with the proposal was that had it been passed, it could never have been enforced. The intervening 16 years would've seen a flood of masters bringing slaves into the territories in order to establish slavery as a de facto institution. Besides, thousands of slaves already lived there by 1784.

Nevertheless, delegates were not unsympathetic to the spirit of Jefferson's proposal, and three years later the Confederation Congress passed the Northwest Ordinance banning slavery north and west of the Ohio River. The ordinance was important for two reasons. It appeared to settle the question of slavery's expansion once and for all, given that the westernmost border of the United States at the time was the Mississippi River, by confining slavery to the South. More importantly, it established a precedent that gave Congress the power to regulate slavery in federal territories.

Most southern delegates voted for the 1787 Northwest Ordinance. But the 1803 purchase of the Louisiana Territory raised questions about its sectional fairness, because much of the new territorial acquisition was north of the Ohio River's southern terminus. Legislators disagreed about whether the 1787 Ordinance applied to the new territory or only to the old northwest. Both President Jefferson, who authorized the purchase, and his successor, James Madison, were uninterested in restricting the westward spread of slavery into the new territory.

The question of whether slavery could extend into the territories was crucial because the way it was answered affected the balance of congressional power. Each state sent two senators to Congress, and at the time that Missouri applied for statehood, a tradition of parity between free and slave states had been established. Supporters of the Tallmadge amendment feared that allowing territories to apply for admission as slave states could upset the balance. Their worry was exacerbated by the fact that many of them already believed the South wielded disproportionate power in the House of Representatives because the three-fifths clause in the Constitution boosted the number of southern representatives beyond what it would be otherwise. So making sure that the South didn't acquire an additional congressional advantage was an issue of some urgency for northern congressmen. As one of them, New York senator Rufus King, frankly admitted, his support of Tallmadge's amendment wasn't motivated by any concern for the welfare of blacks. Instead, his goal was to prevent the South from gaining extraordinary political power over the rest of the nation.

Southern congressmen argued against the amendment on two grounds. Some raised a procedural objection. Tallmadge's ban on slavery was proposed when Missouri was still a territory in the process of petitioning for statehood. The 1787 Ordinance had set the precedent of Congress regulating slavery in territories, but the Constitution allowed states to decide on their own. Missouri, in the process of transitioning to statehood, was argu-ably neither fish nor fowl, and this created a gray zone when it came to the question of who had jurisdiction over the slavery issue.

Other southern congressmen, led by future president John Tyler, argued that northern opponents of slavery should actually welcome slavery's extension into the territories as the best way to put an end to it. This rather bizarre position, called the "diffusion argument," held that spreading slaves more thinly across the nation not only minimalized the threat of a slave revolt but also gradually weaned whites from reliance on forced labor. A rejection of the Tallmadge amendment, Tyler insisted, would "add much to the prospect of emancipation and the total extinction of slavery."[5]

Speaker of the House Henry Clay, who represented the border state of Kentucky, sided with the proslavery opposition, arguing that slaves were materially better off than white northern laborers. Georgia representative Thomas Cobb attacked the amendment furiously, ominously warning that it was "a fire that all the waters of the ocean cannot put out, [but] which seas of blood can only extinguish." Tallmadge, fired up by Cobb's threat of violence, responded with equal fury. "Let it be so!" he shouted. "If civil war must come, let it come!"[6] These back-and-forth volleys were nerve-wracking. But when the vote was taken, neither the North nor the South flinched. The northern-controlled House approved the amendment, but the southern-controlled Senate voted it down. Legislators voted by sec-tion, not political affiliation, and Missouri's application for statehood was held over to the next congressional session.

When Congress convened again in December, the impasse between North and South was broken by Illinois senator Jesse B. Thomas. Earlier, Clay had suggested that Missouri be admitted without any restrictions in regards to slavery, but that the Maine district, the northernmost chunk of Massachusetts which had also applied for statehood, be admitted at the same time as a free state. This would solve the problem of equilibrium in the Senate. Thomas proposed that in addition to the unrestricted admission of Maine and Missouri, the slavery extension debate be settled once and for all by drawing a line at the 36-30 parallel, the southern border of Missouri, and declaring that henceforth any state formed north of the line, excepting Missouri, would be free. Any state carved from the Louisiana Purchase territory south of the line could opt for slavery if it wished.

It's one of the ironies of American history that Thomas's proposal, eventually accepted by Congress and known as the Missouri Compromise of 1820, was credited to Henry Clay, who ever afterwards was honored by his fellow citizens as the "Great Compromiser." Clay proposed the Missouri-Maine linkage of the bill and as Speaker shepherded the whole thing through the House. But the significant proposal, the establishment of a line to perpetually curtail slavery's extension, came from Senator Thomas. In fact, although Clay publicly defended the compromise, he privately doubted that it would work. After it became law, he even told John Quincy Adams that he expected the slavery issue would nonetheless tear the country apart within five years.

Clay's doubts notwithstanding, the immediate crisis was scotched by the Missouri Compromise, and legislators as well as the general public hoped it had put an end to the national tussle over slavery. But Thomas Jefferson, observing from his slave-tended Monticello, wasn't so sure. In the same letter in which he compared slavery to a wolf held by the ears, he wrote that the northern resistance to admitting Missouri as a slave state was a "fire bell in the night" that had been "hushed" for only the time being. He predicted that the compromise's "geographical line" now dividing North and South would "never be obliterated; and every new irritation will mark it deeper and deeper." His "only consolation," he bleakly concluded, was that he would die before the escalating sectional disagreement about slavery made "useless" the "sacrifice" of his "generation of 1776."

THE NULLIFICATION CRISIS

Slavery wasn't the only issue dividing North and South. Twelve years after the Missouri Compromise and six years after Jefferson's death, another sectional crisis erupted. This time, the flashpoint was an 1828 federal tariff that the state of South Carolina refused to recognize as binding.

Southerners had bristled at tariffs ever since Congress imposed the first one in 1791 to protect northern manufacturing from foreign competition. They charged that the duties imposed on European imports made them so expensive that the relatively unindustrialized South was forced to buy most of its manufactured goods from the North.

South Carolinians felt particularly penalized by the 1828 tariff. Throughout the 1820s, the state's fiscal health had spiraled downwards.

By the end of the decade, over 50,000 whites had left the state, taking with them some 30,000 slaves, to look for better economic opportunities elsewhere. Although the main culprits for the economic downturn were the nationwide financial panic of 1819 on the one hand and depletion of soil from intensive farming on the other, South Carolinian legislators loudly and frequently blamed the federally imposed tariff. There was some truth in their complaint. Higher tariffs both increased the price of the manufactured goods southerners needed and reduced the profit margin of the cotton they sold in order to buy the goods. Moreover, the duties kept going up. The tariff of 1816 set a 25 percent tax on imported goods. A new one eight years later jacked it up to 33 percent.

Then in the election year of 1828, in a truly Machiavellian ploy on the part of Andrew Jackson's presidential campaign to beat the incumbent president John Quincy Adams, a new tariff was pushed through Congress. The bill favored the western states, which were being courted by the Jacksonians, while ignoring the interests of New England, a region which they rightly calculated was lost to them anyway. The bill most heavily penalized the South, but the Jacksonians knew that southerners were likely to vote for their candidate come what may. Besides, Jackson's chief political strategist, Martin Van Buren, let it be known that as soon as Jackson was elected, he would relieve the burden imposed on the South by the tariff of 1828, which quickly became known as the Tariff of Abominations.

The problem is that once in office, Jackson seemed perfectly content to leave the 1828 tariff untouched. South Carolinians, already feeling as if they were barely staying afloat economically, predictably simmered in anger, egged on by state congressman George McDuffie, who famously (and misleadingly) told cotton growers that the tariff "plunders you of 40 out of every 100 bales [of cotton] that you produce."[7] South Carolinian John C. Calhoun, Jackson's vice president, turned up the heat when he anonymously published an "Exposition and Protest" that defended the right of a state to nullify federal laws deemed contrary to its interests. The federal government, he argued, existed only because the individual states had covenanted with one another to create it. In other words, Congress and the president were the servants rather than the masters of the ensuing confederation, and if any state concluded that a federal law ran counter to its specific interests, it had the right to declare that law null and void within its borders. State sovereignty, argued Calhoun, was the bottom-line principle of the American experiment.

South Carolinian John C. Calhoun, antebellum America's leading defender of states' rights, insisted that the federal government had no constitutional authority to limit the spread of slavery. He died believing that a rupture between North and South over slavery was inevitable. (Library of Congress)

To exacerbate the situation even more, many southerners associated the tariff, which after all was enacted during the administration of a Massachusetts-born and antislavery president, with abolitionism. By 1831, with the appearance in Boston of the abolitionist newspaper *The Liberator* and the short-lived but gory Nat Turner slave rebellion in Virginia, the South was beginning to feel under siege. Nullification champion Charles Pickney, editor of the *Charleston Mercury*, heatedly insisted that the tariff was the camel's nose under the tent. Submit to it, he warned, and the forced abolition of slavery was sure to follow.

Discontent and the threat of nullification simmered for the next four years, finally prompting Congress to try to mollify the South by passing a new tariff in 1832 which reduced duties on imported goods. But as far as South Carolinian legislators were concerned, it was too little too late. In November 1832, they approved an ordinance of nullification declaring that the tariffs of 1828 and 1832 were unconstitutional and that, beginning the following year, they would be neither obligatory nor enforceable within the state. If the federal government tried to interfere with this decision, legislators warned, South Carolina would secede. To show they meant business, they called for 25,000 militiamen and, recalling one of their federal senators, offered his seat to nullification champion John Calhoun. Calhoun promptly resigned the vice presidency to defend on the floor of the Senate the right of states to ignore federal law.

Jackson's response was swift and strong. He considered nullification tantamount to secession, and sternly warned the people of South Carolina that they were subverting the Constitution and consequently "in direct violation of their duty as citizens of the United States." He cautioned that if they offered armed resistance to federal enforcement of the tariff, they would also be guilty of treason. He was even blunter when warning a South Carolina congressman against the folly of deploying state militia. "If one drop of blood be shed there in defiance of the laws of the United States," he said, "I will hang the first man of them I can get my hands on to the first tree I can find."[8]

Henry Clay, who only four months earlier had been humiliatingly defeated in his bid to deprive Jackson of a second term in the White House, now emerged as a genuinely great compromiser. Together with Calhoun, he brokered a new tariff bill that gradually reduced protective duties over the next decade until they reached the 1816 level of 20 percent. The Compromise Tariff, as it was called, avoided a head-to-head confrontation between South Carolina and Washington, even as it testified to the growing divide between North and South. Calhoun and other champions of state sovereignty had now made the threat of southern secession a perennial feature of political rhetoric. As President Jackson ruefully noted, the Compromise Tariff wouldn't satisfy nullifiers for long, because "they intend to blow up a storm on the slave question." Men like Calhoun, he predicted, "will do any act to destroy the union, & form a southern Confederacy, bounded north, by the Potomac river."[9] The president was absolutely correct. Two years before South Carolina issued its nullification ordinance, Calhoun had written to a correspondent that the real aim of southern opposition to tariffs was to safeguard slavery. Given the growing disparity between the economies and values of the North and the South, Calhoun wrote, southerners "must in the end be forced to rebel or submit."[10] And he didn't consider submission a live option.

But the storm portended by the nullification crisis and anticipated by Jackson and Calhoun was still on the distant horizon. In the meantime,

Clay's smoothing of the troubled waters convinced a young man from Illinois named Abraham Lincoln that the Great Compromiser from Kentucky, the state in which Lincoln himself had been born, was the perfect model of what a statesman should be.

WHIGGERY, LINCOLN, AND ANTISLAVERY

Shortly after Clay lost his bid for the presidency, he launched a new anti-Jackson political party whose members called themselves "Whigs," a term that harkened back to the heroes of 1776. Clay's coalition was bound together by loyalty to a national agenda, the "American System," which emphasized the obligation of Congress to encourage economic growth by financing internal improvements, legislating protective tariffs, and promoting individual entrepreneurship, upward mobility, and a national bank. The trademark policies of Whiggery were in direct contrast to the Jacksonian Democrat ones of battling concentration of federal power, keeping the private sector free of governmental subsidies, favoring agriculture over urban industry, and vigorously opposing the establishment of a national bank.

The Whig Party lasted only 20 years, barely outliving its founder and leading light, Henry Clay. It became a casualty of the sectional divide over the spread of slavery that splintered old political alliances and created new ones in the two decades leading up to the Civil War. As will be seen in subsequent chapters, Whigs with anti-immigrant tendencies tended to drift toward the nativist Know-Nothings, a short-lived but powerful party, while proslavery Whigs went over to the Democrats and antislavery ones to the Republicans. But despite the party's brief lifespan, it posed, while it lasted, the single most powerful political challenge to the Democrats. It was also the party that shaped the career of the man who became the first Republican president.

Clay's American System fit Lincoln, the self-made frontier man, to a tee. (As Lincoln's first law partner once remarked, "He was as stiff as a man could be in his Whig Doctrines."[11]) Although Lincoln had no use for the elitism of conservative Whigs and never displayed any sympathy for evangelical Christianity, he *was* the Whig ideal of an individual who through sheer hard work and iron discipline managed to raise himself above humble origins. Both his personal experiences and his convictions persuaded him that free labor, unimpeded by social or sectional prejudice and occasionally helped along by government-supplied opportunities, was the route to individual happiness and national prosperity. The "legitimate object" of government, he wrote, "is to do for a community of people, whatever they need to have done, but can not do for themselves."[12]

For Lincoln, free labor was the route to a good life, and this meant that slavery was its antithesis. Slavery not only robbed free laborers of opportunities to earn a living for themselves and their families—who, after all, would hire a wheelwright or a carpenter when a slave could be forced do the same work for nothing?—but also reduced slave owners to lives of self-indulgence and helplessness when it came to fending for themselves. The possibility of slavery's expansion into the western territories, a possibility that had been stalled by the Missouri Compromise, could only mean the economic marginalization of potential white homesteaders by huge plantations with dozens of slaves. Slavery, in short, was an obstacle to progress.

Many Whigs and free soilers, as opponents of slavery's extension came to be called, agreed with Lincoln's conviction that slavery was an obstacle to economic progress. But unlike many of them, Lincoln was also convinced from an early age that slavery was deeply, shockingly immoral. Writing one year before his death, he declared, "I am naturally anti-slavery. If slavery is not wrong, nothing is wrong. I can not remember when I did not so think, and feel."[13] There is no reason not to take Lincoln at his word. Although one of his great-uncles owned slaves and Lincoln married into a slave-owning family, his own parents strongly disapproved of slavery and passed on their convictions to their son. Moreover, on a couple of flatboat trips down the Mississippi taken when he was 19 and 21 years old, Lincoln recoiled at the sight of chained and beaten slaves. He shared with most white Americans of his day a racial prejudice that devalued the intelligence and talents of blacks and believed that whites and blacks could never coexist peacefully in the United States. For most of his political career, Lincoln was an advocate, as was his hero Henry Clay, of gradually emancipating slaves and colonizing them in Liberia. But despite his racial prejudice, which he shed to a remarkable degree in the last couple years of his life, Lincoln never doubted that blacks, like whites, were endowed with a fundamental right to happiness, which in turn depended on the opportunities afforded by free labor.

Because slavery disregarded this right by depriving the slave of the fruits of his labor, it was immoral. As was seen in the Prologue, this was the basis of Lincoln's great speech in Peoria.

In 1832, the same year he voted for Clay in the presidential election, Lincoln tossed his own hat in the political arena for the first time. In announcing his candidacy for the Illinois state legislature, he forthrightly declared himself a defender of the American System. "My politics are short and sweet," he said, "like the old woman's dance. I am in favor of a national bank. I am in favor of the internal improvement system and a high protective tariff."[14] Lincoln lost, finishing 8th of 13 candidates— Illinois was never a particularly Whig-friendly state—but he ran again two years later and won the first of four consecutive two-year terms. While in the legislature he studied law and was admitted to the bar, began what became a lucrative legal practice, and by 1836 was acknowledged as a leader of the Illinois House Whigs. In 1837, he made his first recorded public statement about slavery in a resolution he coauthored with a fellow legislator that acknowledged the excesses of abolitionism while condemning slavery as "founded on both injustice and bad policy."[15] Although out of public office throughout the mid-1840s, Lincoln remained active in state Whig politics and loyally campaigned for Whig candidates in every presidential election between 1836 and 1852. In or out of office, he earned a statewide reputation as a hardworking and reliable Whig foot soldier.

The abolitionist movement that Lincoln's 1837 resolution referred to was one of the several reform movements—others included temperance, prison reform, and pacifism—that emerged in the 1830s. Inspired in part by the Second Great Awakening, a wave of religious revivalism that swept through large parts of the nation in the 1820s and 1830s, abolitionists contended that slavery was an evil that violated Christian values. At least in its early years, most members of the movement sought to end slavery through nonviolent "moral suasion" aimed at opening the eyes of slave owners to the wickedness of human bondage. Later, as frustration at the apparent failure of moral suasion built, some abolitionists repudiated nonviolence. One of them, as will be seen in later chapters, was John Brown, the "Pottawatomie butcher" and leader of the raid at Harpers Ferry. Another was ex-slave Frederick Douglass.

Obviously not all who thought slavery immoral or un-Christian considered themselves abolitionists. Free soil Whigs like Lincoln, for example, simply wanted to prevent slavery from spreading to new territory. They were willing, with varying degrees of reluctance, to allow it to continue in states where it already existed just so long as its defenders didn't try to expand it. By contrast, abolitionists were viewed as radicals who preached social equality between blacks and whites, a claim that most whites, northern or southern, couldn't stomach, and who demanded immediate abolition of all slavery. Neither of these perceptions was entirely accurate. Many white abolitionists abhorred slavery but considered blacks their inferiors, and others advocated gradual rather than sudden emancipation. But the public, whose dislike of abolitionism was partly fueled by Southern demagoguery, generally ignored these distinctions.

Many white politicians, including state assemblyman Lincoln, additionally disliked abolitionism because it kept the slavery debate alive at the national level. Since the Missouri Compromise, and notwithstanding the Nullification Crisis blip 12 years later, national legislators had worked hard to keep the vexing issue of slavery off the front burner. The sectional rancor it created risked splintering partisan unity, and in the minds of many statesmen got in the way of more pressing business. Moreover, defensive southern congressmen were increasingly testy over even the mildest criticisms of slavery, and their northern colleagues, for the sake of peace, thought it best to put a lid on them, at least in Congress. In 1836, the House of Representatives went so far as to pass a "gag rule" forbidding on-the-floor discussions of antislavery petitions submitted by constituents. Although some representatives led by fearless old John Quincy Adams tirelessly opposed the rule, it remained in effect until 1844.

But abolitionists in the public forum weren't similarly restrained, and their outcries against slavery prevented the topic from being swept under the rug. William Lloyd Garrison published the first issue of his Boston weekly *The Liberator* on January 1, 1831, and in its inaugural editorial defied the politicians who wanted the slavery issue to go away. "I will be as harsh as truth and as uncompromising as justice," he swore. "I will not equivocate—I will not excuse—I will not retreat a single inch—and I will be heard." Issued until the end of the Civil War, *The Liberator* became the primary voice of abolitionism, irritating, sometimes outraging, but always seeking to convert, readers.

Southern opposition to abolitionism was predictably fierce, fueled by the horrible example of the Nat Turner slave revolt that occurred in

Virginia only a few months after Garrison launched his newspaper. Southern defenses of slavery began to shift from characterizing it as an economically moral evil—Jefferson's wolf—to an institution that was moral as well as in the best interest of blacks. Additionally, especially in the 1830s, hostility to abolitionists was notable in the North as well. Thuggish mobs frequently broke up abolitionist meetings in northern cities with clubs and knives, abolitionist editor Elijah Lovejoy was murdered in 1837 by a proslavery Illinois mob—the same year as Lincoln's resolution in the Illinois legislature—and two years earlier poor Garrison had nearly been lynched by an anti-abolitionist mob in Boston. Still, by the 1840s, over 100,000 people, many women and free blacks among them, had joined local abolitionist societies in the North. Thousands more, though reluctant to actually call themselves abolitionists, declared against slavery or at least its expansion. Despite the congressional gag rule, slavery remained a national political issue. By the 1850s, it had become *the* central and consuming political topic of the day, with southern politicians defensively interpreting just about every piece of legislation that came before Congress as a threat to their "peculiar domestic institution" and northern politicians becoming increasingly weary of their southern blustery defensiveness.

Many abolitionists, following Garrison's lead, refused to get involved in politics. Their thinking was that the executive, legislative, and judicial branches of government were tainted because grounded in a document, the U.S. Constitution, which approved of slavery. Consequently, to work within the political process for the abolition of slavery was to become morally corrupt by association.

But not all abolitionists took this hands-off approach, and in late November 1839 a group of them launched the Liberty Party. As its name suggested, the party's guiding principle, initially expressed more in religious and moral than political language, was the immediate abolition of slavery everywhere it existed in the United States—this despite the fact that the federal government had no constitutional authority to authorize such an emancipation. The party held its first national convention in April 1840, just in time to nominate a candidate, James Birney, for that year's presidential election. Birney received less than 7,000 votes nationwide, but the abolitionist movement now had a political arm. Ohio's Salmon P. Chase, a future member of President Lincoln's cabinet and Supreme Court justice, left the Whigs to throw his lot in with the Liberty

Party. Under his guidance, the party transformed its religious rhetoric into a more practical political platform, which helped determine the outcome of the presidential election four years later.

TEXAS ANNEXATION AND SLAVE POWER

Beginning in the 1820s, the governor of the Mexican state of Coahuila invited North Americans to settle in the huge but underpopulated province of Tejas. His intention was that they would convert to Roman Catholicism, adopt Spanish as their primary language, and embrace Mexico as their mother country. But land-hungry North Americans flooded into the region they called Texas too quickly and in too great numbers, and proved too stubbornly attached to their own culture, for this plan to succeed. By the mid-1830s, over 30,000 of them lived in what increasingly amounted to an English-speaking American colony in Mexico. Those who settled in east Texas also brought with them 1,000 slaves to work the cotton fields.

Tension between the Mexican authorities and the North American settlers was inevitable, not the least because Coahuila passed legislation in 1827 that outlawed slavery, and a six-month war erupted in late 1835 which culminated in the emergence of the independent Republic of Texas. The new nation's territory was huge, encompassing present-day Texas and stretching all the way north to the Canadian border to include large chunks of Colorado, New Mexico, Utah, Oklahoma, and Wyoming.

Almost immediately Texas made overtures to the United States for admission to the Union. But neither Andrew Jackson, president at the time of the Texas War of Independence, nor Martin Van Buren, his successor, was interested. Although adding such a vast territory to the United States was attractive, a war with Mexico, which refused to recognize Texas independence, wasn't. Moreover, the fact that Texas would almost inevitably enter the Union as a slave state was also troublesome, especially for the northerner Van Buren. Finally, Texas had heavy war debts, and the United States, slipping by 1837 into an economic slump that would drag through the mid-1840s, simply couldn't afford to take them on.

In the 1840 presidential election, the nation's economic woes cost Van Buren a second term and took William Henry Harrison to the White House. Harrison was a Whig, the first member of his party to become president. Although not opposed to expansionism, Whig policy had always been to maintain and improve the nation within its existing borders rather than seeking to expand them too rapidly. So the possibility of Texas annexation under a Harrison administration was bleak. But Harrison died after only a month in office, and was succeeded by his Virginia-born vice president John Tyler. Although Tyler had run on the Whig ticket, his opposition to federally funded internal improvements as well as his expansionist ambitions soon became apparent, so infuriating the leaders of his own party that they officially expelled him from it.

As a president without a partisan political base, Tyler, disdainfully called "His Accidency" by his detractors, realized that he needed to pull off something spectacular to win enough popular support for a second term. He chose to concentrate on foreign policy, creating an American presence in Hawaii (then called the Sandwich Islands) and promulgating the Tyler Doctrine, which did for the Pacific what the Monroe Doctrine did for the Americas. More ambitiously, he began secret annexation negotiations with the Republic of Texas. Although Tyler seems genuinely to have believed that acquiring Texas was in the best interests of the entire United States, he wasn't blind to the fact that adding another slave state to the Union would win him the South in a bid for reelection. But he also knew it would be risky to give the public impression that the annexation would benefit the South, first because of free soil opposition to the extension of slavery, and second because many northerners believed that the South already enjoyed an unfair political advantage and was conspiring for even more.

The northern conviction that there existed a conspiratorial "Slave Power" intent on controlling the federal government was yet another indication that the Missouri Compromise, although quelling the 1820 crisis, had done little to ameliorate deep-seated distrust between North and South. Prominent northern statesmen who endorsed the Slave Power thesis included ex-president and congressman John Quincy Adams, Massachusetts senator Charles Sumner, Liberty Party leader Salmon Chase, Harvard president Josiah Quincy, and *New York Tribune* editor Horace Greeley. As will be seen in a later chapter, Abraham Lincoln not only believed in a Slave Power conspiracy, but publicly accused Stephen Douglas of being part of it when the two men vied for the same Senate seat in 1858.

Some northerners were more paranoid than rational in their belief in the existence of a Slave Power conspiracy. But whether or not there was an actual cabal at work, the South did indeed play a disproportionate role in the nation's governance. Although the North had a larger white population (hence the compensatory three-fifths provision in the Constitution) and was more industrially sophisticated than the South, southern-born statesmen seemed to be in near-perpetual control of all three branches of the federal government. The White House was occupied by southerners for 49 of the 72 years between Washington and Lincoln. Additionally, three northern-born presidents during that period (Millard Fillmore, Franklin Pierce, and James Buchanan), accounting for 11 more years, were markedly sympathetic to the South in their administrative policies. Between 1789 and 1861, 20 out of 35 Supreme Court justices were southerners, constituting a majority on the Court at any given time. Twenty-three of 36 Speakers of the House were from the South, and so were 24 of 36 presidents pro tem in the Senate.

Although the South had gained four slave states (Louisiana, Missouri, Arkansas, and Florida) from territory acquired since the founding of the United States to the free North's one (Iowa), southern leaders constantly played the secession card to wrest as many additional concessions from the free North as possible. This had happened so often that by 1860 Abraham Lincoln and many other leaders of his party simply didn't take seriously the South's threat to leave the Union if the Republicans won the White House. Tiresomely familiar and increasingly unbelievable as the threats became, northern legislators and citizens still resented what they perceived as the South's willingness to bully its way to a larger piece of the governance pie than it was due.

By the 1850s, the perception that the South pulled the strings of the nation's destiny was so widely held that even many southern leaders, despite their plaints about the North, believed it. South Carolina senator James Hammond famously crowed in an 1858 speech that "Cotton is King," boasting that the South was invincible because it produced the cotton that the world demanded, that Dixie's cotton revenues from international markets kept northern banks and commercial interests solvent, and that the real slave owners were northern employers who routinely exploited the "hireling class." "The difference between us," he contemptuously told the North, "is that our slaves are hired for life and well compensated," while "yours are hired by the day, not cared for, and scantily compensated."[16] It followed that the expansion of King Cotton and slavery into western territories was not only an economic necessity for the nation. It was also good for the men and women held in bondage.

Southern arrogance of this kind did nothing to soothe ill feelings between North and South, but it did help to contribute to the widespread impression, domestic as well as foreign, that the center of power in the United States lay in the South. Five years before Hammond's King Cotton speech, an article in the Edinburgh-based *Blackwood's Magazine* alleged that the Slave Power exercised "control in and over the United States . . . more absolute than that of any European aristocracy—almost as uncontrolled by public sentiment as an Asiatic potentate."[17]

President Tyler, well aware of northern perceptions of a conspiratorial Slave Power, tread softly in his plans to annex Texas. His secretary of state, fellow Virginian and slave owner Abel Upshur, worked behind the scenes to persuade northern senators that the acquisition of Texas was a national rather than a sectional plum, and by early 1844 had lined up the necessary two-thirds majority for approval of the annexation. But in February 1844 Upshur was killed in a freak accident, and in a colossal misstep that cost him reelection and nearly cost the nation Texas, Tyler appointed John Calhoun to take his place. Calhoun immediately upended all of Upshur's careful diplomacy by turning the acquisition of Texas into a sectional issue. He publicly urged annexation to forestall abolition-minded Britain from interfering with slavery in either Texas or the already-existing slave states of the Union. This change of focus from national to southern interests created an uproar that predictably killed the possibility of Senate approval.

Seeing the way the political wind blew, the president threw his weight behind Tennessee Democrat James Polk in the 1844 election, knowing that Polk was just as ardent an expansionist as himself. Henry Clay, who had opposed the annexation from the start, ran against Polk as the Whig candidate, and in Illinois Abraham Lincoln loyally stumped for him. But during the campaign, Clay, hoping to curry favor with proannexation southern Whigs, allowed that he might endorse the Texas acquisition if it was done "without dishonor"—whatever that meant—"without war, [and] with the common consent of the Union."[18] This was too much for northern Whigs, many of whom either sat the election out or voted for James Birney, once more heading on the Liberty Party ticket. Birney took so many popular votes away from Clay in New York, in fact, that he threw the state's electoral votes to Polk. On Election Day, the Democrat from Tennessee won the presidency by a slim margin of less than 40,000 popular votes, but a more respectable electoral one of 65 votes.

Four days before handing over the White House keys to his successor and one year to the day of Secretary of State Upshur's death, President Tyler, claiming that Polk's election was a mandate from the people for Texas statehood—a debatable claim, given that Polk just barely squeaked past Clay in the popular vote—engineered the annexation of Texas through a joint congressional resolution. Ten months later, on December 29, 1845, President Polk signed the papers that officially made Texas the 28th state of the Union and the 15th slave state.

MR. POLK'S WAR AND MR. WILMOT'S PROVISO

James Polk was the land-hungriest president ever to occupy the White House, remarkably voracious even in a period when the nation's "manifest destiny" to expand geographically was accepted as a given. Not content with the enormous land mass gained through the Texas annexation, Polk also wanted California. When Mexico refused his offer to buy it and New Mexico for $25 million, he determined to seize what he wanted. But he needed a pretext to avoid coming off as a common buccaneer.

A border dispute gave Polk the opportunity he was looking for. The Republic of Texas had maintained that its border with Mexico was determined by the course of the Rio Grande River. Mexico, on the other hand, insisted on the less southern border of the Nueces River. (The border dispute was curiously incongruous with the fact that Mexico had never actually recognized Texas independence.) The disagreement was left unsettled when Texas became a state, with the land lying between the two rivers now claimed by both Mexico and the United States. Seeking to provoke Mexican authorities, Polk ordered Gen. Zachary Taylor to lead a contingent of troops into the disputed territory. On April 25, 1846, a Mexican force responded to what it interpreted as an American trespass, and in the ensuing fracas 16 of Taylor's soldiers were killed. Two weeks later, Polk announced to Congress that Mexico had violated U.S. sovereignty and taken American lives, and asked for a declaration of war. On May 13, Congress gave it to him. Whigs, who generally opposed territorial acquisition, caved again, just as they had when Tyler asked for

One year into the presidency (1845–1849) of James K. Polk, "Mr. Polk's War" with Mexico erupted. The huge landmass won from the war intensified debate over the extension of slavery. (Library of Congress)

a joint resolution to annex Texas. Only 14 of them ultimately voted against the declaration.

But most Whigs, as well as some members of Polk's own party, were convinced that the war was a transparent Slave Power ploy to acquire more land for slavery. After all, they knew that at the time Polk asked for a declaration of war against Mexico, he was negotiating a diplomatic resolution of a border dispute with Britain over the Oregon territory. Why, then, resort to violence in a similar dispute with Mexico? Consequently, even though they voted for what quickly came to be known as "Mr. Polk's War" and to fund field supplies for troops once it was underway, Whigs did so holding their noses. Outside of Congress, northerners such as Frederick Douglass and a young lieutenant who saw combat in Mexico, Ulysses Simpson Grant, also believed the war a pretext for creating a vast slave empire. And even Georgia's slave-owning Alexander Stephens, who wasn't at all adverse to extending slavery into new territories, condemned the war as a "disgraceful and infamous" campaign "against a neighboring people to compel them to sell their country."[19]

The war lasted until early 1848, when the Treaty of Guadalupe Hidalgo gave Polk everything he wanted. Mexico ceded California and the New Mexico territory (virtually all Mexican holdings north of the 31st parallel), a full half of Mexico's total land mass, and in return the United States paid Mexico a paltry $15 million, less than Polk's prewar offer. Along with a final settlement with Great Britain of a boundary dispute over the Oregon-Canada boundary and the formal admission of Texas as a state, Polk's acquisitions from Mexico expanded the United States' land mass by two-thirds. It was the single largest territorial gain in the nation's history.

But the enormous cession began to create congressional storms even before it was acquired. Two years earlier, only three months into the war, Polk triumphantly announced that he fully expected the United States to acquire territory from the conflict. In anticipation of the final settlement, he asked Congress for an appropriation to fund future negotiations. If he expected a swift and uncomplicated thumbs-up from Congress, he was disappointed. Almost immediately, on a stifling August night, a young House Democrat from Pennsylvania, David Wilmot, stood to offer an amendment to Polk's appropriations request that in the months to come would thrust Congress and the nation into yet another sectional conflict over slavery. "As an express and fundamental condition to the acquisition of any territory from the Republic of Mexico," the amendment read, "neither slavery nor involuntary servitude shall ever exist in any part of said territory, except for crime."[20]

The Wilmot Proviso, as the amendment came to be called, was neither spontaneously proposed nor exclusively Wilmot's. It was engineered by a group of northern Democrats to which he belonged who were fed up with what they saw as the southern domination of their party. Connecticut Democrat Gideon Welles, who later turned Republican and served as Lincoln's secretary of the navy, spoke for them when he declared that "the time has come when the Northern democracy [Democrats often referred to themselves collectively as 'the Democracy'] should make a stand. Everything has taken a Southern shape and been controlled by Southern caprice for years."[21] Northern Democrats weren't as a body opposed to slavery. But they were growing impatient with their party's

Pennsylvania congressman David Wilmot became widely known as the author of the Wilmot Proviso, a legislative effort to ban slavery in any of the territory acquired as a result of the Mexican War. (Cirker, Hayward, ed., *Dictionary of American Portraits*, 1967)

southward shift of power. For his part, Wilmot also made it clear to his fellow legislators that his amendment wasn't motivated by any "morbid sympathy for the slave," but rather concern for future settlers in the acquired territory "of my own race and color" who would suffer "dishonor and degradation" if forced to share land with blacks.[22]

Northern Democrats in the House were happy to support their young colleague's amendment, and their more consistently antislavery Whig counterparts were delighted to do so. Southern Democrats opposed it, as did a resentful Polk, who felt he'd been disloyally blindsided by a member of his own party. When the House voted, Wilmot's amendment passed along sectional rather than party lines. Congress adjourned before the Senate could vote on it, but the proviso was reintroduced at the beginning of the next session—the first of many reintroductions—and once again passed the House. But by this time Texas had been admitted into the Union, swinging the balance of slave and free states in the South's direction—15 slave to 14 free states—and the amendment died in the Senate. (The balance was reestablished in 1848 with the admission of Wisconsin. But by that time, southern senators had won over enough northern colleagues to defeat the proviso anyway.) Polk finally managed to get his request for negotiation funds passed, but not before promising to veto any appropriations bill sent to him that had Wilmot's amendment attached to it.

Popular opposition to Mr. Polk's war meant hard times for Democrats in the 1846 midterm elections. In the House, Whigs picked up 38 additional seats, guaranteeing that when the 30th Congress convened in December 1847, agitation for the Wilmot Proviso would be renewed. As one House member in the new Congress complained, wrangling about slavery dominated Congress. "From morning to night, day after day, and week after week, nothing is talked about here, nothing can get a hearing that will not afford an opportunity to lug in something about negro slavery."[23]

One of the Whig freshmen who were thrown into the midst of the House debate was Abraham Lincoln of Illinois. (He had been elected in 1846. But in the mid-19th century, members of Congress took their seats more than a year after their actual election.) Lincoln later admitted that he'd not been too exercised by the 1844 debate over Texas annexation because he thought it made little difference one way or the other when it came to slavery. But when he took his place with fellow Whigs in the House of Representatives, he voted consistently for the Wilmot Proviso every time it came to the floor, and did so out of conviction rather than simple party loyalty.

During his single term in Congress, Lincoln earned the nickname "Spotty" for himself because of his impassioned speeches in the House demanding that Polk divulge the exact geographical spot where the slaying of the 16 American troops that had sparked the war took place. His insinuation, applauded by fellow northern Whigs and some northern Democrats, was that the killing had taken place on Mexican rather than American soil, and that Polk's rationale for war was, consequently, duplicitous. Lincoln's speeches were courageous and, for him, uncharacteristically florid—"the blood of Abel," he declaimed at one point, "is crying to Heaven against" Polk, "a bewildered, confounded, and miserably-perplexed man."[24] They may have delighted some of his fellow Whigs, but they enraged many of his Illinois constituents, who felt that such aspersions upon the chief executive in wartime were unpatriotic if not downright treasonous. His "spot resolutions" would come back to haunt him in 1858 when Stephen Douglas, against whom Lincoln was running for the U.S. Senate, would accuse him of siding with the enemy during the Mexican War.

Lincoln's speech also outraged southern legislators, who saw it as an affront to the many sons of Dixie who fought and died in the Mexican War. The South's disproportionately heavy participation in the conflict also helped fuel southern opposition to Wilmot's proviso. Why, slaveholding southerners reasonably asked, should they be required to give up claims to all the land wrested from Mexico when they had fought gallantly for it? They argued that Wilmot's proviso was basically the application of a Northwest Ordinance–like ban on slavery in the new territories, and that this was an unjust privileging of the free North. If the proviso passed into law, James Hammond warned his fellow southerners, 10 new free states would be created, the senatorial balance between North and South destroyed forever, and the slave states put in serious jeopardy. "Our only safety," he thundered, "is equality of POWER."[25] It was hard to disagree with his logic.

To avoid the disaster predicted by the Wilmot Proviso's opponents, three alternative proposals were discussed. One, endorsed by President Polk, was a simple extension of the Missouri Compromise line through all the territory ceded by Mexico. To his way of thinking, that strategy had served the country well in 1820 and there was every reason to believe that "a similar adjustment of the questions which now agitate the public mind would produce the same happy results."[26] Although this struck many as a reasonable proposal, some southern legislators, believing that the 1820 Compromise had handed their section of the country the short end of the stick, wanted nothing to do with it. The indomitable John C. Calhoun was one of them, and in February 1847 he offered a second alternative consistent with his long-held conviction that ultimate authority rested in the states rather than the federal government. Any new territorial holdings acquired in the name of the United States, he asserted, were actually the common property of *all* the states. Consequently, it was unconstitutional to pass a federal law like the Missouri Compromise that deprived citizens in any state of full and equal access to the territories. This included the right to transport property, including human property, into them.

Map illustrating the Missouri Compromise of 1820. Under terms hammered out by Congress, Missouri entered the Union as a slave state, while Maine entered as a free state. Slavery was banned in the remainder of the territory north of the southern border of Missouri. (North Wind Picture Archives)

Consequently, concluded Calhoun, the new territory should be open to all comers, slaveholders or not. His proposal delighted his southern colleagues, but predictably failed to satisfy his northern ones.

The third alternative to Wilmot's proposed ban on slavery in the Mexican cession was floated by Michigan senator Lewis Cass. He agreed with the spirit of Calhoun's failed proposal but thought it too open-ended. So he defended instead a strategy of popular or local sovereignty, whereby the actual residents of territories, not the federal government, had the right to determine whether they would accept or reject slavery in their midst. Cass didn't make it clear whether local sovereignty kicked in during the territorial stage or only after statehood, nor did he actually offer his alternative as a congressional motion. Instead, he introduced the idea in a letter to the *Washington Union*. But it created enough of a stir to defeat the Polk-backed proposal to extend the Missouri Compromise line to the Pacific prior to Congress's adjournment in the summer of 1848. Polk, ill and dispirited, announced that he would honor the election pledge he'd made four years earlier not to seek a second term. This left a clear field for the presidency, with the fate of the land formally ceded by Mexico in February of that year still undecided. Polk's plan and Calhoun's plan had fallen by the wayside, and Cass's suggestion was still up in the air.

THE 1848 PRESIDENTIAL ELECTION

By the time the presidential election year of 1848 arrived, both major political parties had good reason to reflect on Ralph Waldo Emerson's prediction a few years earlier that even though the United States would win the war with Mexico, victory would be like swallowing arsenic. "Mexico will poison us," the sage of Concord had warned, and events proved him right.[27] The land ceded to the United States as part of the peace settlement had resurrected national rancor over slavery. Traditional political allegiances were giving way to sectional ones, and there was no end to the bickering in sight. Congress was deadlocked, and combative editorials in newspapers north and south kept public opinion fired up. What Polk had seen as a boon to the commonwealth—hundreds of thousands of square miles of additional territory—was becoming a nightmare.

In the hope of holding their respective parties together, both the Whigs and the Democrats wanted to keep the extension of slavery issue out of sight during the presidential campaign season. So, rather remarkably, they competed with one another in playing it safe. The Whigs issued no platform whatsoever, and the Democrats settled for a minimalistic one. Even though Lewis Cass of popular sovereignty fame was the Democratic candidate, the party's platform didn't formally endorse the position, instead resting content with a boilerplate repudiation of the Wilmot Proviso. To offer sectional parity, the Democrats chose William Butler, a Kentuckian and Mexican War general, as Cass's running mate.

Seventy-year-old Henry Clay, the grand old man of the Whigs, was denied his party's nomination, and with it his final chance of achieving the office for which he longed. He was too tainted by his opposition to the Mexican War, and he was also a three-time loser in previous presidential elections. Whig strategists wanted an uncontroversial candidate who had popular appeal and no political baggage, and the man they settled on was Zachary Taylor, a career army officer who had become a national hero in the Mexican War. It was a surprising but canny choice: surprising because Taylor was a leader in a war the Whigs had opposed, canny because while Taylor, a slave-owning southerner, would appeal to southern Whigs and perhaps some southern Democrats, he was enough of a war hero to appeal to opponents of slavery too. Taylor had no previous history with the Whigs, nor any other political party for that matter—in fact, he had never even voted—and during the campaign he maintained a stubborn silence except for promising that he wouldn't veto any decision that Congress made about slavery in the new territories. To round out the ticket, Whigs nominated New York's rather nondescript Millard Fillmore for the vice presidency.

Southern Whigs hoped that Taylor's ties to the South would make him sympathetic to a settlement of the Mexican cession favorable to slave states. Antislavery northern Whigs worried about the same possibility, and their concern led these so-called Conscience Whigs to break from the party and join forces, or fuse, with other antislavery groups such as a faction of New York Democrats nicknamed "Barnburners" and some members of the old Liberty Party. (Liberty Party loyalists ran their own candidate, but received only 2,500 votes in the nationwide election.) The result was the formation of a new political alliance, the Free Soil Party. At their August convention in Buffalo, Free Soil delegates nominated ex-president Martin Van Buren and Massachusetts blueblood Charles Francis Adams as their presidential and vice presidential choices. Van Buren had supported slavery, even if lukewarmly, for most of his political career. But by 1848 he had changed his mind to advocate closing off the new territories to slavery as well as abolishing it in the capital city. Adams, the distinguished son and grandson of American presidents, had a long antislavery pedigree.

The Free Soil Party, unlike the earlier Liberty Party, didn't advocate the nationwide abolition of slavery, but only its containment within the states where it already existed. Its entry into the campaign was pivotal for two reasons. First, Free Soilers were explicitly sectional, even as the Whigs and Democrats were trying to reunite sectionally divided party members. Both Free Soil candidates were northerners, and their supporters were bound together by a single issue: opposition to slavery's expansion, generally identified with the North. Second, the presence of the Free Soil Party injected into the presidential election precisely the topic—slavery—that both Whigs and Democrats had hoped to downplay.

The disgruntlement with Mr. Polk's war that had resulted in state and congressional election victories for Whigs two years earlier, coupled with the fact that the absence of a Whig platform made it difficult to find much ground for criticizing the Whig candidate, took Taylor to the White House. He was the second Whig elected to the highest office in the land, and he would prove to be the last. Cass and Taylor divided the states evenly between them, but Taylor wound up with 167 electoral votes to Cass's 127. The popular vote was much closer. Out of a million and a half votes, Taylor outdistanced Cass by only a little more than 100,000. The reason Taylor's popular numbers were so low—he carried only 47 percent of the votes—was that the Free Soil ticket skimmed off 10 percent, or nearly 300,000, of the total votes cast. In the North, a full 15 percent of all voters went with Van Buren and Adams. But the strong showing of a sectional party dedicated to the containment of slavery was both a sign of how strong antislavery sentiment was growing and a portent of an even stronger sectional and antislavery party that would emerge a few years later. As Massachusetts senator Charles Sumner said, the election of 1848 was but the "Bunker Hill" of the battle against slavery.[28] More battles and, he was sure, ultimate victory, would come later. But for the present, all eyes looked to the new president and the new Congress to do something about the Mexican cession deadlock.

NOTES

The chapter epigraph from Jefferson is from his *Notes on the State of Virginia*, in Paul Leicester Ford (ed.), *The Writings of Thomas Jefferson* (New York: G. P. Putnam's Sons, 1905), IV:300.

1. Jefferson, *Notes on Virginia*, in Ford (ed.), *The Writings of Thomas Jefferson*, IV:298.

2. Ibid.

3. Ibid., 300.

4. Thomas Jefferson to John Holmes (April 22, 1820), in Ibid., X:157.

5. William W. Freehling, *The Road to Disunion: Secessionists at Bay* (New York: Oxford University Press, 1980), 151.

6. David S. Heidler and Jeanne T. Heidler, *Henry Clay: The Essential American* (New York: Random House, 2011), 144.

7. Freehling, *The Road to Disunion*, 256.

8. Daniel Walker Howe, *What Hath God Wrought: The Transformation of America, 1815–1846* (New York: Oxford University Press, 2009), 405, 406.

9. Robert V. Remini, *Andrew Jackson and the Course of American Democracy, 1833–1845* (New York: Harper and Row, 1984), 42.

10. William Montgomery Meigs, *The Life of John Caldwell Calhoun* (New York: G. E. Stechert, 1917), I:419.

11. Allen C. Guelzo, *Lincoln and Douglas: The Debates That Defined America* (New York: Simon & Schuster, 2008), 28.

12. Roy P. Basler (ed.), *The Collected Works of Abraham Lincoln* (New Brunswick, NJ: Rutgers University Press, 1953), II:221. Hereafter cited as CW.

13. CW VII:281.

14. Allen C. Guelzo, *Abraham Lincoln: Redeemer President* (Grand Rapids, MI: Wm. E. Eerdmans, 1999), 65.

15. CW I:75.

16. James McPherson, *Battle Cry of Freedom: The Civil War Era* (New York: Oxford University Press, 1988), 196.

17. Anonymous, "Slavery and the Slave Power in the United States of America," *Blackwood's Magazine* 73, #447 (January 1853): 17.

18. M. P. Hay and Carol Reardon (eds.), *The Papers of Henry Clay* (Lexington: University of Kentucky Press, 1991), 10:91.

19. Allen G. Guelzo, *Fateful Lightning: A New History of the Civil War and Reconstruction* (New York: Oxford University Press, 2012), 63.

20. Chaplain W. Morrison, *Democratic Politics and Sectionalism: The Wilmot Proviso Controversy* (Chapel Hill: University of North Carolina Press, 1967), 18.

21. *Congressional Globe* (January 7, 1847), 29th Congress, 2nd Session, 136.

22. Joel H. Sibley, *Storm Over Texas: The Annexation Controversy and the Road to Civil War* (New York: Oxford University Press, 2005), 125.

23. Eric Foner, *The Fiery Trial: Abraham Lincoln and American Slavery* (New York: W. W. Norton, 2010), 52.

24. CW I:439, 441–42.

25. William L. Barney, *The Road to Secession: A New Perspective on the Old South* (New York: Praeger, 1972), 106.

26. James Polk, "Special Message to Congress, August 14, 1848," in J. D. Richardson (ed.), *A Compilation of the Messages and Papers of the Presidents, 1789–1908* (Washington, D.C.: Government Printing Office, 1908), 4:608.

27. Edward W. Emerson and Waldo E. Forbes (eds.), *Journals of Ralph Waldo Emerson* (Boston: Houghton Mifflin, 1914), VII:206.

28. McPherson, *Battle Cry of Freedom*, 63.

CHAPTER 2

A FALSE PEACE: THE COMPROMISE OF 1850

I go for an honorable compromise whenever it can be made . . . All legislation, all government, all society, is formed upon the principle of mutual concession, politeness, comity, courtesy.

—Henry Clay

If any man has a right to be proud of the success of these measures, it is the senator from Illinois.

—Jefferson Davis

Illinois congressman Abraham "Spotty" Lincoln had made something of a name for himself by repeatedly challenging, on the floor of the House, President Polk's pretext for going to war with Mexico. Perhaps that's why fellow Whig Joshua Giddings, an Ohio representative who was an uncompromising opponent of slavery, tapped Lincoln to draw up a bill proposing the abolition of slavery in the District of Columbia. The slave trade in the nation's capital had long been an embarrassment to northern legislators and a scandal to visiting foreign dignitaries such as Charles Dickens, who in 1842 savaged slavery in his *American Notes*. Lincoln's proposal had two parts. The first was that all children born to slave mothers after January 1, 1850, would be free, subject to a period of apprenticeship to their mothers' owners. The second was that owners wishing to free slaves born before 1850 would be compensated, at fair market price, by the federal government.

Although Lincoln gave notice in January 1849 that he would introduce the bill, it never actually made it to the floor. Cautious members of his own party were too alarmed by it, as Lincoln later recalled, and so he "dropped the matter, knowing that it was useless to prosecute the business at that time."[1] Even so, southern representatives and senators alike were outraged by the mere possibility of such a bill being proposed. By itself, Lincoln's proposal might not have been enough to cause such an uproar. The issue of the slave trade in the nation's capital had come up before. But sectional tension was running high over the question of what to do with the Mexican cession, and Lincoln's proposal was just another coal heaped on an already blazing fire.

President Polk had stoked the blaze in his fourth and final address to Congress in early December 1848. He had scarcely been able to contain his excitement as he spoke about the newly discovered gold mines in California, part of the territory won in the recent Mexican War. The population of the Pacific territory was growing by leaps and bounds as thousands of hopeful prospectors flooded into it. Given the obvious natural wealth of the region, Polk recommended expediting statehood for California as well as the vast New Mexico region. To make sure that the South received its fair share of the newly acquired bounty, Polk once more recommended extending the Missouri Compromise line all the way to the Pacific. More land for the extension of slavery would be made available, and the possibility of continuing the tradition of congressional parity between slave and free states strengthened.

Polk's December recommendation amounted to a bypassing of the often moved and as often defeated Wilmot Proviso, predictably gladdening slave state and irritating free state sensibilities. From then until the end of the congressional session the following March, senators and representatives angrily blustered, shouted at one another, and occasionally backed up harsh words with fists. In the House, the northern majority reaffirmed its support for the Proviso and the admission of California as a free state. All this made Lincoln's proposed bill to abolish slavery in the capital especially offensive to southern congressmen. In it, they saw yet another effort to contain and destroy the southern way of life.

Even though antislavery motions from the House had no chance of getting past the Senate, southern congressmen decided to caucus in order to collaborate on an appropriate pushback to what they saw as northern aggression. The consensus arising from their meeting was that South Carolina's John Calhoun should write and publish an "Address to the People of the Southern States" outlining the South's grievances against northern agitators who denied the South's right to expand slavery into the Mexican cession, a right surely earned on the battlefields of Mexico.

Calhoun's "Address," one of the period's finest pieces of political writing, did nothing to change the minds of slavery's opponents. But like all of Calhoun's work, it struck a responsive chord in the South. His thesis was that the North had a long history of mistreating the South, beginning with the Northwest Ordinance's 1787 banning of slavery and proceeding straight through to legislative proposals like the Wilmot Proviso and Congressman Lincoln's contemplated bill to end slavery in Washington, D.C. The North's aim, argued Calhoun, was to destroy the political power of the South and to emancipate slaves throughout the entire country. If this happened, he warned, anarchy would reign in the South as free blacks gained and whites lost control. This possibility was so horrendous— Calhoun most likely had in mind the blood-curdling 1831 Nat Turner rebellion, in which angry slaves slaughtered nearly 60 whites, many of them as they slept in their beds—that the South "would stand justified by all laws, human and divine," in repelling it, "without looking to consequences" and resorting "to all means necessary for that purpose."[2]

Calhoun and his caucus hoped that the "Address" would stir up enough popular and congressional support either to extend the Missouri Compromise line all the way to the Pacific coast, or to apply the Constitution's protection of slavery in the states to the territories as well. But the South Carolinian's fighting language was too much for some caucus members. Although enthusiastically supported by the likes of Jefferson Davis, the caucus eventually split over the "Address." Forty-six of the 73 southern Democrats signed it, but only 2 of 48 Whigs. Even fire-breathing Georgia congressman Robert Toombs, who in principle agreed with everything Calhoun wrote, thought the document politically ill-timed. So nothing was settled about what to do with California, and opponents and proponents of slavery extension alike hoped that President-elect Taylor would sort the mess out in their favor as soon as he was inaugurated in March.

Their hope was ill-founded.

A CRISIS LOOMS

Zachary Taylor, although running as a Whig, refused to be bound during his presidential campaign by Whig or any other political positions. Should he take the White House, he wanted to be unencumbered by party loyalties and campaign promises. But he had let drop a casual remark that at the time startled many, especially in light of the gold that had been discovered in California. He mentioned that he thought the Pacific coast of little consequence to the United States, since in all probability California and Oregon would become separate nations anyway. It was naïveté like this that prompted seasoned political observer Horace Greeley to explode. "Old Zack is a good old soul," he exclaimed, "but he don't know himself from a side of sole leather in the way of statesmanship!"[3]

By the time he took office in March 1849, Taylor had grown more astute in statecraft. The gold deposits discovered in California were proving to be of enormous value—in December 1848, an emissary from the mines had presented to outgoing President Polk a solid gold tea caddy weighing 320 ounces—and Taylor wanted to make sure that the wealth stayed in the country. Moreover, so many citizens had migrated to California either to prospect or sell provisions to forty-niners that the population was already de facto American, and certainly large enough to qualify for statehood. Finally, the influx of new people into California created social and legal problems that cried out for organized government. Ports were overcrowded and badly in need of supervision, and San Francisco was becoming a hotbed of vice and crime.

Shortly after his inauguration, Taylor sent a representative westward to encourage California officials to apply immediately for statehood. Taylor was well aware that the authority to admit new states belonged to Congress rather than the president. But since California already possessed all the requirements for statehood, the old soldier saw no reason to dilly-dally. With his encouragement, a California Constitutional Convention was held in September, and by early October its delegates had unanimously voted to seek admission to the Union as a free state. Taylor was delighted, and planned to offer the same deal for immediate statehood to the equally slaveless New Mexico region.

In his first annual address to Congress in early December 1849, Taylor made his intentions clear. The speech—read, as was customary, by a clerk instead of the president—was rambling. But when it came to the question of the western territories, it was unequivocal. "Compelled by the necessity of their [chaotic] political condition," Taylor declared, Californians "will shortly apply for the admission into the Union as a sovereign State." He recommended their petition "to the favorable consideration of Congress."[4] Members of both Houses knew that the constitution ratified by the California Convention prohibited slavery, and that Taylor's endorsement meant that California—and, later, New Mexico—would become free states. Only a year before, President Polk had recommended extending the Missouri Compromise line to the Pacific coast, thereby opening up much of the Mexican War–acquired territory to slavery. Now President Taylor had made an end run around both that possibility and the Wilmot Proviso proposal. His loyalty to the nation had outweighed any sectional ones he might have had, sorely disappointing advocates of the Missouri Line solution as well as champions of the Wilmot Proviso.

The 31st Congress convened the same week that Taylor's annual address was read. Senators and representatives alike already knew what he was going to say about California, and the atmosphere in both chambers was charged. The House in particular was primed for a fight over the California issue, although the battle lines were complex and sometimes difficult to discern.

Although the Whigs had done well in the 1846 midterm elections and taken the presidency two years later, they lost the House in 1848. In the 31st Congress, Democrats held a slim majority, with 112 of them to 105 Whigs. Moreover, southern representatives in both parties held more seats than northern ones. But because of the tiny margin between Democrat and Whig seats, the balance of power in the House was held by 13 Free Soil Party members. The Whigs were the obvious party for Free Soilers to align with when it came to congressional votes. But they had grown impatient with what they saw as Whiggish waffling on slavery extension, and they determined to use their voting power to push Whigs toward a stronger stand. The first contest in which they stretched their muscles was the election of a Speaker of the House.

Typically, electing a Speaker was a relatively routine affair. But this time things were different. The Whigs put forward Massachusetts congressman Robert Winthrop, who had ably served as Speaker in the previous congress. The Democrats countered with Howell Cobb, one of the wealthiest slave owners in Georgia but a staunch Unionist. A successful candidate needed 111 votes. On the first ballot, both Winthrop and Howell fell short, mainly because the Free Soilers to a man voted for David Wilmot. Ballots on the next day were equally inconclusive, and the acrimonious rivalry that descended on the House in the days following Taylor's presidential recommendation of immediate statehood for California only complicated the process of deciding on a Speaker.

One especially indignant representative was Robert Toombs. Rising to his full height and striking a classically rhetorical pose, he issued a warning to northern members of the House as well as to the president. "I avow before this House and country," he shouted, "and in the presence of the living God, that if by your legislation you seek to drive us from the territories of California and New Mexico . . . and to abolish slavery in the District of Columbia, thereby attempting to fix a national degradation upon the States of this confederacy, *I am for disunion*." In the midst of the ensuing shouts of censor or approval, Alexander Stephens, Toombs's fellow Georgian, leapt to his feet. "I tell this House that every word uttered by my colleague meets my hearty response," he shouted in his reedy voice. He would rather die, he vowed, than see "the South submit for one instant to degradation."[5] Toombs and Stephens were as different in manner, temperament, and physique as two men could possibly be. Toombs was acerbic, loud, histrionic, and bearish; Stephens small, frail, retiring, and shrill. But when they rose to speak on the House floor in mid-December 1848, they shared the conviction that the South was in grave danger of losing political and literal ground to the North.

In the meantime, day after day of debate and vote after vote failed to break the deadlock over who would be the next Speaker of the House. The list of possible candidates steadily grew; by the time the 41st ballot was reached, at least 30 different congressmen had been nominated. Tempers grew progressively frayed as the struggle continued. Increasingly heated insults were exchanged between legislators, challenges to duels were indignantly offered, and at one particularly heated moment, a fistfight broke out on the floor between several fed-up congressmen. Finally, a tired representative from Tennessee who hoped to draw the interminable process to an end proposed that the body accept a simple plurality rather than a majority. His proposal was seized upon by his equally weary colleagues, and on the 63rd ballot Cobb defeated Winthrop by a mere three votes. The House finally had a Speaker, and he was a southern Democrat.

But the end of the tussle for the speakership didn't calm down Congress. Calhoun and like-minded southern colleagues kept the fire burning by angrily iterating Toombs's and Stephens's threats of disunion, and President Taylor didn't help matters by equally blustery vows to hang traitorous secessionists, in almost the same language that fellow military man Andrew Jackson had used nearly 20 years earlier during the Nullification Crisis. Fire-eaters, so named because of their zeal in defending southern rights, were still a minority among southern congressmen, and most of them were not yet absolutely committed to secession. That would take a few more years. But they were noisy, and their influence was felt. Back in October 1848, for example, bipartisan southerners had convened in Jackson, Mississippi, to plan a convention for the following June, to be held in Nashville, in which they hoped the South would take a united stand against the Wilmot Proviso or any other attempt on the part of the federal government to interfere with the expansion of slavery. Should the North remain insensible to the justice of the South's position, a dissolving of the partnership between them would be the only option left. Mississippi's state legislature enthusiastically appropriated $20,000 to fund the upcoming convention.

Nor were southern congressmen and their constituents the only ones dismayed and angry at the growing sectional rift over California. Northerners, too, were apprehensive. One of them, New Yorker Philip Hone, expressed the anxiety felt by tens of thousands. "Madness rules the hour," he wrote. "Faction, personal recrimination, and denunciation prevail, and men for the first time in our history do not hesitate openly to threaten a dissolution of the Union."[6] Hone was mistaken; disunion had been threatened before, by both South and North, and almost always over slavery. But the threat had never been as palpable as it was in 1850.

CLAY TO THE RESCUE

During the ruckus over electing a Speaker, Henry Clay, still smarting from his party's refusal to nominate him for president in the last election, had noted that "there is no organization in the House, which is in a very curious state." His observation was deliberately understated, because Clay was actually quite alarmed at the polarization he saw taking place over the California issue. "I fear for my Country," he admitted to a friend a few days after Congress convened. "From both parties, or rather from individuals of both parties, strong expressions are made to me of hopes that I may be able to calm the raging elements."[7]

Although he wasn't sure he could pull off another great compromise like the ones of 1820 and 1833—he was, after all, 73 and most likely already suffering from the tuberculosis that would kill him two years later—he was willing to try. So he asked to be excused from regular committee assignments in the Senate in order to devote himself full time to

Henry Clay of Kentucky, founder of the Whig Party and three-time candidate for president, was known as the "Great Compromiser" for his work in engineering the Missouri Compromise and the Compromise of 1850. (Library of Congress)

the crisis at hand. Throughout the rest of December and the early weeks of January, he secluded himself to work out a comprehensive plan that would satisfy all parties enough to keep the Union together. As he later said, he "cut [himself] off from the usual enjoyments of social life"—and Clay was a man who delighted greatly in such things—to "restore the blessings of concord, harmony and peace" to Congress and the nation.[8]

At the time, Clay was widely reckoned to be one of the three greatest living American statesmen. Together with South Carolina's John Calhoun and Massachusetts's Daniel Webster—the three were frequently called the "great triumvirate"—he had guided the nation's affairs for an entire generation. Between them, they represented the three different sections of the nation—North, South, and western border states—whose interests were represented in Congress. The three men had sometimes cooperated and sometimes clashed with one another in matters of state, and Clay wished to partner with his two colleagues again to find a solution for the present crisis. But he knew that Calhoun, with whom he had worked out the Compromise Tariff deal in 1833, was too committed to the South's cause to be of help this time. So he turned instead to Webster, seeking his counsel and his support. Webster listened to what Clay had in mind, found it "great and highly patriotic," and concluded that "Providence" had made the Kentuckian "the means and the way of averting a great evil from the country."[9] Webster promised his backing when Clay was ready to present his proposal to the Senate.

On Tuesday, January 29, 1850, Clay was ready, though even he, given the political climate, must've been a bit apprehensive. He knew that both his personal reputation and the Whig Party that he had founded rested on how successful he would be in resolving the sectional crisis. Taking the floor and addressing the president of the Senate, the Great Compromiser launched a debate that would consume Congress and the nation for the next seven months. "Mr. President," he called out, "I hold in my hand a series of resolutions which I desire to submit to the consideration of this body. Taken together, in combination, they propose an amicable arrangement of all questions in controversy between the free and slave States, growing out of the subject of slavery."[10]

The eight resolutions in Clay's proposal covered all the points of contention that were ripping the nation apart. First and foremost, they dealt with the territories won in the Mexican War. California should be admitted to the Union as a free state. This was what her people desired and what they had written into their proposed constitution. When it came to the New Mexico territory, popular sovereignty, not Congress, should decide whether slavery would be prohibited or allowed. Slavery had been outlawed in the region under Mexican law. But as a U.S. territory, Clay told his fellow senators, slavery was protected by the Constitution until and unless New Mexican residents drafted a constitution that determined otherwise. At this point, Mississippi's Jefferson Davis jumped up to protest that the only thing that would satisfy the South was an extension of the Missouri line all the way to the Pacific, a surprisingly more modest demand than Calhoun had offered in his "Address to the People of the Southern States" and Davis had defended a few months earlier. Clay quite reasonably responded that the South was much better off with an option like popular sovereignty, because it left open the possibility of slavery on either side of the Missouri line. Extending the line would close off the northern sections of the territories to slavery once and for all.

So much for the first two resolutions. The third and fourth dealt with a boundary dispute between Texas and the New Mexico territory. The conflict was weighty because of the possibility of one or more new states being carved from the region. Texas, a slave state, laid claim to a huge portion of New Mexico, thus extending by thousands of square miles slavery's geographical range. If the state lost the territory, not only would the range be forfeited, but the territory could actually declare as a free state in the future. In order to settle the dispute, Clay proposed that Texas redraw its western boundary to give up the New Mexico territory, but that in exchange the federal government assume responsibility for all of Texas's debts accrued before annexation.

The fifth and sixth resolutions returned explicitly to slavery, dealing with the same question of human bondage in the District of Columbia that Lincoln had raised a year earlier. Clay proposed that while slavery should remain in the district until and unless its residents and the residents of Maryland decided otherwise, the slave trade should be abolished. It was scandalous, he said, that any slave trader could march his pitiable merchandise from the Capitol to the White House for all to see. But it would be equally shocking to wrest human property from the hands of residents who had bought and paid for it.

The final two resolutions were widely and correctly seen as attempts to mollify the South over the admission of California as a free state. Clay proposed that a stricter fugitive slave law should replace an older one written in 1793 and that it should be strictly enforced by both state and federal authorities. Moreover, he recommended that Congress go on record as relinquishing any jurisdiction to interfere with interstate slave trade. Such regulation, Clay contended, belonged exclusively to the slaveholding states themselves.

Clay freely admitted that his resolutions, although presented as a compromise that asked both sides to give a little, tilted more toward the South than the North. But he asked his northern colleagues to appreciate that the South had more at stake. Regardless of what moral judgments might be made about slavery, the peculiar institution, he argued, was vital to the South's economic well-being. On the northern side, there was "sentiment, sentiment, sentiment alone." But on the southern side, what was at stake was "property, the social fabric, life, and all that makes life desirable and happy."[11] Clay's reduction of the North's moral case against slavery to mere sentiment was, of course, a gross oversimplification. But it set the tone for looking at slavery as an exclusively political rather than ethical issue, an approach that would be adopted by future defenders of popular sovereignty.

When he sketched out his compromise, Clay knew that it would satisfy neither the southern fire-eaters on the one hand nor abolitionists on the other. His hope was that he could marshal enough support from moderates alarmed at the possibility of disunion to win the day. He was gratified to see that many of them, northerner and southerner alike, seemed sympathetic. So he felt confident when, a week after he proposed the bill, he delivered a two-day speech before the Senate defending the olive branch he offered to both North and South and hoping that the "empire of reason" would triumph over sectional passion. Then he concluded with a bit of passion himself.

> I conjure gentlemen—whether from the South or the North, by all they hold dear in this world—by all their love of liberty—by all their veneration for their ancestors—by all their regard for posterity—by all their gratitude to Him who has bestowed upon them such unnumbered blessings—by all the duties which they owe to mankind, and all the duties they owe to themselves—by all these considerations I implore them to pause—at the edge of the precipice, before the fearful and disastrous leap is taken in the yawning abyss below, which will inevitably lead to certain and irretrievable destruction.[12]

But one person who remained unmoved by Clay's appeal was his fellow Whig, President Taylor. The old general, used to having his orders obeyed by subordinates, had expected his plan for immediate statehood to be endorsed by Clay and Webster, if not out of conviction then out of party discipline. Instead, the one introduced a much more complicated proposal, and the other supported it. Taylor felt that he had been denied the leadership role that was rightfully his, and was hurt and angry. From the moment Clay offered his compromise to the day of his death five months later, the president actively opposed it. Taylor wanted the issue of California decided by itself, and believed that Clay's eight resolutions only muddied the water. But Clay feared that admitting California in the absence of his other resolutions would so alienate the South that the possibility of any kind of Union-saving compromise would vanish.

Clay worked hard to garner both legislative and public support for his resolutions. He urged his followers to organize public rallies in support of the compromise, and each time he received word of one he made sure that his fellow senators heard about it too. His hope, of course, was to put pressure on legislators by convincing them that public fears of disunion demanded action on their part and a broadening of their loyalty from section to nation. For himself, as he angrily said at one point on the floor of the Senate when challenged by a colleague, "I know no foes, no enemies, no opponents, either at the North or at the South. I consider us all as one family, all as friends, all as brethren. I consider us all as united in one common destiny."[13] His clear message to congressmen like Calhoun, Toombs, and Stephens was that their sectional loyalties ought not to trump fidelity to the nation as a whole.

THREE LANDMARK SPEECHES

Clay suspected that he could expect no support from John Calhoun, and he was right. The fiery defender of states' rights was just as worried as his colleague from Kentucky that the nation was facing a crisis. But he was convinced that responsibility for the mess lay at the North's doorstep, and that consequently the burden of fixing it was also the North's.

On March 4, nearly two months into the congressional debate on Clay's resolutions, an alarmingly feeble Calhoun was helped into the Senate chamber by a colleague. He was desperately ill—he would die, in fact, before the end of the month—but had prepared a final speech for his fellow legislators and the American people. Too weak to stand and deliver his own speech, he asked Virginia senator James Mason to read it for him.

Calhoun charged (through Mason) that the "long continued agitation of the slave question on the part of the North" was the sole cause of "the almost universal discontent" that pervaded the southern states.[14] The founders recognized that to keep the Union intact, a geographical equilibrium of representation was essential. But since then, every territorial acquisition of the federal government had been legislatively skewed in favor of the North (not true, by the way) and contrary to the interests of the South. The same familiar pattern was evident in the current dispute over the fate of the California and New Mexico territories.

The injustices endured by the South, Calhoun continued, had already strained political and cultural cords binding North and South—several religious denominations, for example, had already split over slavery—and if things continued in this way, the only thing that would be left to hold the Union together would be force exerted by a despotic federal government.

But Calhoun wasn't totally hopeless. The Union could be preserved, he insisted, if the South received the justice that was her due. Only then could southern states "remain in the Union consistently with their honor and their safety." The North must grant the South equal access to all present and future territorial acquisitions, and must enact a constitutional amendment that would "restore to the South the power she once possessed of protecting herself."[15] It wasn't clear what Calhoun meant by this last point, but he might have had in mind something along the lines of a proposal defended in his *Discourse on the Constitution*. In that posthumously published work, he suggested a constitutional amendment that mandated two chief executives, one from each section of the nation and each possessing veto power. It was an absurd idea, but it showed just how distrustful of the North Calhoun had become.

To anyone familiar with Calhoun's fundamental position—and what American born in the previous 30 years was not?—none of this was new. But the circumstance of their delivery made Calhoun's words especially poignant. They were a dying man's final warning and recommendation to his nation, and as such carried weight, even if the message they conveyed had been heard many times before. Henry Clay, to whom Calhoun's speech was directed, knew that even though his southern colleague's remarks called for a vigorous rebuttal, the response had to be respectful. Daniel Webster, the greatest orator of his day, was just the man for the job.

Less than a week after the dying South Carolinian vicariously delivered his final speech before the Senate, Webster stood to defend Clay's proposals in what became known as the "Seventh of March Speech," perhaps the best-known one of his entire career. Calhoun's earlier speech had a peevishly aggrieved tone, and it threw down a take-it-or-leave-it ultimatum, hardly a recipe for compromise. Webster's, on the other hand, was one that eloquently embraced the importance above all else of preserving the Union, and thus the need for each sectional rival adopting a certain flexibility in its demands. His famous opening words made clear where his own loyalties lay. "Mr. President," he began, "I wish to speak today, not as a Massachusetts man, not as a northern man, but as an American, and a member of the Senate of the United States." It was in that capacity, Webster continued, that "I speak today for the preservation of the Union."[16] Webster, like Clay before him, made it crystal clear that his first loyalty was to the Union, and his second to his state.

Calhoun had laid sole responsibility for the present crisis upon the North. Webster countered that there was blame enough to go around. The North, he acknowledged, had unjustifiably aggrieved the South and disregarded the Constitution by not respecting the slave owner's right to human property. Fugitive slaves absconding to the North were often given shelter and secreted away from both private slave catchers and officers of the law. This, Webster conceded, was wrong. But the South for its part had erred in the opposite direction by abandoning the founders' under-standing of slavery as a necessary evil. Now southerners extolled it as a moral necessity and favorably contrasted it with free labor in the North. This, too, Webster said, was wrong.

A longstanding and progressive history of mutual distrust between North and South had unnecessarily escalated the present disagreement about the status of California and New Mexico into a threat to the nation's unity. As a Whig, said Webster, he personally and politically favored a pol-icy of developing already-held territory rather than grasping for additional land. But now that the United States possessed the huge geographical con-cession wrested from Mexico, the wisest course of action would be to allow popular sovereignty to decide the issue of slavery in it. The South shouldn't be insulted by a northern insistence on prohibiting slavery in California and New Mexico. Nor should the North fear slavery taking much of a foothold there. Climate and geography precluded the cultiva-tion of crops such as cotton, tobacco, or rice that required intensive slave labor.

It was for this bit of land that firebrands on either side of the slavery issue were willing to break apart the Union. They pretend, said Webster, that North and South can separate without violence. Nonsense. "Peace-able secession! ... There can be no such thing as a peaceable secession. Peaceable secession is an utter impossibility." It was also a "moral impos-sibility." The very word "secession" stank in his nostrils. "I dislike it— I have an utter disgust for it, I would rather hear of natural blasts and mildews, war, pestilence, and famine, than to hear gentlemen talk of secession." To avoid it, men of good will should be willing to compromise with one another to preserve for future generations a government "popular in its form, representative in its character, founded on principles of equality, and calculated, we hope, to last forever."[17]

Webster's speech was riveting, delivered with all the oratorical skill that the silver-tongued senator from Massachusetts could muster. Two hundred thousand copies of it were printed and eagerly read, and newspapers in both the North and the South praised it. But Northern abolitionists and abolition sympathizers felt betrayed by Webster's championship of popular sovereignty and savaged him for what they saw as his betrayal of blacks. So it was no surprise when, four days after Webster's speech, one of the Senate's strongest foes of slavery, New York's William Seward, stood before his colleagues to reply to it. Seward was as unbending in his attack on slavery as Calhoun had been in defending it. As a consequence, neither man had any use for Clay's eight resolutions or Webster's defense of them.

Seward may have been a freshman in the Senate, having taken his seat only at the commencement of the 31st Congress, but he was an experienced two-term governor of New York with a long record of opposition to slavery as well as to racial prejudice—not a common pairing even among abolitionists. He had the reputation of being a radical, and was regarded as something of a loose cannon on the slavery issue even by many of his fellow Whigs. Still, they were unprepared for the startling thesis he defended in the Senate on March 11.

Unlike Webster, Seward was an uninspiring orator. He read his speech from a written text, something frowned upon at the time, and he spoke in a monotone that ignored the histrionic inflections expected of mid-19th-century orators. But his argument was anything but monotonous, and it conveyed all the passion with none of the melodrama of Webster's remarks. Seward declared himself absolutely opposed to all legislative compromises, including Clay's, because they necessarily sacrificed integrity for the sake of political expediency. "They involve the surrender of the exercise of judgment and conscience." But even if he could overcome his "repugnance" about compromise in general, the one offered to the Senate by Clay was forever unacceptable because it asked legislators to accept slavery and thereby violate "a higher law than the Constitution," a natural law established by God, which guarantees happiness as every person's right, regardless of his or her skin color. Slavery subverts the natural moral order, and consequently is an institution that directly displeases the Creator. In a nation that claimed to venerate God, slavery could be nothing less than a sin, and to compromise on sin is itself a sin.[18]

That was Seward's philosophical argument against both slavery and compromise with slavery's defenders. His political argument was just as forceful. The intent of the constitutional framers, he asserted, was that states pledged themselves to abide by the will of the majority of citizens in the *entire* nation. The United States, in other words, was an organic whole, not the flimsily connected bundle of individual regions envisioned by Calhounites. Consequently, no state could legitimately secede simply because it disagreed with the national consensus, especially if the consensus also upheld the natural moral order. So the South had neither a philosophical justification for slavery nor a political one for secession.

As a freshman senator from New York and zealous opponent of slavery, William Seward, Lincoln's future secretary of state, denounced Clay's proposed 1850 Compromise as violating a "higher law" against slavery. (Perry-Castaneda Library)

Consequently, declared Seward, he intended to vote for the admission of California, complete with its constitution prohibiting slavery, "without conditions, without qualifications, and without compromise."

This was President Taylor's position, although the chief executive didn't agree with Seward's moral condemnation of slavery, and many in Congress suspected that Seward was driven by ambition to serve as the president's mouthpiece. But they were mistaken. Taylor was horrified by the freshman senator's speech and fussed that the "fine mess" stirred up by "Governor Seward" had to be "disclaimed at once, authoritatively and decidedly."[19] Seward's fine mess would come back to haunt him 10 years later when leaders of the new political party he had helped launch decided he was too radical to serve as their presidential candidate and instead threw their weight behind Abraham Lincoln. The irony is that Lincoln, while expressing himself more moderately than Seward, was sympathetic to both of the New Yorker's arguments against slavery.

THE OMNIBUS

Seward wasn't the only legislator who advocated separating the issue of California's statehood from Clay's other resolutions. Ohio senator Salmon Chase and an up-and-comer, Illinois senator Stephen Douglas, did as well. Chase wanted California immediately admitted as a free state because of his longstanding opposition to slavery. But Douglas was a pragmatist. He thought the only way to break the impasse into which the debate had fallen in the Senate was to consider the California issue in isolation from the others.

But Mississippi senator Henry Foote had an altogether different opinion. Clay had offered his eight resolutions as related but separate items, never intending them to be voted up or down as a single package. But Foote recommended that Clay glue the resolutions together into a giant "omnibus" bill, named after a newfangled contraption that carried passengers and which later generations would shorten to "bus." Clay was reluctant to do so, recognizing all too well that this all-or-nothing strategy could be disastrous. But he eventually agreed, concluding that a presidential veto for the entire package was less likely than a resentful Taylor's picking off the resolutions one by one. So on April 8, Clay asked his colleagues to consider the resolutions as a whole. Knowing that no one would be completely satisfied by everything in the package, he announced: "You may vote against it if you please in toto, because of the bad there is in it, or you may vote for it because you approve of the greater amount of good there is in it."[20] Obviously, he hoped for the second.

Ten days later, Clay was overwhelmingly elected chair of an ad hoc committee, the Committee of Thirteen, charged with examining his resolutions and making an omnibus recommendation to the Senate. Membership included six Whigs and six Democrats. They were a carefully considered cross-section of political and sectional loyalties: southern and border state Whigs, conservative and liberal northern Democrats. In working with them, Clay hoped to solidify support for his resolutions by involving representatives from all factions in the drafting of a new bill. But one senator, Stephen Douglas, declined to serve on the committee. He was convinced that bundling Clay's resolutions into a single package to be voted up or down was a bad tactical move. "By combining the measures into one Bill the Committee [of Thirteen] united the opponents of each measure instead of securing the friends of each."[21] Circumstances would prove him right.

Obstreperous Missouri senator Thomas Hart Benton, fortunately for the committee, also wasn't appointed. In fact, this formidable political lion, who had fought many battles during his three decades in the Senate, objected at once to the omnibus strategy. He too wanted the California question decided separately, and the language he used to make his point was so heated that tempers flared up once more on the Senate floor. When Senator Foote clashed verbal swords with him at one point, Benton, in a blind fury, leapt from his seat and made straight for him. Foote, terrified, pulled a cocked and loaded pistol from his coat and pointed it as his colleague from Missouri. A red-faced Benton, who had been grabbed and held back by another senator, screamed, "Let the assassin fire! A pistol has been brought here to assassinate me!"[22] Another senator wrenched the gun away from Foote, who was obviously grateful for the intervention, and the incident was over. But it was a clear sign that the longer the debate over Clay's resolutions continued, the more likely Congress was to unravel. After his undignified altercation with Foote, Benton launched an anti-Clay campaign on the Senate floor, attacking the Kentuckian at every opportunity and advocating nonstop for the admission of California. Albeit for different reasons, Jefferson Davis also came out heavily against

Clay's omnibus, sticking to his proposal, which by this time had become an *idée fixe*, to extend the Missouri Compromise line to the Pacific Ocean. But in response to them and their supporters, Clay repeated what he'd already said many times: the nation's present crisis was too complex to be remedied by a single, simplistic fix. That's why the give-and-take of compromise, with all parties bending a bit to work out the best solution possible, even if the best solution completely satisfied no one, was necessary.

The Committee of Thirteen met for three weeks, after which Clay retreated to a friend's home to draft its final recommendation to the Senate. It wasn't all that different from Clay's original resolutions. California was to be admitted as a free state. New Mexico and Utah, carved out of the New Mexico cession, were to be organized as formal U.S. territories, with the question of slavery in them determined later by popular sovereignty. Texas would be compensated out of the federal coffer for relinquishing its claim on New Mexico land. The most significant change in the new proposal had to do with the Fugitive Slave Law. As amended by the committee, slave owners claiming runaways now would have to produce documentation proving that the alleged fugitive belonged to them, and fugitives had to be granted trials by jury if they requested them. These amendments were intended to make the law a bit easier for the North to swallow without provoking the South. Just to make sure that southern legislators could live with the changes, the amendments also stipulated that the trial by jury had to be held in the state from which the slave had fled, not the state that offered refuge.

The Senate rumbled on for another six weeks debating the omnibus. Amendment after amendment was offered by various legislators in an effort to make the package more palatable. Diehard opponents from any number of perspectives—men like Missouri Compromise line-extending Jefferson Davis, California-championing Thomas Hart Benton, senators sympathetic to abolition and senators who preached the morality of slavery, not to mention President Taylor—remained stubbornly opposed to it. As the intensity of their objections grew, so did Clay's responses, especially against the president. Even Webster, who had remained Clay's staunch ally throughout the debate, worried that his public sparring with the chief executive was going too far and risking a split in the party.

Toward the end of July, an exhausted Clay mustered enough energy to make a final passionate, three-hour long appeal on the floor of the Senate for his omnibus bill. He castigated diehards on either side who refused to compromise because of misplaced loyalty to principles they considered intractable. He mocked southern threats of secession and chastised abolitionists for what he saw as their intemperate addiction to troublemaking, accusing them of living to stir up contention. He warned his senatorial colleagues that the compromise was overwhelmingly endorsed by the majority of Americans—a claim somewhat exaggerated—and he reminded them that even though the Compromise of 1820 had been excoriated during the congressional debate, there was rejoicing in the land when it was signed into law. He, for one, was glad that his eight resolutions had been gathered together into an omnibus, because they were bipartisan and bisectional, drafted by a committee of legislators who had put aside some of their differences in order to arrive at an agreement that benefited the country. Make no mistake about it, said Clay. The omnibus is well named, because it is the vehicle that will carry the nation into a future that is free, once and for all, of threats of disunity.

As a final rebuke to congressional criers of disunion, Clay made it clear once and for all where he stood. Attached by cords of loyalty and affection as he was to his beloved state of Kentucky, his allegiance to it was nonetheless "subordinate" to his "permanent allegiance to the whole Union." Should Kentucky ever secede, he would never "engage with her in such a cause." But he was confident that Kentucky would never show such disloyalty to the Union. In fact, he was certain that if any other state hoisted the flag of rebellion, "thousands, tens of thousands of Kentuckians would flock to the standard of their country to dissipate and suppress the rebellion."[23] Although he didn't actually say as much, more than one of his colleagues in the Senate must have guessed that the grand old man, if at all humanly possible, would have been in the front ranks of those mustering to put down secessionist revolt.

Clay's speech was a remarkable performance for a man who had recently turned 73 and was in ill health. But he was buoyed by a certain degree of optimism. Just a few weeks earlier he had thought the prospect for his bill bleak. "The Administration, the Abolitionists, the Ultra Southern men, and the timid Whigs of the North are all combined against it," he ruefully noted. "Against such a combination, it will be wonderful if it should succeed."[24] But as the time for a vote approached, he grew more confident that his months of behind-the-scenes lobbying and public verbal jousting had done the trick. He was also heartened by the fact that the Calhoun-inspired convention of secession-minded delegates from slave states that had just met in Nashville had lost much of the previous year's enthusiasm for disunion. The delegates, no longer fired up for secession, rallied behind Jefferson Davis's proposal to extend the Missouri line, a much more moderate outcome than Clay had anticipated. Finally, President Taylor's enmity ended when he became the second American head of state to die in office. He had taken ill after attending a Fourth of July rally, succumbed less than a week later, and was succeeded by Vice President Millard Fillmore. In a single stroke of fate, the president who opposed Clay's compromise was replaced by one who, while generally sympathetic to the South, supported the omnibus as a way out of the sectional crisis. "My relations with the new Chief are intimate and confidential," a relieved Clay wrote to his son.[25] Things looked promising.

But few things in life, and fewer still in politics, are certain. Right before the Senate was scheduled to vote on July 31, a minor disagreement over boundary issues between Texas and New Mexico snowballed into a series of sectional scuffles that picked the package apart, piece by piece. When the vote was taken, the omnibus was defeated. Northern Democrats generally approved of the bill, while southern ones were mixed. Most of Clay's fellow Whigs voted against it, preferring that slavery be totally excluded from all lands won in the Mexican War. The exceptions were border state Whigs, who especially liked the Fugitive Slave Law resolution because slaves from their regions were the most likely to run. "The Omnibus is smashed—wheels, axils [sic] and body," Horace Greeley wrote in his *New York Tribune*.[26]

Opponents of Clay's compromise could scarcely contain their delight at its defeat. Seward literally pranced around the Senate chamber, and Benton joyfully boasted that he had single-handedly "smashed the omnibus to atoms."[27] Clay was crushed. He vowed that he would continue the fight by forsaking the omnibus format and presenting the resolutions separately and distinctly, as he had done originally. But he was physically and emotionally exhausted, and knew that the battle would have to be taken up by someone with more strength and fewer years. He left Washington for Newport, Rhode Island, shortly after the vote to recoup his strength and lick his wounds. In the same editorial that announced the wreck of the omnibus, newspaperman Greeley noted that he had seen its "gallant driver" depart the district, but not before "having done all that man could do to retrieve, or rather to avert the disaster." There was nothing to be done now, Greeley sadly concluded, "but to grin and bear it."[28]

DOUGLAS PICKS UP THE PIECES

Ironically, Clay's removal of himself from the inner workings of the Senate seemed to be exactly what was needed for his resolutions finally to win congressional approval. Stephen Douglas was just one of many who recognized that the Great Compromiser was the chief obstacle standing in the way of his own compromise. "If Mr. Clay's name had not been associated with the bills," he said, "they would have passed long ago. The [Taylor] administration were jealous of him & hated him & some democrats were weak enough to fear that the success of the bill would make him President."[29] But with Clay gone, the ground was cleared for another attempt.

The dust from Clay's departing coach had barely settled before Douglas began picking up the pieces of the smashed omnibus and caucusing with his colleagues to sound out just how far they would back his salvage work. Nicknamed the Little Giant because of his short height but enormous force of personality, Douglas was well suited for the task he took on. A New England native who had followed the nation's westward expansion, he represented a new generation of statesmen—the "Young Americans," as they called themselves—who approached politics as hardheaded and energetic pragmatists. He eventually settled in Illinois, where he practiced law and sat on the state's supreme court for a few months (ever after he was frequently referred to as "Judge" Douglas) before winning election to the House of Representatives and then, in 1847, to the Senate. His capacity for work was as prodigious as his political ambitions. Douglas wanted to be president one day, and he felt confident that rescuing Clay's resolutions would take him a step or two closer to achieving that goal.

At the time of the compromise debate, Douglas chaired the powerful Committee on Territories, a role that put him in a position to wield promises or threats, whichever proved more effective in swaying his colleagues. In the space of just one week, he separated and slightly amended Clay's resolutions and then put together coalitions of Democrats and Whigs that got each one through the Senate. Voted on as a package, the resolutions generated too much sectional controversy to receive the necessary votes. But senators from different parties and different sections could agree with one another long enough to pass them one by one. Northern Democrats coalesced with northern and border state Whigs to pass the resolution to admit California as a free state, to ban the slave trade in the District of Columbia, to settle the border dispute between Texas and New Mexico —the issue that had sunk the omnibus bill—by essentially offering Texas a $10 million bribe, and to leave slavery in New Mexico and Utah to popular sovereignty. Both Democrats and Whigs from the South endorsed strengthening the Fugitive Slave Law. Even though many northern Whigs opposed it, Fillmore pulled political strings to persuade enough of them to abstain from voting, and Douglas wheeled-and-dealed enough northern Democrats to vote favorably, for the resolution to pass. It took the House another month of wrangling before the five bills into which Douglas had refashioned Clay's original eight were approved.

By the end of September, the congressional debate was over and President Fillmore had signed each of them into law, although he had hesitated for two days before putting his signature on the Fugitive Slave Law. The crisis that had threatened to sever the Union along sectional lines, and which had kept the Senate in its longest continuous session ever (304 days), had passed. But what also vanished, at least for a few years, was a strong two-party system, because the crisis, not to mention the public squabbling between Clay and Taylor, the nation's two leading Whigs, splintered the Whig Party even more than the 1848 departure of Conscience Whigs had done. Democrats managed to retain more cohesion, but cracks within their party loyalty had also appeared during the debate. They would widen in the next decade until they literally fragmented the party in the 1860 presidential election and kept its members out of the White House for a generation afterwards. The Compromise of 1850 may have saved the Union, but it changed the political landscape. For the rest of the decade, geographical section more than political partisanship would determine loyalties and allegiances.

A FINAL SETTLEMENT?

On December 2, just two months after the Compromise of 1850 had been struck, Millard Fillmore gave his first annual address to Congress. After

Massachusetts senator Daniel Webster delivers his famous Seventh of March speech during congressional debate about the Compromise of 1850. He spoke "not as a Massachusetts man, not as a northern man, but as an American." It was Webster's finest hour. (Library of Congress)

assuring the assembled legislators that he would "shrink from no responsibility" in his discharge of the duties "solemnly imposed" on him by the Constitution—an oblique reference to the newly enacted Fugitive Slave Law—he expressly turned to the compromise. It represented, he stated, "a settlement in principle and substance—a final settlement of the dangerous and exciting" issue of slavery extension that had nearly torn the country asunder. The legislation, he predicted, was "final and irrevocable." It had saved the nation "from the wide and boundless agitation" that had engulfed it for several years.[30]

Fillmore wanted nothing more than to displace slavery as the front-and-center national issue it had become and return it to the backbench of local and state politics. It was too dangerously disruptive to be allowed to remain in the public eye. The last few years had demonstrated that clearly. So the president's hope was that the Compromise of 1850 had both saved the nation and once and for all removed the danger of future slavery-generated crises. Clay had the same wish. As he told the Kentucky state legislature during a triumphal return to his home state in October, he hoped that his compromise had "pacif[ied], tranquillize[d], and harmonize[d] the country."[31]

A great many Americans shared Fillmore's and Clay's hope. They had been badly frightened by the possibility of disunion, and the expression of their fears in rallies, pamphlets, petitions, and editorials had doubtlessly influenced final congressional approval of Clay's resolutions. Additionally, sheer weariness with the slavery issue on the part of both legislators and private citizens had also made resolution of the crisis and a return to what was perceived as normalcy a welcome reprieve.

But what most Americans failed to see in their jubilancy over the resolution of the immediate crisis was that the slavery debate *was* the new normalcy. Even though the Compromise of 1850 seemed to put the matter to rest, events throughout the decade clearly suggested otherwise. Glimmers of dark clouds were already observable even as Fillmore declared a final settlement to the sectional debate over the extension of slavery. As Stephen Douglas knew, both free soilers and southern disunionists remained dissatisfied with the compromise, and even though they were in the minority, they had loud voices. Charles Francis Adams, the most recent star in an illustrious and ardently abolitionist American family, slammed its Fugitive Slave Law as "the consummation of the iniquities of this most disgraceful session of Congress."[32] Abolitionist William Lloyd Garrison blasted it in his *The Liberator*, accusing Webster and other northern Whigs of "bending the knee" to the Slave Power,[33] while other abolitionists jeeringly called Fillmore the "tool and lickspittle" of the South.[34] And William Seward had already made his views known in his incendiary "Higher Law" speech before the Senate in March 1850.

Hardcore disunionists were also dissatisfied, even though the South was widely perceived as having edged out the North under the terms of the Compromise. Georgian Herschel Johnson sneered that it was "a fecund box of nauseous nostrums," and the editor of one of the leading newspapers in his state announced in an over-the-top way that he "despised the Union and the North" as much as he despised hell.[35] Mississippi governor John Quitman tried to use the Compromise as a pretext for secession, and South Carolina's James Hammond reckoned that sentiment against the new law was so prevalent in his state that "in a few years time it will predominate so far that we will be sustained in open secession against the Union."[36]

Jefferson Davis, who had doggedly resisted the Compromise from the very start, primarily because of its admission of California as a free state—when the second Senate vote came up, the only part of the bill he voted for was the Fugitive Slave Law—icily noted that Stephen Douglas had more reason than any other senator to be proud of the Compromise. He didn't mean it as a compliment.[37]

After the Senate rejected the omnibus version of his bill and Clay fled the district for some badly needed rest and recuperation, he spoke on his way northwards at an impromptu rally in Philadelphia. The crowd that came out to cheer him was so thick that they blocked the route of a real omnibus and brought it to a halt. Despite his recent disappointment, Clay couldn't resist cracking a joke. "That omnibus is like the omnibus I left at Washington," he said. "It didn't get through."[38]

In ways that neither he nor many other Americans could predict, his quip was prophetic. Although his Compromise finally won congressional approval to become the law of the land, it didn't "get through" in the more fundamental sense of offering a long-term solution to the crisis that prompted it in the first place. It was a false peace. James Hammond, and not Henry Clay, got it right. "I see clearly," wrote the South Carolinian, "that the true crisis is not yet, and that he who husbands his strength now can expend it to much more effect a few years hence."[39]

NOTES

The chapter epigraph from Clay is from the *Congressional Globe*, 31st Congress, 1st sess., 660. The chapter epigraph from Davis is from the *Congressional Globe*, 31st Congress, 1st sess., Appendix, 1830.

1. Roy P. Basler (ed.), *The Collected Works of Abraham Lincoln* (New Brunswick, NJ: Rutgers University Press, 1953), II:22. Hereafter referred to as CW.

2. John C. Calhoun, "Address to the People of the South," in Richard K. Cralle (ed.), *The Works of John C. Calhoun: Reports and Public Letters* (New York: D. Appleton, 1864), 312.

3. Allan Nevins, *Ordeal of the Union: Fruits of Manifest Destiny* (New York: Charles Scribner's Sons, 1947), 229.

4. John S. D. Eisenhower, *Zachary Taylor* (New York: Henry Holt, 2008), 106.

5. *Congressional Globe*, 31st Congress, 2nd sess., 28.

6. Allan Nevins (ed.), *The Diary of Philip Hone, 1828–1851* (New York: Dodd, Mead, 1927), 2:880.

7. Fergus M. Bordewich, *America's Great Debate: Henry Clay, Stephen A. Douglas, and the Compromise That Preserved the Union* (New York: Simon & Schuster, 2012), 108, 107.

8. Robert V. Remini, *At the Edge of the Precipice: Henry Clay and the Compromise That Saved the Union* (New York: Basic Books, 2010), 67–68.

9. George Ticknor Curtis, *Life of Daniel Webster* (New York: D. Appleton, 1870), II:397–98.

10. *Congressional Globe*, 31st Congress, 1st sess., 244.

11. Ibid., 246.

12. Ibid., Appendix, 115, 127.

13. *Congressional Globe*, 31st Congress, 1st sess., 405.

14. Ibid., 451.

15. Ibid., 455.

16. Ibid., 476.

17. Ibid., 482, 483.

18. Ibid., Appendix, 262.

19. Remini, *At the Edge of the Precipice*, 118.

20. Ibid., 119.

21. Ibid., 141.

22. Ibid., 121.

23. *Congressional Globe*, 31st Congress, 1st sess., Appendix, 1415.

24. Letter to Thomas Hart Clay (May 31, 1850) in Melba Porta Hay (ed.), *The Papers of Henry Clay* (Lexington: University of Kentucky Press, 1991), 10:736.

25. Letter to Henry Clay (July 18, 1850), in *Papers of Henry Clay*, 10:767.

26. *New York Tribune*, August 2, 1850.

27. *National Intelligencer*, August 1, 1850.

28. *New York Tribune*, August 2, 1850.

29. Remini, *At the Edge of the Precipice*, 154.

30. James Daniel Richardson (ed.), *A Compilation of the Messages and Papers of the Presidents* (Washington, D.C.: Bureau of National Literature and Art, 2007), 5:80, 93.

31. Bordewich, *America's Great Debate*, 358.

32. Holman Hamilton, *Prologue to Conflict: The Crisis and Compromise of 1850* (Lexington: University Press of Kentucky, 2005), 167.

33. *The Liberator*, March 15, 1850.

34. Bordewich, *America's Great Debate*, 359.

35. Thomas E. Schott, *Alexander H. Stephens of Georgia: A Biography* (Baton Rouge: Louisiana State University Press, 1988), 126.

36. Carol Bleser (ed.), *Secret and Sacred: The Diaries of James Henry Hammond, a Southern Slaveholder* (New York: Oxford University Press, 1988), 206.

37. *Congressional Globe*, 31st Congress, 1st sess., Appendix, 1830.

38. Remini, *At the Edge of the Precipice*, 143.

39. Bleser, *Secret and Sacred*, 205.

CHAPTER 3

THE MAKING OF A PERFECT STORM: THE 1854 KANSAS-NEBRASKA ACT

I know it will raise a hell of a storm.

—Stephen Douglas

We arraign this bill as a gross violation of a sacred pledge; as a criminal betrayal of precious rights; as part and parcel of an atrocious plot to exclude from a vast unoccupied region immigrants from the Old World and free laborers from our own States, and convert it into a dreary region of despotism inhabited by masters and slaves.

—*Appeal of the Independent Democrats*

When Henry Clay died in June 1852, he believed that the compromise he had designed and Stephen Douglas had brokered two years earlier had saved the Union. But it was increasingly clear to Clay's admirers and foes alike that the 1850 Compromise, while it diffused an immediate crisis, did little to ameliorate the underlying ill will between North and South. Indeed, the issue of slavery, thanks in large part to the Fugitive Slave Law, was increasingly dividing the nation into two antagonistic regions, both of which fervently believed itself in the right and the other in the wrong.

After leaving Congress and returning to Illinois in 1849, Abraham Lincoln devoted himself to his law practice, content to remain active as a private citizen in local and state Whig politics. Like so many others, he hoped that the 1850 Compromise had put an end to the slavery debate.

Democratic senator from Illinois Stephen Douglas was the architect of the 1854 Kansas-Nebraska Act. Opposition to its doctrine of "popular sovereignty" brought Abraham Lincoln out of political retirement, prompted violence in Kansas, inspired the formation of the Republican Party, and edged the nation closer to civil war. (Library of Congress)

Although he morally disapproved of the peculiar institution and opposed its extension, he didn't think that there was any constitutional way to end it where it already existed. In a public eulogy for Clay delivered a week after the statesman's death, Lincoln excoriated abolitionists who would "shiver into fragments the Union" in order to end slavery as well as Calhounites who "for the sake of perpetuating slavery, are beginning to assail and to ridicule the white man's charter of freedom—the declaration that 'all men are created free and equal.'" But even though Lincoln genuinely believed that abolitionism was dangerous, he believed that the graver threat to the nation was the South's "political eccentricities and heresies." "Pharaoh's country was cursed with plagues," Lincoln reminded his audience, sounding very much like the warning Thomas Jefferson had sounded years earlier in *Notes on Virginia*, "and his hosts were drowned in the Red Sea for striving to retain a captive people who had already served them more than four hundred years. May like disasters never befall us!"[1]

The first of the disasters Lincoln feared descended just two years later: the legislative and national furor over a new piece of legislation that overturned Henry Clay's Compromise of 1850 as well as the Missouri Compromise of 1820, a pact that most northerners regarded as solemnly binding. Illinois senator Stephen Douglas, who introduced the new bill that accelerated the rush to civil war, was perfectly correct when he predicted that it would "raise a hell of a storm."

DESTINY'S PATH

Clay died—ironically, given his perpetually frustrated desire to be president of the United States—in a national election year. There was an oddness to the campaigns of both Whig and Democratic candidates that underscored the fact that the 1850 Compromise had only put a temporary lid on the seething slavery controversy.

No provision of the 1850 Compromise was the cause of more recrimination than the Fugitive Slave Law. Abolitionists were infuriated by its harsh provisions for the capture and rendition of runaways, but even northerners who weren't particularly opposed to slavery despised the law as an infringement of their own civil liberties. It created special federal commissioners authorized to act independently of state legislation, and prescribed severe penalties for local officers of the court who refused to cooperate in the seizure of fugitives. It denied captured slaves the right of trial by jury and habeas corpus, leaving many northern whites anxiously wondering whether their rights might also be in jeopardy soon. The Fugitive Slave Law set up a system of bounties for the arrest and return of fugitives that critics correctly blasted as legalized incentives for corruption. Worst of all in the minds of many northerners, the law obliged "all good citizens" to assist in the capture of fugitives, and threatened resisters with stiff penalties. To the North, this perceived encroachment on white civil liberties was too much to swallow. When coupled with other actions such as the congressional gag on antislavery petitions or the southern-backed legislation that forbade the U.S. postal service from delivering abolitionist literature in the South, the Fugitive Slave Law seemed just another ploy on the part of the Slave Power to dominate the nation.

Nor were northern whites the only ones enraged by the new slave law. Free black communities filled the press with their own angry denunciations of it as well. Frederick Douglass insisted that the law made the whole of the United States hostile to blacks. "There is no valley so deep, no mountain so high, no plain so extensive, no spot so sacred to God and liberty in all this extended country, where the black man may not fall prey to the remorseless cupidity of his white brethren."[2] So-called vigilance committees sprang up in cities across the North to keep an eye open for slave catchers and to obstruct their efforts to seize runaways. Many state legislatures either defiantly enacted statutes that ran around the federal law's requirements or simply ignored them. Civil disobedience was in the air.

Southerners, who had insisted on the Fugitive Slave Law in the first place because they believed the North didn't respect their constitutional right to own property, were infuriated at these latest violations. The more they protested, the more energy President Fillmore put into enforcing the law. And the harder he tried, the more furious northern Whigs grew with him, even as southern ones applauded his efforts. So at the Whig convention of 1852, even though delegates from the slave states pushed hard for Fillmore's nomination, northern delegates pushed back even harder with a candidate of their own: Winfield Scott, the venerable soldier who had commanded U.S. troops in the Mexican War. The battle between the two candidates' supporters raged through 53 ballots at the Whig convention. There was something topsy-turvy about the split allegiance: southern delegates championed a northern doughface candidate, while northern ones, most of whom had opposed the Mexican War, rallied for that conflict's Virginia-born but antislavery hero. Ultimately, Scott received the nomination because a handful of moderate southern delegates, moved by either conviction or sheer weariness, switched their votes.

The Democrats, for their part, were almost as deadlocked in their process of coming up with a candidate. Most southerners favored James Buchanan. Although a Pennsylvanian, his doughface support of all things southern was well known. Northern Democrats, on the other hand, resisted his candidacy, favoring instead Stephen Douglas, the "Little Giant" who had engineered the 1850 Compromise. In a balloting battle nearly as fierce as the one fought by the Whigs in their convention, both men were finally defeated on the 49th ballot by Franklin Pierce, a dark horse from New Hampshire. Pierce was a friend to the slave states and

Democratic president Franklin Pierce (1853–1857) wanted above all to keep his party from splitting over the slavery controversy. But he fragmented both it and the nation when he signed the Kansas-Nebraska Act into law. Afterwards, sectional loyalties replaced politically partisan ones. (Library of Congress)

could be relied upon to continue Fillmore's policy of strongly enforcing the Fugitive Slave Law.

Given the split in the Whig party over selecting a presidential candidate, it was inevitable that Scott's campaign was an utter failure. After his nomination, he lost the support of most southern Whig leaders. Even Georgia's Alexander Stephens, one of the party's stalwarts, deserted Scott and threw in his lot with Democrat Pierce. On Election Day, the Whigs were soundly trounced, even though both they and the Democrats ran on promises to uphold the 1850 Compromise. Although Pierce beat his rival by less than 300,000 votes in the popular vote, he took 254 to Scott's 42 electoral votes. All the slave states except Kentucky and Tennessee went for the New England candidate. In the Lower South, the Whig Party vanished, with the vast majority of its members hastening to the Democrats. Northern Whigs managed to field a candidate in the next presidential election, but they were finished as one of the nation's two major political parties.

One of the reasons the South endorsed Pierce so enthusiastically was his sympathy with expanding the southern boundaries of the United States. Doing so would add new territory for slave-worked plantations without violating the specifications of the 1820 Compromise. The South's desire for more land wasn't driven by hopes of carving out new slave states and gaining control of the Senate so much as by the grim realization that it was necessary for the southern way of life. Slave Power rhetoric notwithstanding, both proponents and opponents of slavery recognized that the only way for the South to maintain itself economically and perhaps even become financially independent of the North was to grow ever increasing quantities of cash crops such as rice, cotton, and tobacco. But intensive cultivation of them depleted the soil so quickly that more and more land—and slaves—were required.

President Pierce lost no time in telling his southern supporters what they wanted to hear. In his inaugural address, he scorned Whiggish "timid forebodings" that dreaded the prospect of empire, insisting that the future of the United States—her security as well as her prestige in the international community—demanded "the acquisition of certain properties." Pierce didn't mention upholding the South's slave economy as a major motive for empire-building, but everyone knew that's what he had in mind, because southerners had been agitating for new slave territories for months. The "path of our destiny on this continent," wrote a Virginian journalist, lay in the acquisition of "tropical America" where the "noble peculiarities of Southern civilization" could flourish and spread. The influential southern journal *De Bow's Review* proudly announced that "we have a destiny to perform, 'a manifest destiny,' over all Mexico, over South America, over the West Indies." Mississippi senator Albert Gallatin Brown was less eloquent but more frank. He wanted to annex Cuba and several Mexican states, "and I want them all for the same reason—for the planting and spreading of slavery."[3]

Everyone agreed that the island of Cuba, which already had a slave economy in place, was the plum. At Jefferson Davis's urging, President James Polk had made a $100 million bid to Spain for the island back in 1848. But Spain was unwilling to sell then, and equally unwilling to sell to Pierce four years later. So behind the scenes and unofficially, the president encouraged adventuresome soldiers of fortune, hailing mainly from slave states, to take the matter into their own hands. These men, more buccaneers than soldiers, were aptly called "filibusters," from the Spanish word for "pirate."

Filibustering efforts to extend American slavery's domain to Caribbean and Latin American countries predated Pierce's administration. As early as 1849, Narciso López, a Cuban who fled the island after an unsuccessful attempt to incite a rebellion against its Spanish rulers, raised a small army in the United States to try again. López was something of a crackpot, but his plans were taken seriously by men who weren't. Both Jefferson Davis and Robert E. Lee turned down the Cuban's invitation to lead his army of mercenaries, but only after giving the offer serious consideration.

López's first filibustering escapade came to naught. President Zachary Taylor, a professional soldier who had no use for amateurish mercenaries, refused to let López's ships leave New York harbor. Undaunted, López relocated to New Orleans, where he raised another army with the help of Mississippi governor John Quitman. Unlike their northern counterparts, southern officials willingly turned a blind eye to López's plans. His small force sailed to Cuba in May 1850, but soon scurried ignominiously back to New Orleans after the Spanish army proved too much for it. A furious Taylor indicted López and Quitman for violating federal neutrality laws, but the charges were eventually dropped after it became clear that New Orleans juries would never convict them. López's dreams of annexing Cuba as a U.S. slave territory ended in the late summer of 1851, when his third attempt at an invasion also failed. Spanish officials in Cuba captured and executed the troublesome buccaneer, along with 50 American soldiers of fortune who had signed on with him. One of them, much to the Fillmore administration's embarrassment, was the nephew of U.S. attorney general John Crittenden.

Filibustering reached its high water mark toward the end of the 1850s with the efforts of Tennessee native William Walker (1824–1860). Unlike López and a handful of earlier filibusterers, Walker's dream of creating a new southern slave empire actually succeeded, at least for a brief while. In 1853, he and a small army of fewer than 50 men managed to capture Baja California and Sonora. Walker immediately declared the "conquered" land a new republic and named himself head of state, but his glory was short-lived. Mexican troops soon forced him to flee back across the U.S. border, where the former president of a republic was arrested as a

private citizen and charged with violating neutrality laws. But like filibusterers before him, he was easily acquitted.

Two years later, Walker was ready to try again. His target this time was
Nicaragua. Within a year he controlled the country, and the Pierce
administration happily granted diplomatic recognition to the puppet
government that Walker put in place there. Shortly afterwards, threatened
by other Central American governments understandably alarmed by his
exploits, Walker issued a decree legalizing slavery in a nation that had abolished it a generation earlier. His hope was to receive military and monetary
aid from a grateful South. But even though he was given both, domestic and
foreign resistance to his government proved too determined, and he was back
in the United States by May 1857. Although indicted by the Buchanan
administration for violating the neutrality laws, Walker was greeted as a hero
by most southerners and more than a few northerners, and predictably acquitted. Refusing to be daunted by his previous failures, Walker embarked on filibustering expeditions to Nicaragua two more times before finally being
captured and executed in Honduras, right in the middle of the 1860 U.S.
presidential campaign. A few months later, in a desperate effort to keep the
Union together, the same John Crittenden whose nephew had been executed
in Mexico with Narciso López proposed to President-elect Lincoln that slavery be allowed in any Caribbean or Latin American country that might be
annexed in the future by the United States. Lincoln rejected the idea.

Shortly after his own election to the presidency, Pierce contacted John
Quitman to encourage him to take up where López had left off. Quitman,
who had military experience from the Mexican War and had twice been
governor of Mississippi, began raising a private army. In the meanwhile,
Pierce worked with congressional leaders to legislate a suspension of the
neutrality laws. But by the time Quitman was ready to sail to Cuba, the
Kansas-Nebraska Act had so splintered the Democrats and upset the country at large that Pierce thought it politically prudent to put the dream of
seizing Cuba on hold. He ordered Quitman to stand down.

Quitman felt betrayed by Pierce, as well he should have, but what he
didn't know is that the president had another card up his sleeve. He had
instructed the U.S. minister to Spain, a French immigrant named Pierre
Soulé who had remarkably little talent for diplomacy, to make Spain an
offer for Cuba. Failing that, Soulé was given vague orders to "detach" the

island from Spain's sovereignty. Pursuant to his instructions, Soulé traveled to Ostend, Belgium, where he met with James Buchanan, then U.S. minister to Great Britain, and John Mason, U.S. minister to France, to discuss possibilities. Their meeting produced a document, later called the Ostend Manifesto, which argued in strong language that the United States had both the legal and the divine right to seize Cuba if Spain refused to sell the island. The story of the meeting and the text of the manifesto soon hit the U.S. press. The *New York Tribune* called the document a "manifesto of brigands" that justified "grow[ing] rich on the spoils of the provinces and toils of slaves."[4] The Pierce administration, trying to do what damage control it could, recalled Soulé, and Secretary of State William Marcy, who had arranged the meeting of the three ministers, publicly disavowed the manifesto. But it was too little too late. In the eyes of the North, the Pierce-Soulé plot to wrest Cuba was just the latest move on the part of the Slave Power to consolidate its control of the nation.

Although annexation of Cuba was a particularly southern priority, the desire for new territory wasn't unique to the slaveholding states of the nation. Westward expansion was a dream shared by most Americans, and certainly by most presidents, during this period. But acquiring land was one thing. Developing it into economically profitable parts of the country was another, and that depended partly on enticing settlers to relocate to the new regions and partly, after the development of the steam-driven locomotive in the 1820s, on building railroads.

Railroad construction in the east took off in the 1850s. By the end of the decade, the United States could boast over 30,000 miles of it, more than any other nation on earth. After the 1848 acquisition of California following the Mexican War, the dream of entrepreneurs and politicians alike was to see the nation united from coast to coast by rail. But building a transcontinental railroad was an expensive proposition. On level ground, the cost exceeded $20,000 per mile. Hilly terrain doubled the expense, and no one could calculate the cost of blasting tunnels through the western mountain ranges. Purchase of land rights, supplies, and accommodations for workers brought big money into local communities, and more than one land speculator, anticipating where the Mississippi River to California track might run, dreamt of making a fortune. Politicians lobbied for the line to bisect the regions they represented, knowing that both private and federal funds would flood the communities through which tracks were laid.

One of the men jockeying for a transcontinental railway was Stephen Douglas. As a new senator back in 1847, he had proposed Chicago as the eastern terminus of a line running straight through to San Francisco. The problem, of course, was that most of the land the line would have to cross belonged to Mexico. But Douglas was undaunted, suggesting that the United States simply annex the land it needed as the railroad was built. His bill was defeated, and the annexation part of it became moot anyway after the Mexican War cessions. But congressional squabbles over where precisely the line should run continued. Southern congressmen favored a route from New Orleans to Texas, while northern ones tended to favor Chicago or St. Louis as the eastern depots. But whatever route was ultimately chosen, a necessary condition for starting to build was federal organization of the territories through which the railroad would run. Otherwise, surveys couldn't be conducted, land deeds couldn't be drawn up, and settlers couldn't establish townships and counties.

STORM WARNINGS

In 1852, congressmen from Illinois, Missouri, and Iowa had schemed for federal organization of the huge landmass, ranging from the Indian Territory (now Oklahoma) to the Canadian border, that was the northern remnant of the Louisiana Territory. Their intent was to use the organization as a stepping stone for the lucrative business of building a railroad through the region they proposed to call "Nebraska," from an Otos Indian name for the Platte River. Their plan would require the forced removal of Indians from land ceded to them by the U.S. government.

Sectional protests immediately sounded. Because the land was part of the Louisiana Purchase, the provisions of the Missouri Compromise's ban on slavery north of 36-30 applied to it. Southerners, knowing full well that states would quickly be carved out of the vast territory, rightly feared that the congressional balance would be tipped in favor of the North. Moreover, Texas congressmen, jockeying for a southern transcontinental route that would run across the breadth of their own state, also protested. Although some of them were old Indian fighters, they insisted with straight faces that the plan was a moral outrage because of its forced removal of Indians. Given this southern opposition, the 1852 proposal to organize the northern territory as Nebraska never got off the ground.

Stephen Douglas decided to revisit the Nebraska issue the following year. He had political reasons for doing so—he wanted the eastern terminus of the railroad to be located in Chicago—as well as personal ones—he had made a small fortune in Chicago real estate, and knew that a railroad would enhance the value of his property. Douglas had picked up a lot of congressional clout since his first attempt, six years earlier, to write legislation on a transcontinental railroad. With the passing of the "great triumvirate"—John Calhoun died in 1850, Henry Clay and Daniel Webster in 1852—Douglas was the undisputed rising star of the Senate. He also chaired the powerful Senate Committee on Territories.

Partnering with fellow Illinois Democrat William Richardson, who chaired the House Committee on Territories, Douglas proposed a new bill that would organize the land north of the old Missouri Compromise line of 36–30 into the Nebraska Territory. The House quickly approved, but the bill got stuck in the Senate when a bloc of powerful southerners objected to it. Known as the F Street Mess because they all boarded together at a house on F Street, the bloc was comprised of two senators from Virginia, one from South Carolina, and the president pro tem of the Senate, Missouri's David Atchison, a rabid and, as events in Kansas would later demonstrate, dangerous champion of slavery. Their opposition had stalled the first Nebraska proposal in 1852, and they had the same objection a year later to the new bill: the provisions of the Missouri Compromise would prohibit slavery in the new territory. Until they were satisfied, the Douglas-Richardson bill had no chance.

Douglas was surprised by their opposition, especially since Atchison, temporarily bowing to the inevitability of the Missouri Compromise's prohibition of slavery in the northern territories, had initially but reluctantly supported it. But his F Street Mess mates evidently convinced him that the 1820 agreement wasn't chiseled in stone, despite what northerners believed, and he soon swayed to their side. If Nebraska prohibited slavery, announced Atchison, his own slave state of Missouri would be bordered on three sides by free territory, and this would so encourage slaves in his state to run that "this species of property would become insecure, if not valueless, in Missouri."[5] In the face of the F Street Mess's disapproval, Douglas realized it was time to rethink his options.

THE STORM HITS

Douglas knew he needed to appease southern senators if the Nebraska Territory was ever to be organized and the transcontinental railroad built in the North rather than the South. But he also knew it was risky to the point of foolishness to antagonize northern colleagues by meddling with the 36-30 boundary established by the Missouri Compromise. He was in one of those situations where damaging fallout was bound to hit him regardless of what he did. So his initial tactic, not surprisingly, was to try to sidestep the whole troublesome issue of slavery by harkening back to one of the provisions of the 1850 Compromise.

In that bill, it will be recalled, the question of whether the New Mexico territory would seek admission as slave or free states was left up to the people who lived in them. Douglas aimed to apply the same policy of popular sovereignty to Nebraska. In January 1854, he made plans to propose a bill for the organization of the territory that suggested that the question of slavery should be a matter of local rather than federal decision. Getting wind that the bill's language wasn't strong enough to suit his southern colleagues, Douglas changed it the next day to state explicitly that it was exclusively up to Nebraska residents to determine whether or not to permit slavery. He tried to save face for this pretty substantive addition by announcing that its omission in the original version of his proposal was a clerical error. But even this wasn't enough to satisfy the members and friends of the F Street Mess, because the ban on slavery established in 1820 still applied to the territory in question. Kentucky senator Archibald Dixon, who had succeeded to Henry Clay's congressional seat, was assigned the task of informing Douglas that his bill had no chance in the Senate unless it explicitly repudiated the Missouri boundary line agreement. Douglas, seeing that the head-on confrontation he'd hoped to avoid was inevitable, knew he had no choice but to agree. "By God, sir," he reportedly replied, "you are right, and I will incorporate it in my bill, though I know it will raise a hell of a storm."[6]

So the bill was rewritten yet again, this time explicitly asserting that the Compromise of 1850's policy of popular sovereignty superseded the 1820 ban on slavery north of the 36-30 line. Anticipating the uproar this would create, Douglas also proposed carving two distinct territories out of the northern remnant, Kansas to the south and Nebraska to the north. It was an obvious stab at maintaining representative parity in the Senate by setting up provisions for one future slave state (Kansas) and one free state (Nebraska). Popular sovereignty would still determine whether slavery would be allowed in the two proposed territories, but chances were good that the more northern one would ban the peculiar institution. But Douglas's bill was silent on the specifics of how popular sovereignty would work. Questions of who would be qualified to vote in a referendum and when it ought to be held—before or after application was made for statehood—were left unresolved. Over the months that followed, this vagueness spelled trouble for the Kansas Territory, just west of the slave state of Missouri.

Douglas planned to formally present his bill to the Senate on Monday, January 23. But well aware of the storm it would raise, he wanted to be sure that President Pierce would back it and use the authority of his office to put pressure on any northern Democrat who might have reservations about it. So Secretary of War Jefferson Davis arranged a meeting in the White House on the preceding Sunday, despite the president's dislike of conducting business on the Sabbath. Douglas and Davis were accompanied by five of the most powerful southern Democrats in Congress.

The meeting with the president was a classic case of arm-twisting. Pierce and his cabinet had already concluded that repealing the Missouri Compromise would shatter the North's loyalty to the Democrats and inflict serious damage on party unity. It's not clear why Pierce ultimately agreed during that Sunday meeting to endorse the bill, but by the time Douglas left the White House, he'd gotten what he wanted, and more. Pierce promised to sign the bill if it came to his desk and to make Democratic support of it a party loyalty test. Perhaps Pierce was worried that refusing to back the bill would alienate southern Democrats and split the party. Perhaps he was actually persuaded by Douglas's argument, the same one the Little Giant subsequently offered to the Senate and the public, that the 1850 agreement to allow popular sovereignty in the New Mexico territory was already a de facto repeal of the Missouri Compromise. But regardless of his reasons, Pierce staked his entire political career on supporting what turned out to be the decade's single most disruptive piece of federal legislation. The fallout from that decision cost him a second term in the White House, created havoc in Kansas, and edged the nation closer to civil war.

When Douglas presented his bill the next day to the Senate (a House version was offered a week later), he sparked a four-month congressional debate that quickly blew up into a sectional fracas. Less than 24 hours after the bill was introduced, a handful of Free Soil congressmen led by Ohio senator Salmon Chase blasted it in *An Appeal of Independent Democrats in Congress to the People of the United States*.[7] Written as a letter to Washington's *National Era*, the antislavery newspaper which serialized Harriet Beecher Stowe's *Uncle Tom's Cabin* in 1850 and 1851, the *Appeal* thunderously condemned Douglas's bill as the advance guard of a wicked campaign to repudiate the "sacred pledge" made in 1820 to contain slavery within definite boundaries.

> We arraign this bill as a gross violation of a sacred pledge; as a criminal betrayal of precious rights; as part and parcel of an atrocious plot to exclude from a vast unoccupied region immigrants from the Old World and free laborers from our own States, and convert it into a dreary region of despotism inhabited by masters and slaves.

The authors of the *Appeal* made it clear that their target was broader than Douglas's bill. In opposing it, they intended to battle the Slave Power they were convinced was its real sponsor. Even if defeated in Congress, they vowed, they would never submit. "We shall go home to our constituents, erect anew the standard of freedom, and call on the people to come to the rescue of the country from the domination of slavery."[8]

The *Appeal*'s eloquent condemnation of Douglas's claim that the 1850 deal he'd brokered superseded the Missouri Compromise rang a chord with northern Whigs and some northern Democrats in Congress. In the first place, many people in the North in fact did regard the 1820 agreement as a "sacred pledge" whose overthrow seemed nothing short of blasphemous. In the second place, Douglas's tactic of claiming that the popular sovereignty granted to New Mexico also applied to Kansas-Nebraska was clever but forced. The 1850 agreement referred precisely and only to territory ceded to the United States as part of the Guadalupe Hidalgo Treaty. The vast Kansas-Nebraska territory, part of the Louisiana Purchase, was completely outside that sphere.

Knowing that he was skating on thin ice, Douglas went on the attack, insisting that opposition to his bill came not from rational and open minds but from "the pure, unadulterated representatives of Abolitionism, Free Soilism, [and] Niggerism in the Congress of the United States"[9]—all foes of the very Union which he, Douglas, was struggling so valiantly to preserve. Douglas was referring specifically to the authors of the *Appeal*, but his ugly charge was broad enough to include anyone, including fellow Democrats, who dared to cross swords with him. Senator Chase, not intimidated in the least by Douglas's bluster, gave as good as he got, retorting that it was Douglas, not "we who are denounced as agitators and factionists," who risked embroiling the nation in sectional strife.[10]

In their *Appeal*, Chase and his coauthors asked citizens to "protest, earnestly and emphatically, by correspondence, through the press, by memorials, by resolutions of public meetings and legislative bodies, and in whatever other mode may seem expedient, against this enormous crime," and protest they did—at least those who lived in the North. The observation galleries of both congressional chambers filled daily with men and women eager to follow the debates. Religious denominations sent petitions to Congress, angry citizens flooded newspaper offices with their letters, and a mere two weeks after the bill was introduced, 26 protesting petitions from citizens in Pennsylvania, Delaware, Massachusetts, Vermont, Ohio, and Indiana were presented to the Senate. It must have awakened nostalgia in some of the old-time legislators for the days when the gag rule had spared Congress such onslaughts of public rage.

One of the more notable private citizens who entered the fray was Harriet Beecher Stowe. In a long newspaper letter published toward the end of February, she argued that the outcome of the debate raging in Congress would "affect the interests of liberty and Christianity" not just in the United States but throughout the entire world. She appealed to sentiment—no mother who loves her child, she insisted, could bear to see inflicted on another's "what she would think worse than death were it inflicted on her own"—but also to the frightening political possibility that the doctrine of popular sovereignty, when applied to the slavery issue, could open the door to reintroducing slavery in the free North. "Slave depots in New York City," she cautioned, were distinct possibilities.[11] In her sometimes purple depictions of slave owner cruelty in her 1852 novel *Uncle Tom's Cabin*, Stowe had fired northern antislavery sentiment. Now she empowered northern women, and mothers in particular, to add their voices to the swelling cry against the possible spread of slavery.

Even though support or opposition to Douglas's bill was largely sectional in both the Senate and the House, a few congressmen ventured to swim against the tide. Whig senator Richard Brodhead Jr. from Pennsylvania argued that there was nothing to fear from the bill's popular sovereignty because the soil and climate of Kansas were incapable of growing the kinds of crops that required slave labor. Most northern Democrats with scruples about slavery eased their minds with the same rationalization. Some Southerners such as South Carolina senator Andrew Butler agreed that slavery would never take foothold in the northern territory, and that the flap over Kansas was much ado about nothing. But he still backed Douglas's bill because he saw no good reason for legislatively preempting the possibility of slavery anywhere.

A handful of southerners, most notably Sam Houston of Texas, opposed the bill. Houston's reasoning, much like President Polk's during the 1850 debate on the Mexican cession, was that the Missouri Compromise's aim of maintaining congressional parity between North and South had worked for an entire generation. "For more than a third of a century," he said, "it has given comparative peace and tranquility," and there was no practical justification for changing course. But he offered a second reason for rejecting the bill. It was a matter of honor, he insisted, to abide by one's agreements, and the 1820 Compromise, given the solemnity with which it had been signed, was especially binding. "The word of one [geographical] section of the Union," he said, "should be kept with the other."[12] Sen. Archibald Dixon from the border state of Kentucky also opposed the bill, although for a less altruistic reason than Houston's. If popular sovereignty became the law of the land, he warned, slaveholders could well be forced to forfeit their human property if the majority of residents in a hitherto slave territory or state decided to abolish the peculiar institution. But, Dixon pointed out, if slaveholders held back from migrating to the territories from fear of popular sovereignty turning against them, the territories would be settled by free soilers whose sovereign will would guarantee a prohibition of slavery. Either way, popular sovereignty was a losing proposition for the South.

Samuel Houston's insistence that legislators were honor bound to remain loyal to the 1820 agreement didn't wash with his southern congressional colleagues or their constituents. The debate over Douglas's bill brought too many old wounds to the surface for that. Some of them had to do with the fury that southerners who had fought in the Mexican War felt over efforts to keep slavery out of the territory won in that conflict. Others went all the way back to the congressional debate that resulted in the Missouri Compromise, feeling that they or their forebears had been dragooned into agreeing to it. In the House, Rep. Phillip Phillips of Alabama voiced this belief when he said that the 1820 legislation was no compromise at all, and that southerners should feel no moral qualms about repealing it. South Carolina senator Andrew Butler agreed. The Missouri Compromise, he contended, had been arrived at because it promised "peace and harmony" between North and South. But "instead of being a healing salve," the agreement had become "a thorn in the side of the southern portion of this Confederacy." "The sooner you extract it," he advised his colleagues, "the sooner you will restore harmony and health to the body politic."[13] Extracting it, in Butler's judgment, meant voting for Douglas's bill, even though Butler personally suspected that Kansas would never be a slave state.

As the debate dragged on week after week, the Little Giant lived up to his reputation as a scrappy fighter. He took on all challengers on the Senate floor, remaining there each day from opening to closing, tirelessly responding to arguments against his bill with logic when he could and bullying when he couldn't. Moreover, he refused to share the spotlight with any other supporter of the bill. It was his alone, and he intended to take all the glory for it. At one point, John Weller, a one-term senator from California, innocently rose to speak in favor of the bill. "Sit down," Douglas snarled at him. "Don't mix in, this is my fight."[14]

Shortly before the Senate voted on the bill, which by this time was variously called the Kansas bill, the Nebraska bill, and the Kansas-Nebraska bill, Delaware senator John Clayton proposed an amendment that prohibited immigrants from other nations voting in territorial elections. Clayton's amendment was a transparent effort to stack the popular sovereignty deck in favor of slavery, since most foreign settlers generally disliked slavery. The amendment was approved, and the Senate, after months of wrangling, was finally ready for the closing debate over Douglas's bill.

Final arguments were heard from both sides during an all-night session on March 3–4. To fortify the weary legislators, a refreshment table complete with a large supply of liquor had been set up in a vestibule, and senators made frequent visits to it as the night wore on. Given the late hour, heated tempers, and general weariness with the whole issue, many of the members drank too much and misbehaved on the floor. "A glance from the Senate gallery at midnight on Friday," wrote a *New York Daily Times* reporter, "revealed the disgraceful fact that more than one of its members had forgotten in their cups, all of their dignity and not a little of the propriety of a deliberative body."[15] Some of the senators, flush with drink, made ramblingly incoherent speeches. Others delivered last-minute fiery broadsides. One speech, from Maine's William Fessenden, so angered Andrew Butler that the South Carolinian twice advanced toward his colleague with clenched fists, restrained each time by fellow senators.

At around 11 o'clock, Douglas, who had made liberal use of the potable refreshments, took the floor and proceeded to harangue his colleagues for the next four hours. He summarized his case for the bill, attacked its opponents—at one point, in response to an exclamation from New York's William Seward, growling, "Ah, you can't crawl behind that free nigger dodge!"—and in general spewed forth with such "violence and vulgarity," in the words of one reporter covering the debate, that it was possible to "convey but a faint idea" of it in print.[16] It was an unworthy performance of a man who aspired to be the successor of Clay, Calhoun, and Webster.

When an exhausted and probably inebriated Douglas finally sat down, Sam Houston made one last effort to persuade his colleagues that the bill under consideration, if passed into law, would churn up the storm Douglas himself had predicted months earlier. "I, as the most extreme Southern Senator upon this floor, do not desire it. If it is a boon that is offered to propitiate the South, I, as a Southern man, repudiate it. I reject it. I will have none of it."[17] But Houston's words had no effect. Minds were made up on either side of the issue, and when the vote was called, the bill passed by 37 to 14. Northern Whigs and Free Soilers unanimously voted against the bill, but they were joined by only 5 of 20 northern Democrats. Nine senators, exhausted by the all-night session, sick and tired of the entire debate, and perhaps not wishing to go on record one way or another, left the Senate before the vote. But even if they had remained and voted nay, the result would've been overwhelmingly in favor of the bill.

The Senate-approved bill went to the House, where the debate continued for nearly three more months and was even more rancorous than it had been in the Senate. Free Soil representative Gerrit Smith, a New Yorker who was one of the nation's wealthiest men and most ardent

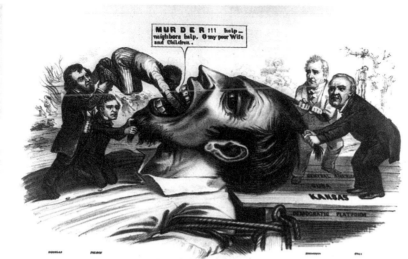

FORCING SLAVERY DOWN THE THROAT OF A FREESOILER

President Franklin Pierce, presidential nominee James Buchanan, Sen. Lewis Cass, and Sen. Stephen A. Douglas force a man down the throat of a giant in an 1856 political cartoon satirizing the Kansas-Nebraska Act of 1854, which allowed popular sovereignty in regards to slavery in the two territories. The act nullified the Missouri Compromise of 1820. (Library of Congress)

opponents of slavery (he would later help bankroll John Brown's raid on Harpers Ferry), mockingly argued that the only conclusion which could be rationally drawn from the debate was that "this Nebraska business must be the work of the devil."[18] Northern Democrats, many of whom were up for reelection in the fall, were wary about voting for the "devil's bill." They knew that President Pierce's wrath would descend upon them if they broke ranks, but they also feared the anger of their anti-Kansas constituents. So they dragged their feet about falling into line behind the bill until Congressman William Cullom, a Kentucky Whig who supported the bill, grew so impatient that he accused them of "strangl[ing] the legitimate legislation of the country." "I should not be a worthy descendent of my mother state," he declared, "if I did not here, in my place, denounce this [hesitation] as a plot against the peace and quiet of the country."[19] But Georgia representative Alexander Stephens, future vice president of the Confederacy and floor manager of the Kansas bill, refused to call for a vote until he was confident he had enough congressmen lined up to pass it.

Finally, on May 22, he did, and debate came to a close. The bill, minus the Clayton amendment, squeaked by on a 115 to 104 vote. Just as in the Senate, Northern Whigs and Free Soilers voted unanimously against it, while nearly all southern Whigs voted for it. While most southern Democrats also voted for the bill, their northern colleagues split pretty evenly. When the bill was returned to the Senate, members accepted the House's rejection of the Clayton amendment, and President Pierce signed the Kansas-Nebraska Act into law on May 30. The Missouri Compromise was dead. Long live popular sovereignty.

Proponents of the bill were jubilant. Alexander Stephens chortled that shepherding it through the House had been the fulfillment of his life's mission, and Douglas crowed that he had single-handedly saved the Union. But in fact the hell of a storm that he had predicted was escalating into a hurricane. Angry citizens across the North held rallies condemning the act. State legislatures in Maine, Rhode Island, Massachusetts, New York, and Wisconsin passed resolutions in defiance of it. Even the free states controlled by Democrats—Pennsylvania, New Jersey, Ohio, and California—declined to endorse it. Instead, realizing the strength of anti-Kansas sentiment among their residents, they prudently chose to issue no statement either for or against the act. The only northern state to pass a resolution of approval was Illinois, Douglas's home turf. But even there, approval was lukewarm, with only slight more than half of the state legislators giving it.

Northern Democrats in the House had been right to worry about the fall elections. Thousands of traditionally Democratic voters in the North either sat the election out to express their outrage or threw their votes to anti-Kansas candidates. Democratic seats in the House fell from 93 to 23. Only 7 of the 44 who voted for Douglas's bill were returned to office. Incumbent Democratic governors in Iowa, Michigan, New York, and Pennsylvania also toppled in the storm Douglas whipped up. Nor did the blowback show any sign of easing up the following spring, when northern Democrats continued to suffer election defeats, losing every House seat for Connecticut, Rhode Island, and New Hampshire. The last was an especially stinging rebuke, since New Hampshire was President Pierce's home state.

Even worse than the electoral rout, a wedge had been driven between northern and southern Democrats that would contribute to the growth of the nation's sectional divide and their own inability to win the White

House for an entire generation after 1856. Still, it was worse for the Whigs, because the Kansas debate that frayed the Democrats pretty much destroyed the Whigs. Too furious with each other to remain united as a single party, northerners and southerners willingly went their separate ways. Many of the former joined a new political party whose members called themselves Know-Nothings, or drifted to other antislavery fusion groups such as the Free Soil Party. The latter gravitated toward the Democrats, who, despite the dissent of a few northern members, had proven themselves skilled at protecting the interests of slaveholders. Connecticut Whig senator Truman Smith, resigning in frustration over the Kansas vote, lamented, "The Whig party has been killed off effectually by that miserable Nebraska business."[20] He was absolutely correct.

The Kansas-Nebraska Act also set in motion a chain of events that embroiled the Kansas Territory in a mini–civil war between proslavery and free soil settlers. Now that the slavery issue was to be decided by popular sovereignty, both defenders and opponents of slavery realized the importance of settling the region with their own kind before any vote was taken. One of the features of Douglas's initial bill had been the establishment of a homestead grant that would encourage settlement in the new territory. But southern senators in no mood to pass any legislation that would encourage free soilers to migrate to Kansas killed that provision, and when a homestead act that would have given settlers 160-acre tracts was passed by the House, they defeated it, too. William Seward, knowing full well that the Senate vote on Douglas's bill signaled the beginning of a race for Kansas that would determine whether the territory became a free or a slave state, saw what was coming. "Come on then, gentlemen of the Slave States," he grimly declared. "Since there is no escaping your challenge, I accept it in behalf of the cause of freedom. We will engage in competition for the virgin soil of Kansas, and God give the victory to the side which is stronger in numbers as it is in right."[21] Massachusetts senator Charles Sumner likewise saw the Kansas-Nebraska Act as a call to arms. "It is the worst bill, inasmuch as it is a present victory of Slavery," he contended, but it was also "the best bill on which Congress ever acted; for it . . . annuls all past compromises with Slavery, and makes all future compromises impossible. Thus it puts Freedom and Slavery face to face, and bids them grapple. Who can doubt the result?"[22] The result, as became clear over the next few months, was that Kansas would bleed.

BLACK CREPE AND BROKEN FENCES

In the very week that the final version of Kansas-Nebraska was approved by Congress and signed into law by President Pierce, something happened in Boston that was a harbinger of the fury that the act would stir. It revolved around the capture of Anthony Burns, a fugitive slave, on May 24.

Burns had escaped from bondage in March 1854 by stowing away on a ship sailing from Virginia to Boston. Once in the North, he found work with a tailor and, believing himself safe, rashly wrote a letter to his brother, who was still a slave. Burns's master intercepted the letter, discovered the whereabouts of his runaway property, and, invoking the 1850 Fugitive Slave Law, had Burns seized by Boston law officers for rendition back to Virginia.

By 1854, Boston was a center of antislavery sentiment—it was, after all, the base of William Lloyd Garrison's *The Liberator*—and it took only two days from Burns's arrest for local activists to organize a massive protest meeting in the city's famed Faneuil Hall, a rallying spot since the War of Independence for public gatherings. The crowd was fired up by one indignant orator after another denouncing both the Fugitive Slave Law and the seizure of Burns. Eventually, a crowd of angry men decided to storm the courthouse where Burns was being held in a cell. They were led by Thomas Wentworth Higginson, a Harvard graduate, Unitarian minister, advocate of women's suffrage and temperance, and ardent abolitionist. Two other men from equally distinguished New England families, Theodore Parker and Wendell Phillips, joined him in leading the crowd. Phillips assured his incensed fellow Bostonians that in resisting a bad law, citizens had a right and a duty to take matters into their own hands. His speech was a replay of the "higher law" oration William Seward made on the floor of the Senate in 1850 when he clashed swords with Henry Clay.

Once at the courthouse, several men from the mob, led by Higginson, made a rush for the door with a makeshift battering ram. Shots rang from marshals and deputies firing out of courthouse windows, Higginson received a cut on his face from a saber-wielding deputy, and other protesters were clubbed to the ground. Although managing to force their way into the building's front hall, the crowd was eventually pushed back, but not before an ex-slave who worked for the Underground Railroad shot a pursuing guard dead.

Fugitive slave Anthony Burns, whose arrest and trial under the Fugitive Slave Act of 1850 touched off riots and protests by abolitionists and citizens of Boston in the spring of 1854. (Library of Congress)

President Pierce was outraged at the vigilantes' disregard for the law and immediately authorized four companies of marines and artillery from nearby Fort Independence to guard Burns. As an extra precaution, Boston's mayor circled the courthouse where the prisoner was held with huge harbor chains. The irony of a public display of chains guarding against the rescue of a slave was not lost on Bostonians.

It was only a matter of days before a judge, in compliance with federal law, ordered Burns returned to his master in Virginia. Burns was marched down to the docks with 2,000 federal troops and state militiamen lining the streets on either side to forestall any rescue attempts. As a sullen crowd of thousands gathered to watch the procession, a marine band mocked them by playing "Carry Me Back to Old Virginny." Angry citizens draped black crepe on doorframes and displayed upside-down portraits of Pierce from windows. All told, the cost of the rendition amounted to tens of thousands of dollars, prompting Higginson to remark that Burns was "the most expensive slave in the history of mankind."[23] Southern newspapers and politicians predictably condemned the attempted rescue of Burns and applauded Pierce for upholding the law of the land. But in the eyes of the North, the rescue was a valiant effort to resist the Slave Power. Henry David Thoreau spoke for thousands when he praised Higginson as "the only Harvard Phi Beta Kappa, Unitarian Minister, and master of seven languages who has led a storming party against a federal bastion with a battering ram in his hands."[24] His insinuation was that other men of letters opposed to slavery would do well to follow Higginson's example and exchange their writing pens for battering rams. As tempers heated and the sectional divide worsened in the wake of the Kansas-Nebraska Act, many men on both sides of the slave debate would come to a similar conclusion.

Meanwhile, back in Douglas's home state of Illinois, a Springfield attorney who thought he'd retired from politics after his single term in the U.S. House was preparing to get back in the game. In a campaign biography of Abraham Lincoln published during his 1860 run for the presidency, readers were told that the 1854 repeal of the Missouri Compromise "aroused Mr. Lincoln as he never had been before. He at once perceived the conflicts that must grow out of it; the angry strife between the North and the South, and the struggles in Kansas." Douglas's act inaugurated a "complete revolution" whose purpose was to shift the "moral sentiment of the country" in the direction of establishing "slavery in the Free States, as well as in the Territories, and the revival of the African slave trade."[25] Lincoln resolved to resist this revolution and challenge the Democratic senator from Illinois who had masterminded it. That Douglas planned to return in August to Illinois to stump for the doctrine of popular sovereignty gave him his opportunity.

Lincoln stewed for a few months before launching the public attack that would culminate in his first great speech, the address at Peoria. He kicked it off with an early September editorial in which he took on an Illinois Democrat named, of all things, John Calhoun, who was a strong defender of popular sovereignty and the newly appointed surveyor general of the Kansas-Nebraska Territory. To get across his sense of outrage at the Kansas Act's repudiation of the Missouri Compromise, Lincoln invented a parable in which he and John Calhoun agreed that a "fine meadow, containing beautiful springs of water" would be Lincoln's, and that the pact between them was "regarded by both as sacred." But in the course of time, Calhoun, greedy for additional land on which to graze his cattle, tore down the fence and exposed Lincoln's meadow "to the ravages of his starving and famishing cattle." When Lincoln protested, Calhoun calmly replied that even though he'd ripped down the fence that originally barred the cattle, it wasn't his intention that they should actually enter the now open field. Instead, he meant "to leave them perfectly free to form their own notions of the field, and to direct their movements in their own way!"[26]

Just in case any reader missed the point he wished to make, Lincoln spelled it out at the end of his editorial. Champions like Calhoun of popular sovereignty were both knaves and fools. They were knaves because they refused to honor the Missouri Compromise's solemnly covenanted latitudinal fence protecting the territories from slavery. They were fools because they actually believed that the average citizen was too thick-witted to see that their real motive in repealing the compromise was the extension of slavery and not, as they claimed, the extension of democracy. Lincoln's years of retirement were over. He was ready to do battle with the knaves and fools.

NOTES

The chapter epigraph from Douglas is from Allan Nevins, *Ordeal of the Union: A House Dividing, 1852–1857* (New York: Charles Scribner's Sons, 1947), 96. The chapter epigraph from the *Appeal* is from William E. Gienapp (ed.), *The Civil War and Reconstruction: A Documentary Collection* (New York: W. W. Norton, 2001), 33.

1. Roy P. Basler (ed.), *The Collected Works of Abraham Lincoln* (New Brunswick, NJ: Rutgers University Press, 1953), 2:130, 132. Hereafter cited as CW.

2. John Blassingame (ed.), *The Frederick Douglass Papers* (New Haven, CT: Yale University Press, 1982), Series 1, 2:295.

3. All quotations are from James McPherson, *Battle Cry of Freedom: The Civil War Era* (New York: Oxford University Press, 1988), 107, 115, 106.

4. Eric H. Walther, *The Shattering of the Union: America in the 1850s* (Lanham, MD: SR Books, 2004), 53.

5. Nevins, *Ordeal of the Union: A House Dividing, 1852–1857*, 92.

6. Ibid., 96.

7. As historian James McPherson points out (*Battle Cry of Freedom*, 124), the authors of the *Appeal* came from Whiggish backgrounds, so their identification of

themselves as "Independent Democrats" is a bit mysterious. McPherson speculates that their name came from Free Soilers' reference to themselves in 1851 as the Free Democracy Party.

8. *Appeal of the Independent Democrats* in Gienapp, *The Civil War and Reconstruction*, 34.

9. Nevins, *Ordeal of the Union: A House Dividing*, 114.

10. *Appeal of the Independent Democrats*, Gienapp, *Civil War and Reconstruction*, 34.

11. Walther, *Shattering of the Union*, 42–43.

12. *Congressional Globe*, 33rd Congress, 1st sess., Appendix, 206.

13. *Congressional Globe*, 33rd Congress, 1st sess., Appendix, 232.

14. Nevins, *Ordeal of the Union: A House Dividing*, 142.

15. *New York Daily Times*, March 7, 1854.

16. Nevins, *Ordeal of the Union: A House Dividing*, 143.

17. *Congressional Globe*, 33rd Congress, 1st sess., Appendix, 340.

18. *Congressional Globe*, 33rd Congress, 1st sess., Appendix, 520. Smith's speech before the House was scathing in its angry sarcasm. Just a snippet gives a good impression of the whole: "Strange! Here is a movement for the immense extension of slavery. Of course, it is not the work of the anti-slavery party … I took it for granted that the pro-slavery party did it. But, it seems it did not … Well, if neither the anti-slavery party, nor the pro-slavery party did it, who was it then, that did it? It follows, necessarily, that it must be the work of the Lord, or the devil. [Laughter.] But, it cannot be the work of the Lord—for the Good Book tells us: 'Where the spirit of the Lord is, there is liberty'—liberty, not slavery. So this Nebraska business must be the work of the devil. [Great laughter.] But logical as is this conclusion, I am nevertheless, too polite to press it."

19. *Congressional Globe*, 33rd Congress, 1st sess., Appendix, 538.

20. William E. Gienapp, *The Origins of the Republican Party, 1852–1856* (New York: Oxford University Press, 1987), 87.

21. Congressional Globe, 33rd Congress, 1st sess., Appendix, 769.

22. David Herbert Donald, *Charles Sumner and the Coming of the Civil War* (New York: Alfred A. Knopf, 1960), 260–61.

23. Edward J. Renehan Jr., *The Secret Six: The True Tale of the Men Who Conspired with John Brown* (Columbia: University of South Carolina Press, 1996), 70.

24. Ibid., 64–65.

25. David W. Bradford (ed.), *Vote Lincoln! The Presidential Campaign Biography of Abraham Lincoln, 1860* (Sacramento, CA: Boston Hill Press, 2010), 114, 115.

26. CW 2:230.

THE REPUBLICANS FIELD A PRESIDENTIAL CANDIDATE

Their election will prevent the establishment of Slavery in Kansas, overthrow Slave Rule in the Republic ..., give ascendency to Northern civilization over the bludgeon and blood-hound civilization of the South, and the mark of national condemnation on Slavery ... and inaugurate a higher and purer standard of Politics and government. Therefore, we go for Frémont and Dayton.

—Frederick Douglass

A candidate must have a slim record in these times.

—Horace Greeley

Fury over the Kansas-Nebraska Act created political and social shock waves that, seven years later, crested in civil war. But its impact was also felt immediately. Writing about the act 30 years afterwards, Republican statesman James G. Blaine recalled that "old political landmarks disappeared, and party prejudices of three generations were swept aside in a day."[1] He exaggerated, but not by much. In the months following the act's passage, the old political landscape, often referred to as the Second American Party System, collapsed. One mainstream political party, the Whigs, imploded and disappeared. Another party, the Democrats, acrimoniously split, largely along North-South sectional lines. And two new political parties emerged from the chaos. One of them, the non-sectional Know-Nothings, seemed unstoppable for a while before it too, like the Whigs and Democrats, splintered on the slavery issue. The other, a decidedly sectional party whose members called themselves Republicans, flourished so well that it fielded a presidential candidate in 1856 and came close to winning.

TWO NEW POLITICAL PARTIES

In the wake of Kansas-Nebraska, party loyalties that had endured for years were increasingly edged out by sectional ones. Disgruntled northern Whigs and free soil Democrats now found themselves more than willing to enter into anti-Kansas coalitions or "fusions" with one another, while southern Democrats began absorbing southern Whigs. The new spirit of ad hoc alliance didn't necessarily mean that old party affiliations were easily renounced. Many Whigs and Democrats continued to believe, at least for a while, that they could hang onto their old political identities. But as the two mainstream parties continued to falter, the Whigs collapsing and the Democrats dividing, the fusions proved to be more than temporary expediencies.

Lincoln was an example of someone who declared himself willing "to fuse with anyone who would unite with him to oppose slave power," but who chose to remain with the Whig Party—or what was left of it—for nearly two years after Douglas's Kansas-Nebraska bill became law.[2] He had retired from politics after his stint in the U.S. Congress, willing if not entirely content to apply himself, as his presidential campaign biography of 1860 said, "more closely than ever to the practice of his [legal] profession."[3] He believed that the Compromise of 1850 had effectively settled the sectional divide over slavery, and that the institution itself had become a "minor question" on its way to a natural extinction.[4] But Kansas-Nebraska's repeal of the 1820 legislation "aroused [him] as he had never been before." He saw clearly that the bill amounted to "a complete revolution in the policy of the government," preparing the way "for a revolution in the moral sentiment of the country, preparatory to the establishment of slavery in the Free States, as well as in the Territories."[5] When Lincoln challenged Douglas in Peoria, his speech made him a leader of Illinois's anti-Kansas community. Henceforth, until his election to the presidency, the essential immorality of slavery and the imperative of keeping it out of the territories, not the economic concerns that had characterized his earlier political career, would be the dominant issues for Lincoln.

Even before the Kansas-Nebraska Act became law, opponents of slavery's extension, sensing the way the wind was blowing, met to form oppositional coalitions. On the night of March 20, 1854, one of these groups of antislavery Whigs, Democrats, and Free Soilers met in a schoolhouse in Ripon, Wisconsin, to plot strategy. They called themselves "Republicans," and their modest gathering is generally credited as the birth of the political party that would become a major player in U.S. politics. In early May, 30 U.S. congressmen who opposed Douglas's bill embraced the new name in homage and imitation of the founding fathers' resistance to tyranny. For them, the Slave Power was the new autocratic threat to freedom. Two months later, an anti-Kansas fusion in Michigan officially adopted the name. "Republican" began to replace the other labels with which oppositional coalitions across the North identified themselves.

The new Republican fusion arrived in Illinois as early as October 1854, the same month Lincoln gave his Peoria speech. Although his address anticipated the platform subsequently adopted by Republicans, Lincoln didn't switch party allegiances for another year and a half. Elected as a Whig to the Illinois State Assembly in 1854, he resigned the following year to make a bid, again as a Whig, for a seat in the U.S. Senate. He eventually withdrew from the contest out of fear that a Douglasite Democrat might win, and threw his weight behind the incumbent, antislavery Democrat Lyman Trumbull. Lincoln's defeat had as much to do with the national decline of Whiggery as it did with the fact that Illinois had never been an especially Whig-friendly state, and by 1856 he was ready to join the state's new Republican party. He helped write its platform, one plank of which called for the restoration of the Missouri Compromise's geographical limitations to slavery's expansion, and delivered the state convention's keynote address, a speech so stirring that the reporters in the crowd later confessed themselves too riveted to transcribe it.

Lincoln may have failed in his stab for the U.S. Senate, but like-minded anti-Kansas candidates in other states did well in congressional and state elections in 1854 and 1855. (Including Trumbull, the man who beat Lincoln in the Illinois contest.) Northern Democrats, viewed as tainted by many of their northern constituents because of their support of Kansas-Nebraska, were decimated. From then until the outbreak of war, southern Democrats on Capitol Hill comfortably outnumbered their northern colleagues, effectively making the party unambiguously proslavery. At the same

KNOW - NOTHINGISM IN BROOKLYN.
"None but citizens of the United States can be licensed to engage in any employment in this city."
Brooklyn Board of Aldermen.

Cartoon captioned "Know-Nothingism" in Brooklyn. "None but citizens of the United States can be licensed to engage in any employment in this city." The Know-Nothing Party, or American Party, gained widespread support in the 1850s. The party's platform called for restrictions on immigrants, including withdrawing their right to vote. When asked about the party's platform, members were supposed to reply that they knew nothing, hence the name. (Library of Congress)

time, 150 anti-Nebraska candidates, running under a number of political labels, were elected to the House. The elections clearly demonstrated that northern opinion was dead-set against the Kansas-Nebraska Act, that Democrats, associated as they were with it, were likely to be in trouble in the upcoming presidential election, and that the anti-Kansas movement was a force to be reckoned with. The midterm elections made something else clear, too. A second new party, whose supporters were commonly known as Know-Nothings, was on the upswing. Unlike anti-Nebraska agitators, Know-Nothings' focus wasn't slavery. Instead, they were zealous nativists whose agenda was anti-immigrationist and anti-Catholic. They won 52 House seats, dominated state elections in Delaware and Massachusetts, and took substantial votes away from mainstream candidates in the Northeast and border states. One dazed Connecticut politician described the political wreckage the Know-Nothings wrought in his state as "havoc."[6]

The American Party, as the Know-Nothing movement pointedly christened itself in 1855, was a fusion of two anti-immigration "secret" fraternities, the Order of United Americans and the Order of the Star

Spangled Banner, which had combined memberships three years earlier to campaign on behalf of "nativist"—that is, Anglo-Saxon Protestant—rights. Know-Nothings, who got their odd name because they were instructed in the movement's early days to say "I know nothing" if an outsider asked them about the "secret" organization to which they belonged, were alarmed by what they saw as the surge of foreigners flooding the nation. Anti-immigration sentiment became widespread in the 1840s, when political revolutions in Europe and the potato blight in Ireland brought tens of thousands of Germans and Irish to the United States. During that decade, Catholic Church membership increased three times faster than Protestant membership, primarily due to immigration. Settling largely along the northern eastern seaboard cities—by 1855, 52 percent of New Yorkers were foreign-born—these immigrants were seen, with some justification, as the sources of increased metropolitan crime and poverty.

As a general rule, Democrats welcomed the influx of immigrants, particularly Irish Catholics, as potential voters. Whigs were more hostile to their presence. By the early 1850s, Know-Nothing dislike of foreigners and Catholics had merged with the temperance movement—German Protestants and Irish Catholics alike were viewed as hard drinkers, yet another alleged sign of their morally destabilizing influence on "native" culture—to build a political agenda that at its high point attracted the allegiance of between 800,000 and 1.5 million supporters. Know-Nothings pledged to vote only for native-born Protestants in local, state, and national elections; demanded a quadrupling of the current five-year waiting period before immigrants could become citizens; vehemently opposed public funding for Catholic schools; and pushed hard for antiliquor legislation. Many northern Know-Nothings were also free soilers. But their focus on combating the "alien" infiltration of American culture and politics overshadowed all other concerns.

The anti-immigration and protemperance positions of the Know-Nothings attracted many Whigs looking for a new political home as their own party disintegrated. American Party leaders, recognizing that many of these old Whigs feared that the new anti-Kansas fusions threatened the stability of the Union, were happy to downplay the slavery issue in an effort to court them. Their success in doing so was one of the reasons for the electoral successes of Know-Nothings in 1854. By 1855, the American Party had grown so strong that it emerged, along with the

Republicans, as a genuine threat to the Democrats. Its swelling numbers weren't lost on the Republicans, who struggled to find ways to appeal to both homeless Whigs and fully committed Know-Nothings without overtly embracing the latter's anti-immigrant sentiments. There was a strategic reason for this balancing act: Republicans needed Know-Nothing votes if they ever hoped to take the White House, but they couldn't risk alienating German Protestants, who, unlike Irish Catholics, were generally sympathetic to the Republican agenda.

Many Republicans were ambivalent about courting supporters of the Know-Nothing movement because they morally disapproved of what it stood for. Lincoln, for one, found their position hard to stomach. "As a nation," he wrote, "we began by declaring that 'all men are created equal.' We now practically read it 'all men are created equal, except negroes.' When the Know-Nothings get control, it will read 'all men are created equal, except negroes, and foreigners, and Catholics.'" That's why, in the event of a Know-Nothing capture of the White House, Lincoln declared that he "should prefer emigrating to some country where they make no pretense of loving liberty—to Russia, for example, where despotism can be taken pure and without the base alloy of hypocrisy."[7] Still, he was too astute a politician to think that the Republicans could get by without courting the Know-Nothings, especially in his own state of Illinois. In the presidential elections of 1856 and 1860, Republicans would have to walk the razor's edge of neither endorsing nor alienating them.

TROUBLE IN KANSAS

Events in Kansas eventually halted the ascendancy of the Know-Nothings and provided the troubled backdrop for the presidential election of 1856. The passage of the Kansas-Nebraska Act decreed that it was up to local populations in the western territories, not the federal government, to embrace or reject slavery. But even before the final congressional vote was taken, proslavers in Missouri and free soilers in New England were preparing to flood Kansas with settlers who would vote to accept or block slavery there. If popular sovereignty was to decide the slavery issue, both sides were determined to be sovereign.

The race was on when several wealthy Boston Brahmans, including Amos Lawrence, one of the wealthiest textile manufacturers in Massachusetts, organized the New England Emigrant Aid Company to bankroll free-state farmers (most originating in the Midwest, as it turned out) who agreed to migrate to Kansas. It's not clear how many company-sponsored settlers actually moved to Kansas, but the towns of Lawrence and Topeka were founded with New England cash and supplies.

In the meantime, proslavers in Missouri, stirred up especially by David Atchison, the state's bellicose U.S. senator, had no intention of letting free soilers get the upper hand in Kansas, even if it meant being "compelled," as Atchison declared, "to shoot, burn, & hang" them.[8] When the Kansas territorial governor appointed by President Pierce announced that elections would be held in November 1854 to send a delegate to Congress, Atchison put together a small army of hard-drinking thugs, who came to be called "Border Ruffians," to flood the balloting places and throw the election to the proslavery candidate. Three months later, they frightened free soilers away from the polls and cast enough illegal ballots to elect a proslavery territorial legislature that promptly passed a draconian set of laws aimed at protecting slavery. Aiding in the escape of slaves was made a capital crime, public protest against slavery became an offense punishable by up to two years' imprisonment, free soilers were barred from serving on juries when the defendant was a proslaver, and in a move that echoed one of the provisions of the despised 1850 Fugitive Slave Law, everyone was required under threat of punishment to report violations of the territory's new slave code. Almost as an afterthought, legislators protected themselves against accusations of having rigged their own election by declaring that there was no residency requirement for Kansas voters. With a stroke of the pen, border ruffians who actually made their homes in other states became residents in good standing.

All this was too much for the territorial governor, who actually had been sympathetic to the proslavery position until he witnessed the hooliganism of the border ruffians. When he complained to President Pierce about them, proslavers threatened his life and Senator Atchison launched a one-man campaign to pressure the president into replacing him with a more pliable governor. Ever willing to support slavery, Pierce did so, but not before angry free soilers in Kansas held their own elections and seated their own territorial government. By early 1856, Kansas had two competing governments, a proslavery one headquartered in the town of Lecompton, and a free soil one located in Topeka.

The hostility between proslavers and free soilers, egged on by hotheaded ideologues on either side, was primed to ignite into a shooting war. But until late 1855, the conflict was mainly one of intimidation and bullying. Things changed when a proslaver murdered a free soil settler. Cries for vengeance rang out, and in response a ragtag army of border ruffians decided to march on the free soil town of Lawrence to burn it down. They were confident (and rightfully so) that the federal troops stationed in the territory wouldn't stand in their way. But what they hadn't anticipated was the stiff resistance put up by the residents of Lawrence. The townspeople were armed with long-range Sharps rifles, popularly called "Beecher's Bibles" because Brooklyn preacher Henry Ward Beecher, who collected and shipped them to Kansas free soilers, said they packed more wallop against proslavers than the Bible. When he realized what his ruffians were up against, Senator Atchison intervened to persuade them to back off, but his motive wasn't to avoid bloodshed so much as to wait for a more opportune time to take the town. The coming of the harsh prairie winter temporarily suspended overt outbursts of anger from either side. But renewed violence would break out the following spring, just in time for the year's presidential campaigns, and the new territory quickly became known as "Bleeding Kansas."

Even before spring, fallout from the uproar in Kansas began to rupture the Know-Nothings. Two blatantly rigged elections, the bloodthirsty screeching of congressional hooligans like Atchison, and the regularly reported depredations of border ruffians who increasingly were viewed as little more than common outlaws helped to create a rift when American Party leaders met in early summer of 1855. Know-Nothing northerners, appalled at the crisis in Kansas, refused to follow their southern colleagues in endorsing the Kansas-Nebraska Act. The party split into two rival factions, spelling an end to the rise of the movement. Although the two factions would both run presidential candidates in 1856, their respective members, courted by both the Republicans and the Democrats, began drifting to one or the other of them. Within another five years, the Know-Nothings had been absorbed. Their disappearance was almost as meteoric as their ascendancy had been.

CONVENTION SEASON

Although he wanted another four years in the White House, it became increasingly obvious that Franklin Pierce wouldn't receive the Democrat nomination in 1856. His doughface favoring of the South that culminated in his signing the Kansas-Nebraska bill into law had too angered northern opinion and damaged his party for him to be a viable candidate. So even though Pierce insisted on throwing his hat into the ring at that year's Democrat convention, everyone but he knew that the contending parties would all field new candidates in the election.

The American Party held its convention first. Meeting in Philadelphia in late February, some of the delegates who had walked out over the slavery issue at the previous summer's national meeting tried to persuade the convention to repudiate the Kansas-Nebraska Act. When they failed, they left again, this time for good, and established a splinter Know-Nothing organization called the *North* American party.

The remaining delegates to the February convention overwhelmingly selected former president and ex-Whig Millard Fillmore as their candidate, and ex-Democrat Andrew Jackson Donelson of Tennessee, a nephew of the former president for whom he was named.

Fillmore was also the nominee of what was left of the Whig Party. This was quite a turnabout from four years earlier, when he had been the second chief executive, after John Tyler, to be refused renomination by his own party. His unabashedly prosouthern policies, his signing the laws that made up the 1850 Compromise, and especially his high-handed insistence that resisters to the Fugitive Slave Law were traitors was simply too much for northern Whigs to stomach. So in 1852, his party's nomination went to Gen. Winfield Scott, who was decisively trounced by Franklin Pierce.

Soon after leaving office, both Fillmore's wife and daughter died, leaving him grief-stricken and at loose ends for a time. But by 1856, he was ready to get back in the game. The political landscape had drastically changed in just the short three years he had retreated to private citizenship; his old party, the Whigs, had all but disappeared. But Fillmore, like so many other conservative ex-Whigs, found that his political principles were entirely compatible with Know-Nothingism. Fillmore loathed and feared foreigners. "I have for a long time," he declared, "looked with dread and apprehension at the corrupting influence which the contest for the foreign vote is exciting upon our election."[9] This concern was in perfect accord with a party that called for a prohibition of Catholic officeholders and a 21-year residency requirement for citizenship, and whose national slogan was "Americans Must Rule America." Even better, Fillmore was more than willing to avoid the messy slavery debate that had split both the Know-Nothings and the Whigs. Know-Nothingism, he insisted, was "the only hope of forming a truly national party, which *shall* ignore the constant and disturbing agitation of slavery."[10] In the mind of a doughface like Fillmore, "ignoring" slavery actually meant supporting it, and the southern proslavery faction that now controlled the American Party knew it. Its members were delighted with his nomination.

Democrats held their convention at the beginning of June in Cincinnati, the first time a major political convention convened west of the Appalachians. Like the American Party, most Democrats wanted above all else a ticket that would bypass the divisive issue of slavery and keep the Union together. Although the Kansas-Nebraska Act's flashpoint doctrine of popular sovereignty couldn't be disowned—it was, thanks to Douglas, a position the entire nation associated with the Democrats— what the party *could* do was select a candidate who wasn't immediately implicated in its passage. That not only put an end to Pierce's chances (to this day he remains the only *full-term* president not renominated by his party), but also those of the act's architect, Sen. Stephen Douglas. Moreover, even though the Democrats needed to court as many Know-Nothing votes as they possibly could, they also realized that a huge percentage of their potential supporters were Irish Catholic immigrants. So in addition to publicly defending popular sovereignty and cautiously limiting their use of the word "slavery" to fewer than 10 times in their longish party platform, they condemned nativism.

Powerbrokers in the party initially approached Charles "Pathfinder" Frémont, the dashing explorer of the far west, to be their candidate. But their insistence that he would have to strongly back the Kansas-Nebraska Act and the 1850 Fugitive Slave Law proved a deal breaker for Frémont. The task then was to find a candidate whose position on slavery would appease southern Democrats without sounding so proslavery as to alienate northern Democrats. The man they settled on was James Buchanan, who had the good fortune to have served as ambassador to Great Britain during the congressional debate and national fracas over the Kansas Act. Buchanan, like Pierce before him, was definitely a southern sympathizer. But his absence from the country in 1854 gave him a semblance of clean hands. As a bonus, he was from Pennsylvania, a state that any presidential contender needed to win.

Buchanan had another advantage, or at least something that many Democrats saw as an advantage: with the exception of the Ostend Manifesto embarrassment, he was boringly uncontroversial. Possessed of a rather colorless personality that matched his unadventurous bureaucratic career, he was at 65 the oldest among the men who were that year's contenders for the White House. A lifelong bachelor, his entire adult life had been devoted to public service in one capacity or another. He had served as congressman, senator, secretary of state, and diplomat. Known (not necessarily admiringly) as "Old Public Functionary," he came across as the stereotypical civil servant. Unlike Douglas or Pierce, Buchanan would stir up no violent dislike among voters. Although both of his party rivals gave him a run for his money at the convention, delegates opted for a safe nominee and gave him the nod on the 17th ballot, with John C. Breckinridge of Kentucky as his running mate. The two men complemented each. Breckinridge was from the South, while Buchanan was from the North. Buchanan was an old man, and Breckinridge was in his mid-thirties. Buchanan was drab and musty, Breckinridge handsome and gallant.

A week after the Democrats brought the gavel down on their convention, delegates from the North American Party, the anti-Kansas wing of the Know-Nothings, opened theirs. The hope of party leaders was to fuse with the Republicans and thereby pose a real threat to the Democrats in the upcoming election. The fly in the ointment was that Republican leaders, while happy to receive Know-Nothing votes in the general election, were unwilling to align themselves publicly with Know-Nothing nativism. But at the same time, Republicans worried that the North Americans might snap up John Frémont, a favorite of both parties. So a scheme was concocted, with bribes passing from Republicans to floor delegates at the North American convention, to support Nathaniel Banks, anti-Kansas Speaker of the U.S. House of Representatives, for the nomination. The plan was that when the Republicans held their own convention, overlapping a few days with the North American one, they would nominate Frémont as their candidate, Banks would announce his withdrawal from the race and throw his weight behind Frémont, and rank-and-file supporters of the antislavery Know-Nothings would fall into line. As events turned out, this is exactly what happened. The only glitch in the plan was that no one bothered to let the North American vice presidential nominee, Pennsylvania's William Johnston, in on it. It took quite a bit of persuasion to convince him to withdraw his candidacy as well.

Despite their deep-seated political differences, the American Party nominee and his Democrat rival agreed on one thing: Republicans were a danger to the unity of the nation, and Fillmore and Buchanan would take every opportunity in the months ahead to warn that the election of a "Black Republican" to the White House would lead to the secession of slaveholding states. Buchanan assailed Republicans as "disunionists," insisting that "the charge must be re-iterated again and again" until it sunk into the popular mind.[11] Fillmore, who indiscriminately lumped Republicans and abolitionists together, agreed. Following tradition, the two candidates didn't campaign actively on their own behalf. But their campaign managers made sure that the disunionist message was hammered home again and again in rallies and broadsides. Both the American and the Democratic campaigns against the Republicans from first to last exploited the public's anxiety about the possibility of secession. The tactic proved especially effective with northern Whigs.

The vehemence with which the Know-Nothings and Democrats attacked the Republicans was a clear indication that their new party was the one to watch. The Republicans' strong opposition to the extension of slavery made them unabashedly sectional (even though they frequently and disingenuously claimed that southern hostility rather than their own political convictions made them so). Some of them, such as Ohio's Benjamin Wade and Pennsylvania's Thaddeus Stevens, were outright abolitionists; others, like New York's William Seward, were only a bit less radical in their opposition to slavery. But most Republicans tended to be moderate in their antislavery sentiments, calling neither for an end to the peculiar institution nor for establishing social and legal equality between blacks and whites. Many of them objected to slavery on moral grounds, but even more of them because they feared that extension of slavery into the territories stepped on white settlers' opportunities for upward mobility. Yet regardless of their individual motives, what tied all Republicans together was hostility to the Kansas-Nebraska Act. They were so willing to fuse with any and all like-minded opponents of the bill that they even hesitated to call their national convention, which convened toward the end of June, "Republican."

But Republican identity wasn't based solely on an anti-Nebraska position. More positively, most Republicans, and certainly Abraham Lincoln, were convinced advocates of free soil and free labor, a commitment they shared with the earlier Free Soil Party. The opportunity to improve one's economic and social standing through free labor was, for most Republicans, a defining principle of the American experiment. The upward mobility they championed wasn't aimed at the accumulation of great wealth, but rather the economic independence enjoyed by the worker who has managed to graduate from wage earner to middle-class entrepreneur. Ownership of capital in a small business, shop, or farm was the ultimate goal; yeomanry and entrepreneurship, not plutocracy, the ideal.

According to the Republican model, willingness to work hard had to be accompanied by opportunity, and westward expansion into the undeveloped territories offered the best opportunity in the 1850s. So Republican opposition to slavery's expansion was based as much (and probably more) on the desire to keep Kansas available for white settlers as on a repugnance to human bondage. Slave-worked plantations gobbled up huge tracts of land that otherwise could be claimed and worked by free men trying to improve their lots in life, flooded the market with slave-produced goods that undersold freely produced ones, sapped initiative from slave owners accustomed to living off the labor of others, and provided a dangerous example to nonslaveholders. What the Republicans wanted instead was free men, free soil, free labor—and, in 1856, Frémont.

The basics of the party's platform had been agreed upon four months earlier at an organizational meeting held in Pittsburgh, the first national Republican powwow. All the attendees were from northern states with the exception of Maryland's Francis P. Blair. Under the chairmanship of none other than David Wilmot, the platform committee branded slavery "a relic of barbarism," demanded that Kansas be admitted to the Union as a free state, voiced undying opposition to the Slave Power, and touted northern free labor as vastly superior to the slave system of the South. A full four-fifths of the platform document was devoted to the slavery question, and at the convention itself, delegates were told that they were assembled "to give direction to a movement which is to decide whether the people of the United States are to be hereafter and forever chained to the present national policy of the extension of slavery."[12] Although the Republicans were in favor of protective tariffs, a policy that went hand-in-hand with their championing of free labor, no mention of it was made in the platform lest it alienate undecided Democrats, whose party traditionally opposed tariffs. The platform did, however, advocate federally funded internal improvements such as a transcontinental railroad.

The most likely possibilities to head the Republican presidential ticket were William Seward and Salmon Chase, both of whom enjoyed national reputations as long-standing opponents of slavery. Both of them also longed for the presidency. But ultimately they backed off, fearing that in this first national election for the Republicans, whoever the party picked was almost certain to lose. So they preferred to bide their time until the 1860 election, when the party would be more strongly established and in a better position to take the White House.

With Seward and Chase out of the running, it was pretty clear by the time the convention met that the party's nominee would be the same man who had been courted by both the Democrats and the North Americans: John Frémont. His only real challenger was the elderly Supreme Court justice John McLean, a man who so desperately wanted to be president that he'd been a contender in all three of the other political conventions.

The eagerness with which three political parties wooed Frémont might seem strange, given that he had almost no national political experience. His only service was a scant three months as U.S. senator from California. But as was the case with William Henry Harrison and Zachary Taylor, two past presidents who had come to the office with no experience to speak of, Frémont's lack of a record was seen as an asset. As Republican editor Horace Greeley noted, candidates with records so slim that they had no past to defend and no outstanding political feuds to worry about were ideal for the fraught times.

But Frémont's record was far from blank. He'd taken a consistent anti-slavery stand since shepherding California's 1849 admission into the Union as a free state. More impressive so far as popular opinion went was his romantic life as an explorer and surveyor in the American West. Adulated as the "Pathfinder" for his efforts to chart a navigable rail line through the Rocky Mountains, Frémont exuded an air of virile self-confidence and rugged determination. It didn't hurt that he was extremely

John C. Frémont, an explorer of the far west known as the "Pathfinder," was the first Republican candidate for the presidency. A handsome and popular man, he was nominated more for his celebrity than his qualifications. (Library of Congress)

handsome and, at 43, the youngest man up to that time to run for president. At the convention, Republican delegates nominated him on the first ballot by a huge margin, with New Jersey's William Dayton selected as his running mate. In his acceptance letter, Frémont came out against the Slave Power and in favor of the thesis that the founding fathers had opposed slavery's extension, exactly the positions Lincoln had taken in his Peoria speech. "Nothing is clearer in the history of our institutions, than the design of the nation, in asserting its own independence and freedom, to avoid giving countenance to the extension of slaver," wrote Frémont. But, he warned, "The influence of the small but compact and powerful class of men interested in slavery, who command one section of the country, and wield a vast political control as a consequence in the other, is now directed to turn back this impulse of the Revolution and reverse its principles."[13] These two sentiments spelled out the fundamental Republican position in this and the subsequent presidential election in 1860.

SEVEN DAYS IN MAY

The Democrats' ameliorative strategy in the 1856 presidential campaign was to divert attention away from the harsh phrase "slavery extension" to the more benign "popular sovereignty." Given that the entire nation had focused on little else than slavery since the Kansas-Nebraska debate began, it was naïve on their part to think that they could soft-pedal the issue. But even if it hadn't been, events in the District of Columbia and in the Kansas Territory during a single week in May guaranteed that slavery would be the single most important topic of the entire election.

Although the 1855–1856 winter had temporarily cooled tempers in Kansas, things began to heat up again with the coming of spring. The free state legislature in Topeka elected its own governor in January, and in March appointed two men to travel to Washington to petition Congress on behalf of the territory's free soilers. Such impertinences infuriated pro-slavery legislators in Lecompton, who resolved to enforce with an iron fist the draconian slave code they had passed the preceding year. If doing so provoked free soilers to rash responses, so much the better.

In late April, proslavers got what they wanted when an especially zealous proslavery sheriff was shot by a free-stater. The proslavery press in Kansas shrieked that the sheriff's "murder"—in fact, he was only wounded—cried to the heavens for vengeance. "War to the knife, and the knife to the hilt!" thundered the *Atchison Squatter Sovereign*.[14] Missouri senator David Atchison, always ready for a fight, obliged by leading another band of ruffians into the territory who promptly murdered two free-staters and tarred and feathered a third. (Actually, unable to find a large enough supply of feathers, they substituted cotton balls, an unintended but appropriate symbol of the ruffians' allegiance to the South.) In the meantime, a band of armed Alabama vigilantes arrived in Kansas hoisting a banner that read "The Supremacy of the White Race," and a proslavery judge ordered every single one of the Topeka legislators arrested and charged with treason. Free-staters, armed with Beecher's Bibles, hunkered down in preparation for an all-out war in Bleeding Kansas.

While all this was occurring, the debate on whether Kansas should be admitted as a free or a slave state continued to rage in Washington. Not surprisingly, Congress was deadlocked, with the House controlled by Topeka-supporting Republicans and the Senate by Lecompton-championing Democrats, and insults flew back and forth with a rage unusual even for the turbulent times. Dire warnings about flowing blood, knifes to the hilt, and secession were the order of the day from both pro-slavers and free soil men. But on May 19, the purple rhetoric of violence and vituperation ratcheted up to a new level when the Republican senator from Massachusetts, Charles Sumner, stood before his colleagues and began a harangue entitled "The Crime against Kansas" that was so lengthy it carried over into the next day.

A few days before he delivered the speech, Sumner had told Salmon Chase that he intended to pour out all the "outrage" that he felt in his soul over the escalating violence in Kansas. But "outrage" was too mild a word for what Sumner spewed. He shouted that proslavery action in Kansas was the moral equivalent of sexual assault, "the rape of a virgin territory, compelling it to the hateful embrace of slavery." He described one of the authors of the 1850 Fugitive Slave Act as an adulterer who "polluted" himself with his mistress "the harlot, Slavery." He singled out South Carolina senator Andrew Butler for especially vile recrimination, cruelly mocking a speech defect of his southern colleague's by characterizing his speech as a "loose expectoration" that let fly nothing but blunders. Moreover, Butler's state suffered from "shameful imbecility," as witnessed by its ardent defense of slavery and its never-ending threats of secession. Nor did Stephen Douglas escape Sumner's venom. Although a northerner, the Little Giant was nothing but "the squire of slavery, its very Sancho Panza"—a particularly cutting allusion to Douglas's short stature and stout girth—"ready to do all its humiliating offices." When Douglas furiously protested, Sumner shot back that "the noisome, squat, and nameless animal, to which I now refer, is not the proper model for an American Senator."[15] All in all, Sumner's two-day diatribe was a shameful attack that outraged Democrats and shook even fellow Republicans who agreed with their Massachusetts colleague's condemnation of slavery. But it clearly demonstrated just how intense the congressional debate over Kansas had become.

Westward, in Kansas Territory, the fury that had been building for the past two months exploded on May 21, the day after Sumner ended his verbal assault on the Senate floor, when a proslavery mob of nearly 1,000 armed men attacked the free soil town of Lawrence. They blocked all the roads leading out of Lawrence with cannon and armed men, and then riotously proceeded to destroy two printing presses, burn the home of the governor elected by the Topeka free state legislature, loot stores and homes, and set fire to the Free State Hotel, a fortress-like structure whose walls were so solid that they withstood an initial artillery bombardment. The ubiquitous Senator Atchison was present at the "sacking of Lawrence," as newspapers quickly christened it, and was fired up to spill blood. "If a man or a woman dare to stand before you," he instructed his raiders, "blow them to hell with a chunk of cold lead!"[16] Fortunately, only one life was lost, and that belonging to a drunken proslavery invader who managed to get himself crushed by one of the Free State Hotel's collapsing walls.

The very next day, another wall fell, this time on Senator Sumner back in the District of Columbia. The insulted Senator Butler of South Carolina happened to have a nephew, Preston Brooks, who was a member of the House. Brooks wasn't a man to be trifled with. He had a fiery temper and an enduring dislike of northerners. A Mexican War veteran, he walked with a cane because of an old hip wound from a duel he had fought 15 years earlier.

Sumner's harangue against Butler and the South was the talk of Capitol Hill, and a furious Brooks believed it was his duty to defend both his uncle and South Carolina. It wouldn't do to challenge Sumner to a duel, because such contests were only fought between social equals, and Brooks declared that Sumner's vile speech revealed him to be more beast than human. So the only appropriate response was to beat him senseless, much as one would an unruly cur.

On May 22, Brooks and two House colleagues strode into the Senate chamber after business had finished for the day. Sumner was still seated at his desk. Walking up to him, Brooks said, "Mr. Sumner, I have read your speech twice over carefully. It is a libel on South Carolina, and Mr. Butler, who is a relative of mine." He then rained down a succession of blows from his cane on Sumner's head and shoulders. When a few senators who were still in the chamber tried to intervene, Brooks's two companions threatened them with drubbings of their own. The assault on Sumner ended only when Brooks's cane shattered. Carried unconscious from the Senate, Sumner wouldn't fully recover from the horrible beating for three years. Afterwards, Brooks boasted to anyone who would listen that the senator from Massachusetts bellowed like a calf as he was being thrashed.

Brooks's attack on Sumner stunned the North and, for the most part, delighted the South. The poet William Cullen Bryant wondered in print if antislavers were now to be "chastised"by Southerners "as they chastise their slaves."[17] Brooks's southern colleagues in the House vied with one another asking him for the "sacred relics" of his shattered cane, and jubilant southerners sent him dozens of new walking sticks to congratulate him for his stand against what the *Richmond Enquirer* called "vulgar abolitionists in the Senate."[18] Neither the Senate nor the House formally punished or even censured Brooks, although a federal court fined him $300 in penalties. To prove to the North that his South Carolina constituents approved of his actions, Brooks defiantly resigned from Congress, immediately stood for reelection, and was enthusiastically returned.

Two days after Sumner's thrashing, the storm of violence shifted back to Kansas. John Brown, a Bible-quoting abolitionist thought slightly mad even by some of his supporters, was the captain of an armed band of free-staters in the conflict-torn territory. Hearing about the pending attack on Lawrence, he and his men set out to help defend the town, but were too late to prevent the violence. At about the same time they heard of Lawrence's sacking, they also learned of Brooks's beating of Sumner. An outraged Brown vowed vengeance. Counting up the number of free-staters he believed had been murdered in the past few months, Brown pledged to kill as many proslavers. On the night of May 24–25, he struck. Accompanied by seven of his band, including four of his own sons, he kidnapped five men from their settlements along the Pottawatomie Creek and mercilessly slaughtered them with broadswords. Neither Brown the "Pottawatomie butcher" nor his accomplices were ever legally prosecuted for the bloody massacre, although federal troops unsuccessfully tried to capture them throughout early June.

The three acts of violence following closely on one another's heels, the sack of Lawrence, the beating of Sumner, and Brown's brutal retaliation, helped to solidify northern support for the Republicans in the 1856 presidential race as well as sharpen southern calls for secession. It also made the candidacies of Fillmore, who wanted to ignore the slavery issue, and Buchanan, who as a Democrat had to own the Kansas-Nebraska Act, more problematic. When Fillmore learned of Sumner's beating, he angrily declared that it "has done more for Frémont than any twenty of his warmest friends ... The Republicans ought to pension Brooks for life."[19] He could just as well have said the same thing about the border ruffians' attack on Lawrence and Brown's butchery at Pottawatomie.

THE RACE IS ON

In keeping with the rather fanciful conceit of the day that public office was a gift from the American electorate and not something to be bargained for, none of the presidential candidates actively campaigned. They all wrote letters and were happy to speak to visitors, but they left the active task of canvassing for votes to their managers.

One of the disappointments, not to mention embarrassments, for the Pathfinder's campaign was the refusal of his nationally famous father-in-law, Missouri senator Thomas Hart Benton, to support his bid for the presidency. Benton took seriously the threats of secession if the Republicans won the White House. Hotheads like Brooks, Georgia's Robert Toombs, or Virginia governor Henry Wise (who threatened to muster the state militia in the event of a Republican victory) could be written off as all smoke and no fire. But much steadier statesmen such as former president John Tyler also predicted that disunion would follow a Republican win. As an old Democrat who had fully supported Andrew Jackson's stern response to South Carolina during the Nullification Crisis, Benton felt he had no choice but to oppose any political party whose electoral victory threatened the Union. Unlike his fellow Missouri senator Atchison, he was no friend of slavery. But neither was he willing to fragment the country over it. So he both endorsed and campaigned for Buchanan.

What Frémont lost in his father-in-law, he partially made up for in Abraham Lincoln. Although still mostly known only in his home state, Lincoln had become one of the most influential Republicans in Illinois, and his endorsement went a long way toward boosting any Republican candidate there. Lincoln's initial choice for the nomination had been old John McLean, primarily because Lincoln believed the judge could draw conservative Whigs away from Buchanan. But when the convention nominated Frémont—the same convention, by the way, in which Lincoln came in second in the balloting for the vice president slot—he wholeheartedly threw himself into campaigning for the Pathfinder. Turning the Springfield law office he shared with William Herndon into what became the state's Republican campaign headquarters, Lincoln reckoned that he gave over 100 speeches in support of Frémont and other Republican candidates during that election season. He especially reached out to the state's old Whigs in an effort to convince them that voting for

Fillmore instead of Frémont would only help Buchanan, because Fillmore had no chance of carrying Illinois. "This is as plain," Lincoln pithily wrote in an election letter that was lithographed and distributed across the state, "as the adding up of the weights of three small hogs."[20] Lincoln campaigned so industriously for Frémont that he let a good deal of his law practice slide. Looking back after the election was over and done, he realized that he "lost nearly all of the working part of last year giving my time to the canvass."[21]

During the race for the presidency, the Republicans predictably played up their opposition to slavery's extension, basing their case primarily on the claim that introducing slave labor to the territories eliminated the "free soil" needed for "free labor." A *Springfield Republican* editorial nicely described the electorate that the party especially wished to reach. "Those who work with their hands," wrote the editor, "who live and act independently, who hold the stakes of home and family, of farm and workshop, of education and freedom—these are . . . the very heart of the nation."[22] The most popular Republican slogan in 1856 was predictably alliterative: "Free labor, free press, free men, free soil, free Kansas, and Fremont!" A shorter version, minus the references to Kansas and Frémont, had been the rallying cry of the Free Soil Party in the last two presidential races.

But at least one nationally prominent Republican publicly expressed an additional reason besides free soil and free labor for opposing slavery. On October 25, New York politician William Henry Seward, who had tossed the bombshell of his "higher law" speech from the Senate floor in 1850, delivered another one in Rochester in which he posited an "irrepressible conflict" between champions of liberty and defenders of slavery. The conflict, he contended, wasn't simply a political or economic one. It was also—and fundamentally—moral, a question of whether the "principles of equal and exact justice to all men" will be upheld or debased. When it came to the great war between good and evil in which the slavery debate was a battle, Seward declared that there could be no compromise.

In his Peoria speech two years earlier, Lincoln had made similar points about the immorality of slavery, but he hadn't threatened slaveholders with talk about an irrepressible conflict between good and evil. Seward's speech, on the other hand, was deliberately provocative. It predictably infuriated Democrats—the *New York Herald* labeled Seward an "arch agitator" more dangerous than any abolitionist[23]—and dismayed Republican strategists who hoped to win over moderate or even conservative Whigs. It was exactly the sort of red flag they needed to avoid if they were to defeat Buchanan. But there was at least one man who solidly applauded Seward and who proclaimed that a Republican win would be a moral victory in the great conflict that could "inaugurate a higher and purer standard of Politics and Government."[24] He was the black abolitionist Frederick Douglass.

Instead of Seward's kind of rhetorical saber rattling, more moderate Republican strategists thought it wiser to focus on the dashing figure of Frémont. Campaign biographies of him extolled his pathfinding courage and often included engravings of his handsome figure. The Quaker poet John Greenleaf Whittier wrote heroic poems praising him, and a pamphlet featuring songs about him and his wife Jessie was widely distributed. Lithographic reproductions of his likeness were printed by the tens of thousands, and towns across the nation were encouraged to change their names to Frémont (astoundingly, at least 12 did). Enthusiastic crowds chanted "We follow the Pathfinder!" and "We are Buck hunting!" at Republican rallies. One Republican wag wrote a campaign song that called Buchanan out for his alleged spineless kowtowing to the Slave Power:

> No more I'm James Buchanan—I sold myself down South.
> Henceforth I'll do what my masters please
> And speak what they put in my mouth!
> But don't let that alarm you, forgive his slavish tone.
> Can you ask a man to stand up straight who was born without a
>   backbone?[25]

The insinuation behind the verse was that Frémont, an independently spirited man of the west, had more than his share of the backbone needed to "stand up straight" in defiance of southern powerbrokers.

In response to all this effusiveness, more than one Democratic editor reasonably pointed out that it took a few more qualifications than charisma and mountain climbing to be a good chief executive, and that Frémont seemed to possess none of them. Fillmore's Know-Nothing nativist supporters darkly (and falsely) added that he was a Catholic. And both Democrats and Know-Nothings made frightening predictions of slave insurrections in the South, miscegenation in the North, and a breakup of the Union if the Black Republicans won the day.

VICTORIOUS DEFEAT

Election Day on November 4 was cold and gloomy throughout most of the North. But extraordinarily large crowds of northerners—no fewer than 83 percent of eligible voters—turned out to cast their ballots. In New York City, so many voters showed up that they often had to stand in line for two hours or longer at the polls. Voting in the free states was up by a full 7 percent from the previous presidential election.

Part of the large turnout was attributable to the enthusiastic perception of many northerners that the Republicans would keep the Kansas Territory free without falling into abolitionist extremism. But voting also hit record numbers in the North because many free soil Whigs, Democrats, and Know-Nothings, frightened by what *they* perceived as the radicalism of the Republicans, came out to vote against them. Voters in Lower North border states such as Pennsylvania and Illinois proved particularly wary of the Republicans. It was the fear of what would happen to the Union if a Republican won the White House, so effectively cultivated by both Buchanan and Fillmore, which cost Frémont the election and gave the victory to Old Public Functionary.

In terms of electoral votes, Buchanan was the clear winner, with 174 to Frémont's 114 and Fillmore's paltry 8. Buchanan carried 14 slave states and 5 free ones (including, embarrassingly for Frémont, California), Frémont 11 free states, while Fillmore, losing even his own home state of New York, managed to win over only Maryland. In raw numbers, Buchanan topped Frémont by a mere 500,000 votes. The final tally was 1,838,169 popular votes for Buchanan, 1,335,264 for Frémont—editor Horace Greeley claimed that at least 100,000 of them came from outrage over the Sumner beating—and 874,534 for Fillmore. But when looked at sectionally, the numbers showed that Frémont carried a full 60 percent of the North's popular vote compared to Buchanan's 36 percent and Fillmore's 4. In the South, Buchanan and Fillmore predictably took all the votes, with the Democrat at 56 percent and the Know-Nothing at 44.

The upshot was that Frémont, an inexperienced candidate from a brand-new political party, had come astoundingly close to winning the highest elected office in the land. Had he carried the four free border states that went for Buchanan—New Jersey, Pennsylvania, Indiana, and Illinois—he would've won the election, and done so without any support

Democrat James Buchanan, although known as a "doughface" sympathizer with the South, was his party's nominee in the 1856 election largely because he was untainted by the Kansas-Nebraska controversy. He won the election but proved to be one of the nation's worst presidents. (Library of Congress)

at all from the slave states. Frémont's performance in the North is especially impressive when weighed against the fact that Buchanan's Democrat predecessor Franklin Pierce took 14 of 16 northern states in 1852, 9 more than Buchanan carried. Moreover, the Republicans achieved considerable success in congressional, state, and local elections across the northern states. As one recent historian notably put it, the Republican loss of the White House was actually a "victorious defeat."[26]

The presidential election of 1856 verified the deep sectional divide in the nation. In effect, the national debate over slavery created two presidential races in 1856: a Northern one which pitted Frémont against Buchanan, and a Southern one between Buchanan and Fillmore. Only 1,200 votes were cast for Frémont in the South, and those were write-ins since he wasn't on any of the ballots. The South may not have formally seceded from the Union, but it was plain to many observers that the rift between North and South was so deep as almost to be a de facto split, one that would be stretched to the breaking point four years later.

Buchanan was angered and humiliated by the fact that he'd been so decisively rejected by the majority of northerners, and his less-than-gracious victory speech, delivered from the porch of his estate outside Lancaster, Pennsylvania, both reflected his pique and demonstrated beyond a doubt his doughface sympathies. "The people of the North," he chided, had foolishly supported a "dangerous party"—the Republicans—that vilified the "southern people [who] still cherish a love for the Union."[27] It was an amazingly petulant remark for a president-elect who properly should have focused on mending fences and encouraging collaboration across party lines.

Another Democrat, President Pierce, was also bitter and humiliated by his failure to receive his party's renomination, and it showed when he delivered his final message to Congress on December 2, less than four weeks after Buchanan's victory. Pierce was too loyal a Democrat to say anything negative about Buchanan. But he angrily condemned antislavery agitation in the North, joining his voice to the chorus of those who insisted that opposition to the Kansas-Nebraska Act endangered the Union. He disdained to mention the Republicans by name, but it was clear to anyone who heard or read his speech that he had them in mind. They were troublemakers who needed close watching.

One week later, at a Republican gathering in Chicago, Abraham Lincoln responded to one of the more extraordinary accusations Pierce had made in his congressional message: that free soilers sought to disregard the Constitution by overthrowing slavery in states where it existed. On the contrary, countered Lincoln, it was the Democratic Party that exhibited disloyalty to the principle of "the equality of men" on which the nation was founded. "The late Presidential election," he said, "was a struggle, by one party, to discard that central idea, and to substitute for it the opposite idea that slavery is right." It was a theme he'd introduced in his Peoria speech, and it would become central to his thinking and campaigning over the next four years.

Now that the election was over, said Lincoln, there was much work to do. Republicans needed to take seriously the anxieties about disunion that had prodded Whigs in Illinois and elsewhere to vote for Fillmore instead of Frémont. Doing so was important because it would build a stronger base for the next presidential campaign. But it was also important because mending broken relations was simply the right thing to do. In words that sound a lot like the plea for reconciliation between North and South that Lincoln would make in his 1861 inaugural address, he now recommended peace between Republicans and Whigs.

> Can we not come together, for the future? Let everyone who really believes, and is resolved, that free society is not, *and shall not be*, a failure, and who can conscientiously declare that in the past contest he has done only what he thought best—let every such one have charity to believe that every other one can say as much. Thus let bygones be bygones. Let past differences, as nothing be; and with steady eye on the real issue, let us reinaugurate the good old "central ideas" of the republic. We *can* do it. The human heart *is* with us—God is with us.[28]

It was a sentiment whose generosity and nobility revealed the caliber of the man Lincoln was and the statesman he one day would become.

NOTES

Chapter epigraphs are from Philip S. Foner and Yuval Taylor (eds.), *Frederick Douglass: Selected Speeches and Writings* (Chicago: Chicago Review Press, 1999), 342; and Joel Benton (ed.), *Greeley on Lincoln* (New York: Baker & Taylor, 1893), 133.

1. James G. Blaine, *Twenty Years of Congress: From Lincoln to Garfield* (Norwich, CT: Henry Hill, 1886), I:118.

2. Roy P. Basler (ed.), *The Collected Works of Abraham Lincoln* (New Brunswick, NJ: Rutgers University Press, 1953), 2:341. Hereafter cited as CW.

3. David W. Bradford (ed.), *Vote Lincoln! The Presidential Campaign Biography of Abraham Lincoln, 1860* (Sacramento, CA: Boston Hill Press, 2010), 112.

4. CW 2:514.

5. Bradford, *Vote Lincoln!*, 114, 115.

6. Michael F. Holt, *The Political Crisis of the 1850s* (New York: W. W. Norton, 1978), 157.

7. CW 2:323.

8. James McPherson, *Battle Cry of Freedom: The Civil War Era* (New York: Oxford University Press, 1988), 146.

9. Frank Severence (ed.), *Millard Fillmore Papers* (Buffalo, NY: Buffalo Historical Society Publications, 1907), 2:348.

10. Michael F. Holt, *The Rise and Fall of the American Whig Party: Jacksonian Politics and the Onset of the Civil War* (New York: Oxford University Press, 1999), 911.

11. McPherson, *Battle Cry of Freedom*, 158.

12. Allan Nevins, *Ordeal of the Union: A House Dividing, 1852–1857* (New York: Charles Scribner's Sons, 1947), 460.

13. Tom Chaffin, *Pathfinder: John Charles Frémont and the Course of American Empire* (New York: Hill and Wang, 2002), 440.

14. Stephen Oates, *To Purge This Land with Blood: A Biography of John Brown* (New York: Harper & Row, 1970), 123.

15. *Congressional Globe*, 34th Congress, 1st sess., Appendix, 547.

16. Eric H. Walther, *The Shattering of the Union: America in the 1850s* (Lanham, MD: SR Books, 2004), 91.

17. William E. Gienapp, "The Crime Against Sumner: The Caning of Charles Sumner and the Rise of the Republican Party," *Civil War History* 25 (1979): 230.

18. Ibid., 222.

19. Tyler G. Anbinder, *Nativism and Slavery: The Northern Know Nothings and the Politics of the 1850s* (New York: Oxford University Press, 1992), 236.

20. CW 2:374.

21. CW 2:413.

22. Bruce C. Levine, *Half Slave and Half Free: The Roots of Civil War* (New York: Hill and Wang, 1992), 208.

23. John M. Taylor, *William Henry Seward: Lincoln's Right Hand* (Washington, D.C.: Brassey's, 1991), 107.

24. Chaffin, *Pathfinder*, 445.

25. Walther, *The Shattering of the Union*, 111.

26. William E. Gienapp, *The Origins of the Republican Party, 1852–1856* (New York: Oxford University Press, 1987), 413.

27. Jean H. Baker, *James Buchanan* (New York: Henry Holt, 2002), 72–73.

28. CW 2:385.

CHAPTER 5

LINCOLN VS. DOUGLAS

I tell you that this doctrine of Lincoln's declaring that the negroes and white men were included alike in the Declaration of Independence, made equal by Divine Providence, is a monstrous heresy.

—Stephen Douglas

I should like to know if taking this old Declaration of Independence, which declares that all men are equal upon principle, and making exceptions to it, where will it stop? If one man says it does not mean a negro, why may not another say it does not mean some other man?

—Abraham Lincoln

Few men were more responsible for the Republican capture of the White House in 1860 than James Buchanan. As president, his policies, feuds, and public statements helped fragment the Democratic party, alienate northern opponents of slavery, and encourage the slave states in their push for an extension of slavery into the Kansas Territory. Although a Pennsylvanian, Buchanan's political and regional sympathies were with the South, and he made no effort to disguise them.

These sympathies were apparent at the very beginning of his administration in his cabinet appointments. Four of the men he selected were wealthy slave owners who would throw in their lot with the Confederacy four years later. The other three were northern Democrats; but, like Buchanan, they were doughfaces. In both his cabinet selections and in the hundreds of patronage positions that were his to award, Buchanan basically ignored free soil Democrats.

He didn't ignore Republicans. Buchanan was convinced that the new party whose "victorious defeat" in the presidential election was both a shock and an embarrassment to him was dangerous, and he took it upon himself to discredit Republicans as often as possible. As he wrote to a friend shortly after his election, "The great object of my administration will be to arrest, if possible, the agitation of the Slavery question at the

North and to destroy sectional parties"—with Republicans as his primary targets. His first public volley was launched in his inaugural address, in which he declared that only the sovereign will of the people ("a principle as ancient as free government itself"), not congressional mandate, could determine the issue of slavery in the territories. In saying this, he not only gave his stamp of approval to the extension of slavery, he also leapt over an ambiguity in the popular sovereignty doctrine that left unanswered the question of whether territorial (as opposed to state) legislatures even had legal authority to address the slavery question at all. But, he continued, the matter would soon be mooted by a "pending" decision from the Supreme Court. He assured his audience that he would "cheerfully submit" to whatever judicial decision was made.[1]

DRED SCOTT AND LECOMPTON

The decision Buchanan referred to was in the case of *Dred Scott v. Sandford*, which had been moving its way through the courts since 1846. Over the years it had become a closely watched legal battle because much was riding on it. The plaintiff was a Virginia-born slave named Dred Scott who was suing for his freedom on the grounds that his master, an army officer, had relocated with him to the free states of Illinois and Wisconsin, and that residence there granted him de facto freedom. As free citizens of the United States, Scott claimed, he and his family were being held in bondage illegally.

The Supreme Court announced its decision two days after Buchanan's inauguration. But the president-elect knew the outcome before he delivered his inaugural address. Before his inauguration, Buchanan had written privately to Justice Robert Grier, a fellow Pennsylvanian, urging him to vote against Scott. Buchanan's solicitation of Grier's vote was improper, but understandable. He knew that the southern majority on the Court would rule against Scott, and didn't want the decision to appear as though it were made exclusively on sectional lines. Appreciating what was at stake, Grier obliged. In his own written opinion, Chief Justice Taney demolished Scott's case by notoriously declaring that no black, not even a free one, could ever be a citizen of the United States; that slaves had the legal status of property and were devoid of any rights that white men were obliged to honor; and that the Fifth Amendment's protection of

Dred Scott was the plaintiff in one of the most important cases of constitutional law in U.S. history. The Supreme Court ruled in 1857 that neither Scott nor any other black person, free or enslaved, possessed civil liberties. In his debates with Stephen Douglas, Lincoln cited the Supreme Court's decision as evidence of what he and others believed to be a Slave Power conspiracy. (Library of Congress)

property meant that bringing slaves into the territories—or into states, for that matter—couldn't be prohibited. This in effect declared the Missouri Compromise's ban on slavery north of the 36-30 unconstitutional and nullified the doctrine of popular sovereignty. It's no surprise, then, that Buchanan announced in his inaugural address that he would "cheerfully submit" to the Court's decision. He had engineered it by putting pressure on Grier.

Reaction to the Court's decision was predictable. Southerners applauded it, most having already made up their minds that the Missouri Compromise's blocking of slavery from the western territories was unconstitutional. Fire-eaters positively gloated. Robert Barnwell Rhett bragged, "We have been simply a step in advance of the highest tribunals in the country, in declaring what was the law of the land, and seeking honestly and faithfully to enforce it."[2] Most northerners, on the other hand, were furious. The *New York Independent* called the decision the "moral assassination of a race," while the *Ohio State Journal* denounced it for transforming the territories into "one great slave pen." State legislatures in New England and Pennsylvania condemned the decision and vowed to resist it. Republicans in particular were infuriated, not the least because the decision seemed to nullify their party's core issue of nonextension. Abraham Lincoln angrily declared: "I am refusing to obey it as a political rule." Speaking for his fellow Republicans, he warned that "Somebody has to reverse that decision, since it is made, and we mean to reverse it." But, he prudently added, "we mean to do it peaceably."[3]

Part of the political fallout from *Dred Scott* hit Stephen Douglas as well. He was up for reelection to the U.S. Senate in 1858, and he had his eye on the White House in 1860. To be successful in either campaign, he had to avoid alienating both free soilers and slavery supporters. To appease the South, he endorsed the Supreme Court ruling. But to appease the North, he held onto a version of popular sovereignty, arguing as early as summer of 1857 that even though the Court's decision established that slaveholders had the legal right to bring slaves into the territories, citizens had the right to withhold local protection for slave property. It was a clumsy attempt to hold together two policies that didn't fit well, but it would be defended by Douglas again and again in his debates with Lincoln the following year.

Buchanan's conniving for a Supreme Court ruling that favored slave owners did a good deal of harm to party unity among the Democrats. His effort later the same year to force an obviously rigged Kansas territorial constitution through Congress inflicted even more damage.

By the time Buchanan took office, the pro- and antislavery factions vying for control of Kansas had issued contradictory laws concerning slavery in the territory. The slave state legislature in Lecompton legalized it; the free state one in Topeka banned slaves, as well as free blacks, from the territory. The situation was chaotic.

In October 1857, the Lecompton government held elections to select territorial legislators as well as a delegate to the U.S. Congress. Voting fraud on the part of proslavers was so egregious that the territorial governor, the third assigned by Washington to the troubled territory, threw out thousands of ballots. His action riled powerful leaders in the South. Buchanan, fearing their anger, withdrew his support from the governor, who promptly resigned. In the meantime, the illegally elected but unfazed Lecompton legislators met to draft a constitution to submit to Congress as part of the federal requirements for admission to the Union. The document explicitly recognized the slaves already in the territory as the legal property of their owners. Knowing that the proposed constitution could never pass a territory-wide referendum, the delegates approved it themselves and sent it directly to Washington.

Although Buchanan extended official recognition to the Lecompton rather than the Topeka government, this streamlining of the democratic process was too much even for him. In response to his objections, the Lecompton legislature pulled a sleight of hand. It agreed to hold a referendum on slavery, but not on the drafted constitution. Kansans could vote either for or against slavery, period. But since the constitution already upheld the right of white Kansans to own property in the form of slaves, the referendum, regardless of how it went, wouldn't abolish slavery in the territory.

Predictably, as a result of stuffed ballot boxes and the boycotting of the election by most free-staters, slavery in the territory was upheld by a vote of 6,143 to 569. When the Topeka government held its own election less than a month later, the tally was 10,266 against and only 162 for slavery. Over the objections of Stephen Douglas, chairman of the Senate Committee on Territories, Buchanan accepted the Lecompton vote, incredibly charging that free state Kansans were "mercenaries of abolitionism" who had tried to create a "revolutionary government."[4] He also let it be known that he expected Democrats to support the Lecompton constitution as a test of party loyalty.

But Douglas refused to be cowed. Up to the Lecompton debacle, he'd been a loyal party man. He had even swallowed his 1856 hopes for the Democratic presidential nomination because party strategists thought that Buchanan, untainted by the Kansas-Nebraska controversy, had a better chance of winning the general election. But the administration's endorsement of the obviously rigged Lecompton constitution was a direct challenge to the doctrine of popular sovereignty in which Douglas sincerely believed and on which he had hung his political hat. So he came out swinging against the president, furiously declaring: "By God, sir, I made Mr. James Buchanan, and by God, sir, I will unmake him!"[5]

On the Senate floor, Douglas appealed to southern Democrats to reject Lecompton by inviting them to consider a reversal of the case. Suppose, he said, a convention of free-staters forced through a fraudulent constitution that forbade slavery. "Would Southern gentlemen have submitted to such an outrage?"[6] Douglas's appeal to southern self-interest was grounded in the principle of popular sovereignty: if the will of the people was ignored, no one, slave owner or free soiler, was safe. But after the *Dred Scott* decision, proslavery Democrats no longer needed popular sovereignty. Jefferson Davis disdainfully dismissed Douglas's argument as "a siren's song."[7]

At the end of the day, Senate Democrats fell in behind Buchanan and approved the Lecompton constitution, even though they knew it didn't reflect the will of the people of Kansas. But it got held up in the House, despite the fact that the Buchanan machine went into overdrive to push it through by vigorously threatening some reluctant congressmen and bribing others. The debate on the floor was so fierce that in early February 1858, more than 30 representatives scuffled in a North vs. South free-for-all. After that, right up to the outbreak of the Civil War, members came armed to the House chamber. As South Carolina's James Hammond observed, the only congressmen who attended sessions without a revolver and a knife "are those who have two revolvers."[8] The House eventually rejected the constitution, and Kansas only entered the Union—as a free state—in 1861.

Buchanan for his part vowed to break Douglas. He had the senator stripped of his leadership of the Committee on Territories and began removing Douglasites from patronage positions and replacing them with his own men. The ensuing acrimonious public feud between the party's two most public figures widened the rift between northern and southern Democrats to such an extent that the 1860 presidential election in effect was lost two years before it was actually held. Additionally, it nearly cost Douglas his bid for reelection to the U.S. Senate in 1858.

A HOUSE DIVIDED

In June 1857, Stephen Douglas, still trying to appease both sides of the slavery debate with his strained contention that popular sovereignty was compatible with the *Dred Scott* decision, gave a speech in Springfield, Illinois, in which he defended the Supreme Court ruling. Lincoln, by then a leader in the state's Republican party, responded two weeks later with a speech of his own denouncing the decision. (He would later astutely claim that Douglas tried to sell his position "as the best means to *break down*, and to *uphold* the slave power. No ingenuity can long keep those opposing elements in harmony."[9]) Rebutting Taney's insistence that the nation's founders never intended blacks to be given legal rights, Lincoln asserted that the Declaration of Independence's guarantees of life, liberty, and happiness applied equally to all men, black or white. The founders, he said, "defined with tolerable distinctness, in what respects they did consider all men created equal"—not equal in *all* respects, but certainly equal when it came to life, liberty, and happiness.[10] In the hands of slavery's defenders, however, the guarantee of "certain inalienable rights" had incrementally eroded. "One after another [proslavers] have closed the heavy iron doors upon [the black man], and now they have him, as it were, bolted in with a lock of a hundred keys."[11]

Lincoln spoke out against Douglas partly because he genuinely disagreed with the Democrat's stand on slavery extension, but also because he was alarmed at the possibility that Douglas's opposition to Lecompton had won him the admiration and support of a few powerful Republican leaders back east. Horace Greeley, editor of the *New York Tribune*, was especially effusive in his praise of Douglas and publicly urged Illinois Republicans to support his bid for reelection. Lincoln was thunderstruck by the endorsement. "What does the *New York Tribune* mean by its constant eulogizing, and admiring, and magnifying Douglas?" he wondered. It looked to him as if eastern Republicans intended to "sacrifice us here in Illinois."[12] From Lincoln's perspective, cozying up to Douglas simply because he ruffled Buchanan's feathers was a losing proposition because it betrayed the principles upon which the Republican Party was built. Douglas had said time and again that he didn't care if slavery was voted up or down in the Kansas Territory, just so long as the final decision was based on local popular will. For him, moral judgments had no place in politics. But to Lincoln, this calculated moral indifference to slavery was symptomatic of the kind of spiritual decay that legitimated it in the first place. As he would say a few months later, "the difference between the Republican and the Democratic parties on the leading issue of this contest . . . is that the former consider slavery a moral, social and political wrong, while the latter *do not*." In fact, continued Lincoln, invoking popular sovereignty when it came to slavery forced Democrats into the bizarre position of having to declare "that slavery is *better* than freedom" if the

New York Tribune editor Horace Greeley infuriated Lincoln by suggesting that Illinois Republicans ought to endorse Democrat Stephen Douglas's bid for reelection to the Senate. Greeley was impressed by Douglas's opposition to the Kansas Lecompton Constitution. Lincoln believed Douglas's moral indifference to slavery was anti-Republican. (National Archives)

majority of (white) people claimed it was.[13] Did eastern Republicans really want to throw their weight behind a man who embraced such a cynical point of view? Doing so, as one Republican editor put it, risked inviting an "ominous wooden horse into our camp."[14] Another Illinois Republican put the matter more pithily. "A penitent prostitute may be received into the church," he said, "but she should not lead the choir."[15]

Almost exactly one year after his Springfield speech, Lincoln, who had been working assiduously to build a Republican base in Illinois, was named the state party's "first and only choice" to challenge Douglas for his U.S. Senate seat. Lincoln's acceptance speech (a longish one for him, lasting 30 or 35 minutes) was a bold statement of Republican values—too bold, in the eyes of some of his associates who, reading it beforehand, feared that it might alienate cautious Illinois Whigs whose votes were essential for a

Republican win. But Lincoln refused to water it down. He realized full well that he had to steer a middle course that avoided both the moral indifference of Douglas and the fervent radicalism of abolitionism. But he also knew that he had to demonstrate to voters that the Republican Party remained relevant despite the *Dred Scott* decision. So his acceptance speech was carefully crafted to strike a defiant tone in its defense of Republican principles without frightening away potential supporters. Afterwards, in defending his speech, Lincoln said that if only one thing would ever be remembered about him, he hoped it would be his remarks at Springfield.

The speech began with a biblical allusion (Matthew 12) that immediately captured the audience's attention and would be repeated and reprinted many times throughout the campaign. Lincoln noted that the slavery debate embroiling the nation "will not cease, until a crisis shall have been reached and passed. 'A house divided against itself cannot stand.' I believe this government cannot endure, permanently half *slave* and half *free*." Lincoln went on to insist that he didn't expect the house to fall. The Union, he declared, would endure. But he did expect it would "cease to be divided. It will become all one thing, or all the other."[16] Lincoln was recycling here, having used the "house divided" image as early as 1843, and the "half slave, half free" phrase in 1855. It showed a firm continuity in his thinking on the slavery issue.

Although it attracted the most public attention, the opening of Lincoln's speech was but a short prelude to the two main points he wanted to make. The first was a calling out of the Democrats on what he believed to be their plot to extend slavery across the entire country. In his opinion, the leading conspirators were Douglas, the champion of the Kansas-Nebraska Act; former President Pierce, who signed the act; Chief Justice Taney, who wrote the majority opinion in *Dred Scott*; and President Buchanan, who endorsed the Lecompton constitution. Lincoln admitted that he couldn't prove the conspiracy, but he believed he *could* make a strong circumstantial case.

> [W]hen we see a lot of framed timbers, different portions of which we know have been gotten out at different times and places by different workmen— Stephen [Douglas], Franklin [Pierce], Roger [Taney], and James [Buchanan], for instance—and when we see these timbers joined together, and see they

exactly make the frame of the house ... we find it impossible to not *believe* that Stephen and Franklin and Roger and James all understood one another from the beginning, and all worked upon a common *plan* or *draft* drawn before the first lick was struck.[17]

Although Lincoln's accusation of a deliberate collusion turned out to be false, the charge resonated with northerners who already believed that the Slave Power dominated national politics. Lincoln returned to the accusation at the outset of his campaign debates with Douglas, although he eventually softened it (although not to his opponent's advantage) by declaring that Douglas was a pawn rather than a ringleader in a southern-led plot to nationalize slavery.

The second point Lincoln hammered home in his speech was that Douglas's claim to be neutral on the issue of slavery was a ploy to lull the nation into an easily manipulated complacency. "We shall *lie down* pleasantly dreaming that the people of *Missouri* are on the verge of making their State *free*; and we shall *awake* to the *reality*, instead, that the *Supreme* Court has made *Illinois* a *slave* State."[18] Douglas-admiring Republicans needed to wake up. Despite Douglas's feud with Buchanan over Lecompton, "clearly, he is not now with us—he does not pretend to be—he does not promise to ever be."[19] In a way, Lincoln's "house divided" allusion at the beginning of his speech was as much a warning to the Republican Party as to the nation. The following March, three months after the Illinois senatorial campaign ended in a Republican defeat, Lincoln still believed it would have been a colossal mistake for his party to have endorsed Douglas. As he told a gathering in Chicago, "if we, the Republicans of this State, had made Judge Douglas our candidate for the Senate of the United States last year and had elected him, there would today be no Republican party in this Union."[20]

Although Lincoln was unanimously and enthusiastically endorsed by Illinois Republicans, he was little known outside of the state, while his incumbent rival had a national reputation. But Douglas sensed he was facing a hard fight. "I shall have my hands full," he told an associate when he heard that Lincoln was to be his opponent. "He is the strong man of his party—full of wit, facts, dates—and the best stump speaker ... [I]f I beat him, my victory will be hardly won."[21] Douglas was actually girding himself to fight a two-front war. He was also up against Buchanan, who wrathfully vowed to call in every debt owed him by Illinois Democrats to block the rebellious senator's reelection.

The campaign began in early July with the two men speaking on consecutive nights in Chicago. Douglas, who went first, unsurprisingly reaffirmed the doctrine of popular sovereignty. "If there is any principle dearer and more sacred than all others in free governments, it is that which asserts the right of every people to form and adopt their own fundamental laws, and to manage and regulate their own internal affairs and domestic institutions." Then he introduced two themes that would become refrains throughout the entire campaign. The first was that, contrary to Lincoln's assertions, the founders had no difficulty at all with a "house divided" when it came to the question of slavery. The Union had endured for over 70 years with a division of opinion between North and South, and there was no reason why it couldn't continue to do so. Douglas's second theme was that Lincoln and the Republicans were the true threats to the Union, because they wanted to grant blacks "equality with the white race," and that abomination would inevitably lead to a "war of extermination" between North and South. Douglas assured the crowd that he personally had no problem with granting the "negro" "every right and every privilege which his capacity would enable him to enjoy." But he nonetheless belonged to an "inferior race" and did not deserve legal equality with a white man. Nor had the founders intended otherwise when they wrote the Constitution.[22]

The following night, Lincoln took on Douglas in a speech that was one of the finest he ever gave. He dismissed popular sovereignty by pointing out that it was rendered irrelevant by *Dred Scott*. Although he confessed that "I have always hated slavery, I think, as much as any Abolitionist,"[23] he avowed, as he would time and again over the course of the campaign, that he didn't think the free states had a right to interfere with it in the slave states. So much for Douglas's hysterical evocation of a war of extermination. Douglas also erred, continued Lincoln, in his assertion that the founders approved of slavery. The record showed that, at best, they tolerated it. Finally, Lincoln rejected the charge that he and the Republicans agitated for complete equality between the races. All they asked for blacks was an equal share of the rights guaranteed to all by the Declaration of Independence. To deny this was nothing less than a thinly disguised return to the "king-craft" which "always bestrode the necks of the people."

Invoking a familiar metaphor, Lincoln declared it "the same old serpent that says you work and I eat, you toil and I will enjoy the fruits of it."[24] (In his very last debate with Douglas three months later, Lincoln would return to this image.) Then he wrapped up his speech on a note intended to put the contest between himself and Douglas in a wider perspective. "Let us discard all this quibbling about this man and that man—this race and that race and the other race being inferior, and therefore they must be placed in an inferior position ... Let us discard all these things, and unite as one people throughout this land, until we shall once more stand up declaring that all men are created equal."[25]

After this initial crossing of swords, Lincoln's campaign strategy was simply to pursue Douglas around the state, grabbing the last word by following up everywhere his rival spoke with a speech of his own. But after he tagged along after Douglas to Springfield for a second round of public addresses, unfriendly newspapers jeered that Lincoln was always in Douglas's shadow, lacking sufficient substance to cast one of his own. Lincoln's campaign managers, worried about public perception, urged him to challenge Douglas to a series of face-to-face debates. For his part, Lincoln balked, content to continue following his opponent around the state. But he finally agreed to sound Douglas out. The Little Giant initially dismissed the suggestion. As far as he was concerned, there was nothing to be gained by debating Lincoln. But he changed his mind on second thought, agreeing to seven different rounds, one each in seven of the state's nine districts. (The two men had already spoken in the other two districts when they exchanged speeches in Chicago and Springfield.) Douglas also insisted on setting the format for the debates, just as he had in Peoria back in 1854. One party would speak for an hour, the other would respond for an hour and a half, and the first would have one-half hour for rebuttal. The order of speaking would rotate at each location. The race was on.

FIRE ON THE PRAIRIE

It's difficult today to conceive of how much excitement the contest between Douglas and Lincoln churned up. People traveled for miles to hear the two candidates square off. Although attendance at the debates shrank as the debates wore on and wintery weather began to set in, even the most sparsely attended had audiences of over 1,000 people. At the best attended ones, the crowd surged to somewhere between 15,000 and 20,000 people. They swarmed on the towns in which the two men debated, camping out in tents or sleeping in buckboards when there were no more rooms to rent. They were wildly enthusiastic and often rowdy in support of their respective candidates, frequently interrupting the speeches with shouts of agreement or disagreement, good-natured jokes, and ill-tempered heckling. Many of the debates were preceded by loud and gaudy parades. There was plenty of drinking, not a few fistfights, and probably more than one pickpocket working the crowds. But perhaps the most startling thing of all was the crowd's willingness—even eagerness—to listen to the debates for a full three hours, enduring blistering heat and choking dust when the debates began in late August and cold winds and wet weather as they wound up in mid-October. As a reporter covering the debates for the *New York Evening Post* remarked in wonderment, "the prairies are on fire."[26]

Two men more different in temperament, style, and appearance couldn't be imagined. Lincoln was unusually tall, Douglas unusually short. Lincoln was so thin that he looked almost unhealthy. Douglas was so stout that he sometimes looked bloated, especially after he'd been drinking heavily, something he tended to do more and more as the campaign wore on and his exhaustion level rose. Douglas looked every inch the powerful and urbane senator. He was always elegantly dressed, often in an immaculate blue suit with silver buttons. Lincoln, on the other hand, looked like the backwoods lawyer he was, sporting "a rusty frock-coast with sleeves that should have been longer" and pants whose shortness "permitted a very full view of his large feet."[27]

Their styles of delivery mirrored their different personalities. Douglas's rhetoric was passionately effervescent. He strode back and forth across the stage as he spoke, theatrically waving his arms and clenching his fists, speaking quickly but grammatically in a bass voice so deep that one listener compared it to the full-throated "roar of a lion."[28] By contrast, Lincoln spoke slowly and rarely moved about. Occasionally he extended a forefinger to make a point, and he had the habit of occasionally bending his knees and jerking upwards for emphasis. Sometimes he fumbled with his glasses, good-naturedly asking the crowd to bear with him. His voice was at the opposite range of Douglas's, a twangy tenor that could become piercingly high when he got excited. Sometimes he betrayed his lack of formal schooling with a lapse of grammar. Always the lawyer, Lincoln also tended to interrupt the flow of his main remarks with long sidebars that risked confusing his auditors.

Thematically, nothing new was revealed during the debates. The two men's positions were already pretty well known before they squared off against one another, and neither of them changed his mind. The people who flocked to hear them most likely came to cheer on their candidates rather than to pick up new information about the differences in their plat-forms. But the very familiarity of the positions defended by Douglas and Lincoln indicated just how much a part of the national consciousness they had become in the preceding decade. In a very real way, the Illinois-based debate between the two senatorial candidates was a microcosm of the nationwide one on slavery.

The broad position defended by Douglas was, of course, his doctrine of popular sovereignty, salted with frequent self-congratulations on his val-iant opposition to Lecompton. Whether or not a state or territory opted for slavery, he maintained, was entirely its business, not the federal govern-ment's, and this position was entirely compatible with the Supreme Court's *Dred Scott* decision. Slavery was a political, not a moral, issue. Legislators, whether local or federal, had no business trying to mandate morality. The continuation of the Union wasn't jeopardized by slavery, but rather by its opponents.

But of course the debates weren't just venues for explanation. They were also opportunities for attack, and the Little Giant took advantage of them. He hammered on Lincoln's opposition to the Mexican War, insinu-ating that it was little short of treason. He played the race card again and again by insisting that Lincoln preached a racial equality between blacks and whites that would eventually lead to miscegenation. He argued that Lincoln preached sectional warfare, maintaining that the real agenda of "Black Republicanism" had become clear when John Brown slaughtered proslavers in Pottawatomie, Kansas. Lincoln, in short, was nothing more than a disguised abolitionist.

For his part, Lincoln focused repeatedly on two themes. The first was that slavery in general and the extension of slavery into the territories in particular was a moral, and not just a political, issue. Slavery was wrong, period. Lincoln and his fellow Republicans were ready to put up with its presence in the slave states as a constitutionally guaranteed legal right. But its formal legality didn't negate its immorality. Attempts on the part of Douglas or anyone else to see it as morally indifferent were both wrong-minded and pernicious. Lincoln's second theme was that the Declaration of Independence, which was at least as important a founding document as the Constitution, promised basic civil rights to all men, not excluding blacks. At the founding of the nation, slavery had been tolerated as a temporary concession to the southern states with the assumption that it would eventually die out and in the meantime wouldn't spread.

In between defending these basic points, Lincoln took his share of potshots at Douglas. He argued that as the champion of the Kansas-Nebraska Act, Douglas wasn't at all neutral on the issue of slavery in Kansas, despite disingenuous efforts on his part to claim otherwise. The Little Giant's doctrine of popular sovereignty threatened the growth of white labor and white prosperity in the territories. Lincoln charged, with good reason, that Douglas's claim that the Republicans advocated racial equality was at best a misreading and at worst a deliberate distortion of their position. And as already mentioned, he returned in the first few debates to the Slave Power conspiracy charge that he'd raised in his House Divided speech.

The exchanges between Lincoln and Douglas focused squarely on the slavery issue. Other issues that divided Republicans and Democrats such as federally funded internal improvements or protective tariffs came up only insofar as they related to slavery and its extension. From first to last, slavery was the main topic over which the two candidates wrangled. It was also the topic that their audiences wanted to hear about.

But the slavery question that was the focus of the entire campaign was grounded in an even more fundamental issue: whether ethical considerations ought to inform public policy. Douglas believed that the two ought not to be mingled. Lincoln, on the other hand, had the intuition that without a moral framework, public policy risked sanctioning evil. As one of the more perceptive historians of the debates notes, "at the deepest level, what Lincoln defended in the debates was the possibility that there could be a moral core to a democracy."[29] The stakes in the campaign were high, involving not only the issue of slavery but the very nature of deliberative democracy.

The first debate was held on August 21 in the north-central town of Ottawa. Douglas had the podium first, but Ottawa was strong Republican territory. Like most of the nation, Illinois was divided by section on the slavery issue. The northern part of the state, settled by westward-migrating New Englanders, leaned toward an antislavery position. Southern Illinois, home to many relocated Missourians, Kentuckians, and Tennesseans, was proslavery, or at least anti-Republican.

Ottawa's normal population of 9,000 doubled as thousands of people poured in. Newspaper accounts of the event described the land surrounding the town as dotted with hundreds of campfires the night before the debate. The next hot and dry morning, the crowd congregating around the speakers' podium kicked up suffocating clouds of dust. But excitement was high, even more than at a county fair. Local militia members marched in formation, brass cannon boomed, and political banners festooned buildings. The entry of the two candidates was equally stirring. A half-mile procession of cheering supporters accompanied Lincoln. Douglas, for his part, made a grand entrance in an elegant carriage drawn by white horses.

Despite being in a part of the state sympathetic to his message, Lincoln didn't shine in this initial debate. Douglas immediately took the offensive, hammering his opponent with pointed questions about his positions on the renewal of the slave trade, the Fugitive Slave Law of 1850, the admission of new slave states to the Union, and the extension of slavery into the western territories. He also took the occasion to repeat the racial accusation he'd made in Chicago a month earlier. Republicans, he charged, wanted to turn Illinois into an enclave of freed slaves and even to mix the races. But this would be disastrous. "I do not question Mr. Lincoln's conscientious belief that the Negro was made his equal and hence his brother. But for my part, I do not regard the Negro as my equal, and positively deny that he is my brother or any kin to me whatever."[30]

Perhaps thrown off balance by Douglas's assault, Lincoln began by quoting at length from past speeches he'd made to try to set the record straight. It made for a tedious opening, but he soon hit his stride. He told the crowd that Douglas had allowed himself to be bound by a judicial decision—*Dred Scott*—even though Democrats had a history of disputing Supreme Court decisions with which they disagreed, and that this disclosed his secret goal of nationalizing slavery. In response to the racial equality issue, Lincoln worked hard to persuade his listeners that natural rights were dependent on neither race nor ability. If they were, then whites could be enslaved as easily as blacks.

"I have no disposition to introduce political and social equality between the white and the black races," he told the crowd. "There is a physical difference between the two, which in my judgment will probably forever forbid their living together on terms of respect, social and political equality." Like so many other opponents of slavery in his day, Lincoln favored efforts to colonize freed slaves in Liberia. In fact, he'd been a member of the Illinois State Colonization society since the early 1840s. So, in agreement with Douglas, he was "in favor of the race to which I belong having the superior position." But there was one marked difference between the two men's opinions about blacks. "There is no reason in the world why the Negro is not entitled to all the natural rights enumerated in the Declaration of Independence." When it came to "the right to eat the bread which his own hand earns, he is my equal and Judge Douglas's equal, and the equal of every living man." At this point, one of Douglas's supporters in the crowd hollered out that Lincoln was a fool. "Well, that may be," Lincoln retorted, "and I guess there are two of us."[31]

According to the rules of the debate, Douglas got the last word, and he used his final half hour to accuse Lincoln of helping to write a Republican Party platform statement in 1854 that expressed abolitionist sentiments. Douglas's charge against Lincoln was unfounded, and it so angered the usually unflappable Lincoln that he tried to interrupt Douglas on three different occasions. Fellow Republicans seated on the speaker's stage next to him finally cautioned him to sit quietly. "What are you making such a fuss for?" they hissed. "Douglas didn't interrupt you, and can't you see that the people don't like it?"[32]

Reporting on the first debate, the *Chicago Times*, a Democratic paper, chortled, "Lincoln's Heart Fails Him! Lincoln's Legs Fail Him! Lincoln's Tongue Fails Him!" Another, alluding to Lincoln's congressional challenge of Mr. Polk's War, jubilantly proclaimed "Lincoln Again Routed! He Can't Find the Spot."[33] Although a bit rough, Lincoln's performance hadn't been that bad. But even his own campaign handlers thought he needed to punch it up in future debates by taking the offensive. Instead of allowing Douglas to pepper him with questions, he needed to throw a few of his own at the senator. So for the second debate, scheduled one week later at Freeport in the northern part of the state, it was decided that Lincoln would hit Douglas where it hurt by challenging him on the compatibility of his simultaneous defense of popular sovereignty and

Dred Scott. The hope was that this would draw attention away from Douglas's Ottawa accusation that Lincoln was a race-mixer.

A crowd of about 15,000 showed up for the Freeport debate, despite the overcast, damp weather. Lincoln had the podium first this time around. He began by offering short responses to the seven questions Douglas had pelted him with in Ottawa. But anyone in the audience who thought that Lincoln was up against the ropes was soon undeceived, because he then moved from defense to offense by asking Douglas what came to be known as the "Freeport Question." It was actually four related questions, the middle two of which invited Douglas to clarify his stand on slavery's extension. Do you believe that the people of a territory can exclude slavery prior to writing a state constitution? Do you approve of the *Dred Scott* decision?

When Douglas stood up to address the rowdy crowd, he was struck in the shoulder by a well-aimed watermelon rind. Looking back afterwards, he might have taken it as a bad omen, because his response to Lincoln's question almost certainly destroyed his chance of becoming president in the 1860 election. It wasn't that Douglas was unprepared for the question and fumbled his response. He'd been asked something like it ever since the Supreme Court ruled on *Dred Scott*, and he'd already publicly stated his opinion on several occasions, the first time in May 1857, two months after the decision. But he knew, just as Lincoln did, that he had to tread carefully this time. If he answered "yes" to the question asking if territories could exclude slavery, he upheld popular sovereignty and pleased most northern free soilers but alienated southern defenders of slavery. If he answered "no," he both jettisoned popular sovereignty and angered northern opponents of slavery. If he answered "yes" to the second question about the *Dred Scott* decision, he denied popular sovereignty while alienating northern opponents of slavery. If he answered "no," he salvaged popular sovereignty, perhaps pleasing the North but surely angering the South. Either way, it was a bad position to be in.

As he had done on earlier occasions, Douglas grabbed both horns of the dilemma by insisting that *Dred Scott* and popular sovereignty were compatible. Regardless of what the Supreme Court determined, regardless of what federal law was on the books, the people of a territory "have the lawful means to introduce [slavery] or exclude it as they please, for the reason that slavery cannot exist a day or an hour anywhere, unless it is supported by local police regulations."[34] These regulations are made by local or state legislators, who in turn are directed by the will of the people they represent. So there's no incompatibility between the Supreme Court decision and the Kansas-Nebraska Act's defense of local self-determination. The first claimed that slave owners had the right to take their property into the territories, but the other recognized that the enforcement of that right was contingent upon the local will of the people.

Douglas's response to the Freeport Question satisfied few in the boisterous crowd, who reacted so angrily that he petulantly accused them of "vulgarity and blackguardism." Nor did it appease many others in the North or South following the debate in the newspapers. Eastern Republicans who had been tempted to adopt Douglas as one of their own began to draw back, and southern defenders of slavery, who thought their position had been once and for all ratified by the Supreme Court, felt betrayed by what they saw as Douglas's waffling. Virginia's James Mason adopted biblical language with which to blister Douglas. "You promised us bread, and you have given us a stone; you promised us a fish, and you have given us a serpent; we thought you had given us a substantial right; and you have given us the most evanescent shadow and delusion." In less scriptural tones, Jefferson Davis accused Douglas of championing a chameleon-like policy that was "shadowy and fleeting" to fit circumstances. After Freeport, southern and northern Democrats split even further, leading one northern Democratic editor to lament that "There is no such entity as a Democratic party."[35]

A good two weeks lapsed before the candidates met again. Both of them used the time to travel throughout Illinois giving stump speeches in towns and villages. They were working their way southwards, because the third debate was to be held in Jonesboro, the county seat of the poorest and most illiterate county in Illinois. If Ottawa and Freeport had been Lincoln country, Jonesboro belonged to Douglas. Some 40 percent of the residents in that part of Illinois were transplants from slave states.

The crowd that gathered for the debate was one of the smallest of the entire campaign. No more than 800 people lived in Jonesboro. About 1,500 local folks showed up to hear Lincoln and Douglas, a modest number when compared to earlier turnouts but still a doubling of the town's normal population. Nothing new was said by either candidate. Douglas rehashed his claim that Lincoln and the Black Republicans were "inviting a warfare between the North and South, to be carried out with ruthless vengeance,"[36] a charge which Lincoln heatedly denied. But such an internecine conflict, Douglas assured the crowd, was absolutely unnecessary. The proof lay in the fact that the Union had managed to survive despite sectional disagreements over slavery, and the basis of that endurance was the constitutional right of states to decide the slavery issue for themselves. Lincoln returned to his favorite claim, that the founders didn't envision slavery remaining a permanent institution, but instead intended it to follow "the course of ultimate extinction." For them, blacks enjoyed the same inalienable rights as whites.[37] Douglas, in a passionately purple piece of rhetoric, denied this, declaring that the framers of the Declaration of Independence in no way intended to include "the Negro or savage Indians, or the Feegee, or the Malay, or any other inferior or degraded race, when they spoke of the equality of men."[38]

If Lincoln felt dispirited by the proslavery crowd at the tiny and rather shabby village of Jonesboro, he was revitalized by the next debate on September 18, held in Charleston, located in the mid-eastern part of the state. Lincoln was greeted by the townspeople as a favorite son, which in some respects he was. Charleston was in the same county that his family had settled in after leaving Indiana when he was 19. In fact, his stepmother, Sarah Bush Johnston Lincoln, still lived in the area. The crowd numbers were also back up, with an estimated 15,000 people in attendance. Excited by the charged atmosphere, Lincoln's and Douglas's supporters had their candidates enter in grand style, Lincoln with a mile-long parade headed by a brass band, Douglas in a procession that featured 32 young women on horseback, each representing one of the states in the Union. Not to be outdone, the Lincoln procession also featured a wagonload of young women holding a banner that read "Girls Link-on to Lincoln."

The Charleston debate reiterated the points of contention that by now had grown familiar to anyone following the Lincoln-Douglas exchanges. But there were two noteworthy moments, both contributed by Lincoln. One was a high-toned announcement of the moral stakes involved in choosing between the candidates. The second was an embarrassingly low-toned response to Douglas's increasingly shrill race-baiting.

The high-toned moment came when Lincoln, deriding Douglas's promise that the Kansas-Nebraska bill would put an end to the slavery controversy once and for all, announced that there were only two ways of settling the issue. The first, endorsed by him and his fellow Republicans,

The Coles County Court House in Charleston, Illinois, in which Lincoln often practiced law and before which he made a short speech in the evening after his fourth joint debate with Douglas, September 18, 1858. (Library of Congress)

was the plan intended by the founders: keep slavery out of the territories, "restrict[ing] it forever to the old States where it now exists" until it collapses under its own weight and becomes extinct. The second way, endorsed by Douglas and the Democrats, was to "cease speaking of it as in any way a wrong" but instead to "regard slavery as one of the common matters of property, and to speak of negroes as we do of our horses and cattle." The upshot of this alternative would be to "plant slavery over all the States."[39] These were the two choices facing the nation and Illinois voters. In framing the alternatives in such uncompromising terms, Lincoln may have frightened away a few fence-straddling Whigs. But he couldn't have made his viewpoint any more clear. The Republican position on slavery was a principled expression of the "ancient faith" to which Lincoln had paid homage back in his Peoria speech eight years earlier. The Democratic position, by contrast, was self-servingly immoral and contrary to the found-ers' hallowed vision of what the country might be.

Unfortunately, Lincoln's moral high ground was leveled to some extent by one of the few public occasions in which he indulged in racist banter. Douglas had accused him of wanting to offer citizenship to blacks in clear contravention of the *Dred Scott* decision. Lincoln responded by insisting that he had never argued for "making voters of the negroes, or jurors, or qualifying them to hold office, or having them to marry with white peo-ple." But then, smarting at the sexually charged innuendoes of race-mixing that had become Douglas staples, Lincoln went too far. "I do not understand that because I do not want a negro woman for a slave I must necessarily want her for a wife," he said. "My understanding is that I can just leave her alone." The only white person he knew who desired such union with blacks, he sarcastically observed, was an old friend of Douglas's, whose taste in mulatto women was well known. The very fact that Douglas and his followers were so worried about the possibility of miscegenation suggested that they must all feel especially tempted to cross the color line themselves. Lincoln offered them his "most solemn pledge that I will to the very last stand by the law in this state that forbids the marriage of white folks with negroes." It was a moment unworthy of him.[40]

The final three debates were all in the west of the state, an especially pivotal region because it was thickly populated with old-line Whigs who both candidates were energetically wooing. Lincoln knew that it would be foolish to expect their votes simply because he had once been a Whig himself. Many of them were wary of his position on slavery, seeing it as too radical. By the same token, Douglas had to convince them that his uncomfortable melding of popular sovereignty and *Dred Scott* wouldn't lead to the nationalization of slavery claimed by the Republicans.

The fifth debate was held at Galesburg on October 7, a cold day so windy that banners and posters went flying and the two candidates were hard-pressed to make themselves heard. Despite the bad weather, the larg-est crowd of any of the debates, some 15,000–20,000 strong, had gathered. The location of the debate was the grounds of Galesburg's Knox College, founded in 1837 by antislavery reformers. Students and faculty both were involved in the Underground Railroad, the loosely structured series of routes and safe houses along which runaway slaves made their way northward to freedom.

The speakers' platform for the debate was built against the wall of one of Knox College's buildings, in part to shield the candidates from the wind. Douglas and Lincoln had to climb onto the platform through a window, prompting Lincoln to quip, "Well, at last I have gone through college."[41] Douglas's retort, if there was one, was not recorded. But college officials heard and apparently took Lincoln's joke to heart. Two years later, they conferred upon him the institution's very first honorary doctorate, just as he was gearing up for his race for the presidency.

Given that both the college and the town were notoriously abolitionist-friendly, Douglas knew he had his work cut out for him. But never lacking in pluck, he came in primed to fight, accompanied by 11 railroad cars of raucous supporters. In addition to the usual give-and-take on by now familiar themes, Douglas condemned Lincoln's claim that the Declaration of Independence established a legal equality between the races as a "monstrous heresy." Lincoln once again appealed to a moral argument by responding that he and Douglas had quite different notions of what the word "equality" meant. Douglas believed "that the owner of slaves and the owner of horses should be allowed to take them alike to new territory and hold them there." This "equality" was "perfectly logical if the species of property is perfectly alike, but if you admit that one of them is wrong, then you cannot admit any equality between right and wrong."[42] Lincoln believed it wrong to think of men as property; Douglas did not. That was the difference between them. Douglas, exhausted from the campaign and unnerved by the crowd's obvious hostility to him, acted badly, losing his temper and shaking his fist within inches of Lincoln's face. It was a bad day for him.

Still smarting from Lincoln's repudiation of the claim that humans can be property, Douglas returned to the theme in the penultimate debate, held on October 12 in the town of Quincy, just across the Mississippi River from Missouri. The Supreme Court, he insisted, established once and for all that slaves in fact are property, legally transferable anywhere in the land but subject to local ordinances—this last bit Douglas's signature mashing together of *Dred Scott* and popular sovereignty. The moral rightness or wrongness of slavery is a matter for private conscience, not legislation. Lincoln, pulling out his trademark claim that slavery is a moral wrong that required legislative amelioration, reminded his audience that neither he nor his fellow Republicans wished to disturb the institution in states where it existed. But he and they did feel a moral obligation to "prevent its growing any ... so that in the run of time there may be some promise of an end to it."[43] By this time in the campaign, the estimated 15,000 in the audience were so well acquainted with each man's position that the most exciting moments of the day were likely when benches on the speakers' platform collapsed not once but twice under the weight of the local dignitaries (and their wives in all their finery) sitting on them.

The final debate three days later was in a location fitting for the conclusion of a series of exchanges about slavery. The town of Alton, southwest of Quincy, was the place where abolitionist newspaperman Elijah Lovejoy had been murdered 21 years earlier by a proslavery mob. Douglas and Lincoln squared off in Alton's brand-new city hall, and attendance was encouraged by a special railroad deal, a $1 round-trip fare from St. Louis, 15 miles to the south in the slave state of Missouri. Despite the offer, only about 5,000 people showed up. The novelty had obviously worn off, and the coming of cold weather disinclined people to travel long distances.

By this point in the campaign, the wear on Douglas was beginning to show. His voice was increasingly hoarse, his mood testy, and the prodigious amount of liquor he normally consumed had steadily increased as a stimulant against weariness. Lincoln was also exhausted, and as a teetotaler couldn't rely on brandy or whiskey for stimulation. But the presence in the audience of his wife Mary and their son Robert, neither of whom had seen him in any of the previous debates, seemed to energize him, and he delivered what may have been his best speech of the entire campaign.

In his remarks, Lincoln acknowledged that even though he was in a region of the state with strongly sympathetic ties to the South, he refused to soften his position on slavery. Slavery, he told the crowd, was simply wrong. Disagreement about that was the real crux of disagreement between him and Douglas, and it would continue to be a source of contention "in this country when these poor tongues of Douglas and myself shall be silent." Make no mistake about it: the debate over slavery was but one episode in the "eternal struggle between right and wrong ... one of them asserting the divine right of kings, the same principle that says you work, you toil, you earn bread, and I will eat it. It is the same old serpent, whether it comes from the mouth of a king who seeks to bestride the people of his nation ..., or whether it comes from one race of men as apology for the enslaving of another race of men."[44] Douglas tried to deflate

Lincoln's lofty prose by claiming that his opponent's opposition to popular sovereignty was every bit as autocratic as the divine right of kings he condemned. But it was too little, too late. Lincoln's remarks were the ones that most attendees at this final debate took home with them, regardless of whether or not they concurred.

The debates were over, but Election Day was still two weeks away. Douglas and Lincoln made the most of those two weeks, delivering as many speeches in as many locales as they could drag themselves to, repeating the same principles and hurling the same accusations against each other that were so familiar to voters by this point that they were scarcely worth repeating. Both men felt confident as the campaign came to a close.

THE OUTCOME

November 2, the day Illinoisans went to the polls, was cold and wet. Still, record numbers turned out, more than had voted in the presidential election two years earlier. The large turnout was due at least in part to the rigorous campaigns run by Lincoln and Douglas. Together, the two of them had traveled nearly 10,000 miles and delivered 200 speeches since July. Although they campaigned up and down Illinois, both concentrated their major efforts in the middle of the state, the so-called Whig Belt, where votes were up for grabs and would determine the election's outcome.

Until the Seventeenth Amendment was passed in 1913, U.S. senators were elected by state legislators rather than directly by citizens. So the contest between Douglas and Lincoln was actually decided by who voters sent to the Illinois legislature on Election Day. Election outcomes in the north and south of the state were predictable, most counties in the first electing Republicans, and counties in the second going Democrat. But with 13 incumbent Democrats not up for reelection, some Democrat-strong districts electing multiple representatives, and most of the state's Whigs who'd gone with Fillmore in 1856 voting for Douglas, the final tally of Illinois legislators when the election dust settled was 54 Democrats and 46 Republicans. Even though Republicans had an edge when it came to the total number of popular votes cast, Lincoln knew there was no way that the Democratic-controlled state legislature would hand over Douglas's seat to him. When Douglas learned the outcome, he responded

Abraham Lincoln, the Republican candidate for U.S. Senate, and Stephen Douglas, the incumbent Democratic candidate, debate in their home state of Illinois in 1858. Although Lincoln ultimately lost the election, the publicity surrounding the debates gained him national attention and helped him to win the Republican nomination for the presidency in 1860. (AP/Wide World Photos)

with a one-line homage to the popular sovereignty doctrine he'd defended throughout the entire campaign: "Let the voice of the people be heard."

Losing a hard-fought political campaign is always painful. But Lincoln's defeat was especially bitter for three reasons. In the first place, he knew that he'd lost to Douglas despite the Buchanan machine's all-out efforts to bribe and bully Illinois Democrats from supporting the Little Giant. Second, he felt betrayed by the state's Whigs rallying behind Douglas. Lincoln's House Divided speech had rattled them badly enough. But New York Republican William Seward delivered a widely reported speech just a week before the Illinois election whose belligerence positively frightened them. The sectional disagreement over slavery, Seward declared, was "an irrepressible conflict between opposing and enduring forces." Southerners were "betrayers of the Constitution and Freedom forever." But with the birth of the Republican Party, "a revolution has begun"—and revolutions, Seward triumphantly declared, "never go backward."[45]

Finally, Lincoln was humiliated by his defeat in an election cycle when his party did quite well nationally. Republicans won significant victories in Michigan, Wisconsin, Indiana, Ohio, and Pennsylvania. Victories were also won throughout New England, where Whigs and many Democrats, equally disgusted by Buchanan's support of the Lecompton constitution, joined forces to elect Republican candidates. Nationally, Republicans gained 18 seats in the House of Representatives, including one each from the four Lower North states of Pennsylvania, New Jersey, Indiana, and Illinois that went for Buchanan in 1856. Democratic-held seats dropped from 53 to 32, with most of the Democrats elected or reelected being Douglas supporters and Buchanan opponents.

What Lincoln didn't appreciate immediately after his defeat was that a good deal of the enthusiasm that accounted for Republican successes elsewhere had been generated by his 100-day battle with Stephen Douglas. Verbatim accounts of their debates had flashed across the nation through 50,000 miles of telegraph wire, inspiring voters in other states to cast their ballots for Republican candidates and giving Lincoln the national coverage he'd never had, not even during his two years as a U.S. congressman. He was the David who'd taken on and bloodied the mighty Goliath. And even though he couldn't know it at the time, his loss of the senate seat prepared the way to the White House two years later.

NOTES

The chapter epigraph from Douglas is from Harold Holzer (ed.), *The Lincoln-Douglas Debates: The First Complete, Unexpurgated Edition* (New York: Fordham University Press, 2004), 247. The epigraph from Lincoln is from Roy P. Basler (ed.), *The Collected Works of Abraham Lincoln* (New Brunswick, NJ: Rutgers University Press, 1953), 2:500. Hereafter cited as CW.

1. Jean H. Baker, *James Buchanan* (New York: Henry Holt, 2004), 81, 83.

2. Michael A. Morrison, *Slavery and the American West: The Eclipse of Manifest Destiny and the Coming of the Civil War* (Chapel Hill: University of North Carolina Press, 1997), 194.

3. CW 2:495.

4. Baker, *James Buchanan*, 102.

5. Don E. Fehrenbacher, *Prelude to Greatness: Lincoln in the 1850's* (Stanford, CA: Stanford University Press, 1962), 56.

6. Allan Nevins, *The Emergence of Lincoln* (New York: Scribner, 1950), 1:278.

7. Bruce C. Levine, *Half Slave and Half Free: The Roots of the Civil War* (New York: Hill and Want, 1992), 213.

8. David M. Potter, *The Impending Crisis, 1848–1861* (New York: Harper & Row, 1976), 389.

9. CW 3:340.

10. CW 2:405–6.

11. CW 2:404.

12. CW 2:430.

13. CW 3:92.

14. Fehrenbacher, *Prelude to Greatness*, 61.

15. Leonard L. Richards, *The Slave Power: The Free North and Southern Domination, 1780–1860* (Baton Rouge: Louisiana State University Press, 2000), 12.

16. CW 2:461.

17. CW 2:465–66.

18. CW 2:467.

19. CW 2:468.

20. CW 3:367.

21. Allen C. Guelzo, *Lincoln and Douglas: The Debates That Defined America* (New York: Simon & Schuster, 2008), 75.

22. Ibid., 76, 78.

23. CW 2:492.

24. CW 2:500.

25. CW 2:501.

26. Holzer, *Lincoln-Douglas Debates*, 1.

27. David Herbert Donald, *Lincoln* (New York: Simon & Schuster, 1995), 215.

28. Guelzo, *Lincoln and Douglas*, 102.

29. Ibid., 311.

30. Holzer, *Lincoln-Douglas Debates*, 54–55.

31. Ibid., 66.

32. Ibid., 79.

33. David Zarefsky, *Lincoln, Douglas, and Slavery: In the Crucible of Public Debate* (Chicago: University of Chicago Press, 1990), 55, 57.

34. Holzer, *Lincoln-Douglas Debates*, 106.

35. Levine, *Half Slave and Half Free*, 213.

36. Holzer, *Lincoln-Douglas Debates*, 149.

37. Ibid., 156.
38. Ibid., 151.
39. Ibid., 227, 228.
40. Ibid., 189.
41. Ibid., 235.
42. Ibid., 258.
43. Ibid., 290.
44. Ibid., 359.
45. Nevins, *Emergence of Lincoln*, 1:409.

CHAPTER 6

FROM WIGWAM
TO WHITE HOUSE

I feel as though I heard the cannon thunder all over the North.
—Carl Schurz

Mr. Lincoln is the next president. We must try to save the Union.
I will go south.
—Stephen Douglas

In the early fall of 1859, two events occurred which significantly shaped the contours of the following year's presidential campaigns.

In September, James Buchanan announced that he wouldn't seek another four years in the White House. It was a prudent decision on the part of a president whose doughface policies had fragmented his own party along sectional lines, whose endorsement of the Lecompton constitution backlashed into Republican victories in the 1858 elections, and whose administration was tainted by charges of kickback corruption. With Buchanan gone, the Democrats just might have a chance in the 1860 presidential race. It also meant that Stephen Douglas had a good shot at his party's nomination.

The next month, on October 16, abolitionist John Brown of Pottawatomie infamy launched his ill-fated raid against the federal arsenal at Harpers Ferry, Virginia. His hope was to steal the weapons housed in it, take to the mountains, and incite slave rebellions throughout the Upper South. It was a hare-brained scheme, and within 36 hours Brown and his ragtag band had been subdued by marines under the command of Colonel Robert E. Lee. Brown was hanged as a traitor six weeks later.

Brown's raid served only to deepen the angry suspicion with which northern opponents and southern proponents of slavery viewed one another. Abolitionists in the North such as Henry David Thoreau, Ralph

Waldo Emerson, Louisa May Alcott, William Lloyd Garrison, and John Greenleaf Whittier praised Brown as a hero and martyr. So did a lot of others who, although not considering themselves abolitionists, disliked slavery. Most southerners saw him as a murderous insurrectionist and were shocked and enraged by the public sympathy shown him north of the Mason-Dixon Line. Slave state legislatures promptly approved emergency appropriations to strengthen their militias in anticipation of future raids by other fanatics.

Democrats, sensing a political opportunity, were quick to argue that the violence at Harpers Ferry was but a hint of the bloodletting that would flood the nation if Republicans ever took the White House. Jefferson Davis insisted that the Republicans were, at heart, a party "organized on the basis of making war" on the South.[1] Stephen Douglas, already gearing up for his presidential bid, thundered that Harpers Ferry was the "natural, logical, inevitable result of the doctrines and teachings of the Republican party."[2] One charge in particular was repeated in scores of Democratic newspapers and speeches: John Brown's raid was Seward's "irrepressible conflict" come home to roost.

Republicans, for their part, strenuously disavowed Brown's actions, either out of genuine conviction or political expediency. Most of them, however, tempered their condemnation of Brown's resort to violence with expressions of sympathy for his hatred of slavery. This was the line taken by William Seward, for example, and it was also endorsed by Abraham Lincoln in early December, after Brown's execution. Speaking in Leavenworth, Kansas, with an eye already on the Republican convention less than six months away, Lincoln declared that "Old John Brown has just been executed for treason against a state. We cannot object, even though he agreed with us in thinking slavery wrong. That cannot excuse violence, bloodshed, and treason." But Lincoln then offered Brown's execution as a warning to southern fire-eaters. If the South tried to secede in the event of a Republican becoming president, "it would be [the federal government's] duty to deal with you as old John Brown has been dealt with."[3]

Buchanan's decision not to run and Brown's failed insurrection added urgency to the presidential race that was gearing up. Both events created the impression that a new level of crisis as well as opportunity had been reached. With Buchanan out of the running, many northern Democrats hoped to field a candidate that could keep both their party and the nation from splitting apart. Many southern Democrats, on the other hand, saw Brown's raid as the final bit of evidence that the North, including northern Democrats, couldn't be trusted. In their eyes, secession became an even more viable option. And Republicans, keeping an eye on both these trends, plotted the strategy they hoped would take them to the White House.

"A SLIP AND NOT A FALL"

A betting man might have wagered that Abraham Lincoln's political career was finished after he failed to unseat Stephen Douglas. It was, after all, his second unsuccessful bid for the U.S. Senate, and his sole term as a Congressman had been undistinguished. He seemed fated to remain a party organizer, not a public office holder.

Lincoln seemed to have concluded as much himself shortly after the Illinois senate race was over. The grueling campaign left him physically and emotionally exhausted, and his loss to Douglas as well as his failure to bring old Whigs on board his campaign still rankled. As he ruefully remarked a couple of months later, "it hurts too much to laugh and I am too big to cry."[4] And on top of everything else, he was broke, or at least thought he was, complaining to a friend that he had neglected his law practice during the campaign to the point where he was "absolutely without money now for even household purposes."[5] He didn't regret debating Douglas, he told someone else, because it allowed him to speak his mind on slavery, "the great and durable question of the age." But it was time to call it quits. "I now sink out of view, and shall be forgotten."[6]

Lincoln's funk lasted only a little while. He eventually decided that his defeat by Douglas was a "slip and not a fall"[7] (an allusion to Psalm 121:3). His confidence was boosted when a friend and leading state Republican who had just returned from the east assured him that his reputation had spread beyond Illinois and that he could be a serious national player if he worked to make himself better known. Other Republicans told Lincoln the same thing. He pretended to laugh them off—"Just think of such a sucker as me as president!"[8]—but they struck a responsive chord all the same. Lincoln began corresponding with Republican leaders across the nation about election strategy, arranged for the publication of his debates with Douglas, and started stumping outside of Illinois for Republican candidates and Republican causes. He was back in the game.

Between late 1858 and 1860, Lincoln traveled some 4,000 miles to make nearly 25 speeches in Ohio, Wisconsin, Indiana, Iowa, and the Kansas Territory. Much of what he said was a replay of the positions he'd defended in his debates with Douglas, who himself was touring a lot of the same ground Lincoln covered in a pre-presidential campaign effort to sell his popular sovereignty doctrine. Everywhere he went, Lincoln tried to encourage antislavery audiences to put aside their local disagreements long enough to focus energy on the national issue that tied them all together: the desire "to prevent the spread and nationalization of slavery."[9] He reassured audiences again and again that he and the Republicans had no intention of interfering with slavery where it already existed, but only with its extension into the western territories. But the arguments he gave to defend this position made it clear, as his exchanges with Douglas two years earlier had, that he believed slavery to be morally reprehensible for at least two reasons. First, it ignored the humanity of blacks, relegating them to the moral status of animals and the legal status, thanks to the *Dred Scott* decision, of property. "When men are spoken of, the negro is not meant; when negroes are spoken of, brutes alone are contemplated."[10] Second, slavery degraded both blacks and whites because it eroded the possibility of free labor, "the just and generous, and prosperous system, which opens the way for all—gives hope to all, and energy, and progress, and improvement of condition to all."[11]

In October 1859, Lincoln received an invitation from Henry Ward Beecher of "Beecher's Bibles" fame to give a public lecture at his church in Brooklyn. By the time Lincoln arrived there in late February, the venue had been relocated to the basement-level Great Hall of Cooper Union. The speech Lincoln delivered there, one of the most important of his life, is known as the Cooper Union Address.

Lincoln labored harder over this speech than any he ever delivered. He realized that the stakes were enormous. Although it took him a couple more months to admit he had an eye on the November presidential election—"The taste *is* in my mouth a little," he finally confessed in April[12]—his Cooper Union Address was clearly intended to show eastern voters that he was a viable candidate. In order to do that, he had to address the slavery issue firmly but not fanatically. If he succeeded, he had a shot at the nomination. If he bombed, he was just another backwoods politician in an ill-fitting suit.

The speech, delivered before a packed audience of 1,500, was a gauntlet masterfully thrown at the slaveholding South on the one hand and an invitation to reconciliation, or at least toleration, on the other. Lincoln struck at the heart of the sectional divide over slavery—"Their thinking it is right, and our thinking it is wrong, is the precise fact upon which depends the whole controversy"—by going to great pains to refute the pro-slavery claim that the framers of the Constitution approved of owning other human beings. On the contrary, said Lincoln, laying out his case as carefully and precisely as if he were in a courtroom, the majority of framers tolerated slavery only out of expediency, fully believing and desiring that it would eventually die out. This aversion to slavery was reiterated in subsequent legislative decisions, beginning with the 1787 Ordinance that forbade the extension of slavery into the Northwest Territory.

Lincoln repeated that Republicans had no intention of interfering with slavery in southern states. But, he maintained, this wasn't enough to satisfy slaveholders, because they wanted nothing less than the "nationalization of bondage." They "want us to stop calling slavery wrong and join them, in acts as well as words, in calling slavery right." If they don't get their way, continued Lincoln, they threaten to break apart the Union, all the while blaming northern opposition to the extension of slavery as the cause of the split. But this is an absurd position, tantamount to a highwayman holding a gun to the head of his victim and muttering, "Stand and deliver, or I shall kill you, and then you will be a murderer!"

In contrast to the fire-eaters' loud demands for secession, Lincoln insisted that Republicans would do everything possible to work for a peaceful resolution of the sectional tension. "Even though the southern people will not so much as listen to us, let us calmly consider their demands, and yield to them if, in our deliberate view of our duty, we possibly can." This was said in part to distance the Republicans from John Brown, whose raid was still fresh in everyone's mind. But Lincoln closed his address with words intended to rebuke would-be secessionists and to suggest that there are limits to Republican forbearance. "Let us have faith that right makes might, and in that faith, let us, to the end, dare to do our duty as we understand it."[13]

The success of the Cooper Union Address was stunning. An excited reporter who covered the event enthused that "no man ever before made such an impression on his first appeal to a New York audience."[14]

Following his triumph, Lincoln embarked on a two-week tour of New England, introducing himself in nearly a speech a day to a part of the nation that was already Republican-friendly and receptive to his message. Along the way, he repeated his objections to slavery and emphasized its corrosive effects on free labor. Every person, he argued, had a right to improve their lot in life through hard work, and this applied to the black man as much as the white one. "I want every man to have the chance—and I believe a black man is entitled to it—in which he can better his condition," he told a crowd in New Haven, Connecticut.[15] Referring to a shoemaker's strike under way in Massachusetts, Lincoln refused to speculate about who was in the right and who in the wrong. But "I know one thing," he declared. *"There is a strike!* And I am glad to know that there is a system of labor where the laborer can strike if he wants to! I would to God that such a system prevailed all over the world."[16]

By the time Lincoln returned to Springfield in mid-March, his was a national name. When the book edition of his debates with Douglas appeared around this time, it sold well, going through four separate editions in as many weeks. It was clear to everyone that Lincoln would play a prominent role in determining the Republican platform and ticket at the upcoming national convention. But he didn't yet lead the pack when it came to potential nominees. He was still, as one of his contemporaries said and he himself acknowledged, everyone's second choice to Republicans like William Seward or Salmon Chase.

CONVENTION SEASON

If anyone had any doubts that the election year would be rancorous, the feud that embroiled the House of Representatives when the 36th Congress convened in December 1859 should have cleared them up. Assembling three days after John Brown was hanged, the first order of business was to elect a Speaker. After the 1858 midterm elections, the Republicans held a plurality, although not a majority, in the House, and they nominated Ohio congressman John Sherman, a brother of future Union general William Tecumseh Sherman. Soon after the nomination, it came to light that Sherman had endorsed (without actually reading, as he later admitted) Hinton Rowan Helper's 1857 antislavery tract *The Impending Crisis of the South*, which urged nonslaveholding whites in the South to repudiate the institution on the grounds that they were economically hurt by slavery. Despite the fact that Helper backed up his argument with data from the federal census, southern congressmen exploded with fury, repudiated his conclusions, and with the help of Upper South Know-Nothings blocked Sherman's nomination through 44 hotly debated ballots. Congressmen from all sides began bringing weapons with them to House sessions. Some southerners expressed the wish to fight out the sectional disagreement with pistols there and then. Francis Wilkinson Pickens, the governor of South Carolina, assured his state's congressmen that if it came to a physical showdown, he would immediately dispatch an armed militia regiment to Washington.

After two months of increasingly tense wrangling, Sherman stepped aside. It had become clear that the South would never accept him as Speaker. Even a few compromise Douglas Democrat candidates whose names had come up in the course of the debate were rejected by Lower South Democrats. With Sherman out of the running, the Republicans nominated a first (and only) term congressman from New Jersey, William Pennington, whose relative anonymity proved acceptable to a majority of representatives. When he took the oath of office in February, the *New York Times* noted with relief that "if the Union had been cracked in the contest, the seams were again sealed."[17] Before the year was out, the seams would burst.

THE DEMOCRATS SPLIT

Six months after John Brown's raid and two months after the House deadlock ended, the Democrats held their national convention in Charleston, South Carolina. The very location gestured at the influence southern Democrats exerted over the party and their determination to nominate a candidate and write a platform that best represented the interests of the slaveholding states.

In addition to the southern Democrats' readiness to assert their region's interests at the convention, there was a small but vocal group of fire-eaters convinced that the only way to guarantee slavery was to break away from the Union. Led by South Carolinian Robert Barnwell Rhett and Alabaman William Lowndes Yancey, they believed that conciliation with the North, especially if a Republican took the White House in November,

was impossible. In an 1859 Fourth of July speech, Rhett spoke for this faction by calling Republicans (and, presumably, all other free soilers) "plun-
derers and fanatics" and warned that submitting to their "rule" would
smear white southerners as a "weak and conquered race."[18] To avoid such
submission, Rhett and Yancey planned to disrupt the Democratic convention by alienating the northern delegates with unacceptably prosouthern
demands, splitting the party, throwing the election to the Republicans,
and using the victory as a pretext for secession. As events turned out, this
is exactly what happened, although not because of the fire-eaters' schem-
ing. The Democrats simply proved too divided over the slavery issue to
create a united political front.

Stephen Douglas's assumption going into the convention was that the
nomination was his for the taking. With Buchanan out of the running,
he was unquestionably the best known Democrat in the nation. It was
Douglas's third stab at the nomination (he'd tried in 1852 and 1856),
and this time he was determined to win the prize. But politically astute as
he was, he didn't fully appreciate the damage his defense of the Freeport
Doctrine and his opposition to the Lecompton constitution had inflicted
on his credibility with the southern wing of his party.

As sweltering heat in the 90s and bad and crowded accommodations
frayed delegates' already strained tempers, Yancey and his cohorts came
out swinging. They insisted that the party platform include a demand for
the federal protection of slavery in the territories, and procedurally they
demanded the right as a section to veto nominees, a transparent tactic to
block Douglas's nomination. Yancey even went so far as to call for the
renewal of the Atlantic slave trade. After all, the westward expansion of
slavery guaranteed by *Dred Scott* meant that southerners would "want
negroes cheap" to work the land. "If slavery is right per se," Yancey rea-
soned, "if it is right to raise slaves for sale, does it not appear that it's right
to import them?"[19] The logic of his point notwithstanding, its moral
cynicism proved too much for most northern Democrats, who felt they
were being bullied yet again by the Slave Power. George Pugh, a delegate
from Ohio, stood to warn Yancey that Democrats from the northern states
"were not children under the pupilage of the South," nor were they at
the "beck and bidding" of slaveholders. "Gentlemen of the South,"
he declared in response to Yancey's demands, "you mistake us—you
mistake us—we will not do it!"[20]

HON. WILLIAM L. YANCEY.

Alabama secessionist William L. Yancey labored behind the scenes in the 1860 presidential election year to splinter his own Democratic Party. His aim was to throw the presidency to "Black Republican" Lincoln as an incitement for the South to rebel. (Library of Congress)

Nor did they. Seven days into the convention, northern Democrats defied the South by just managing to squeak through Douglas's popular sovereignty as a plank in the party platform. Fifty-one delegates from the Lower South, led by Yancey, stormed out in protest. The convention continued without them, but even without their disruptive presence sectional differences stalemated the proceedings. Fifty-seven ballots later, Douglas still hadn't managed to receive the necessary two-thirds majority required by party rules. His nomination was blocked each time by southern delegates who, although not part of the Yancey-Rhett crowd, still opposed Douglas. The convention finally adjourned with no nominee. Delegates agreed to reconvene six weeks later in Baltimore to try again.

When the Democrats met again in June, the sectional fighting began anew. New squabbles surfaced about whether or not the Yancey walkouts from the Charleston convention should be reseated. But the major bones of contention remained the same. For many northern delegates, it was

"Douglas or nobody," an ultimatum totally unacceptable to the southern ones. Moreover, the popular sovereignty provision in the platform stuck in the craw of proslavery Democrats. The upshot was that southern Democrats, and not just Yancey's followers, bolted again, this time twice as many as had left the Charleston convention. Reassembling in a building across town, they held a rump convention and in quick order—it took only one ballot—nominated Kentuckian John Breckinridge, Buchanan's vice president, as their presidential candidate. Southern-born Joseph Lane, general in the Mexican-American War and Oregon senator, was selected as his running mate. In the meantime, over at the other convention, Stephen Douglas finally got the nomination he wanted from the northern Democrats. Ex-governor of Georgia Herschel Johnson was chosen as his running mate.

The separate platforms of the Douglas and Breckinridge parties coincided in several respects. Both, for example, advocated the acquisition of Cuba, urged the construction of a transcontinental railway, maintained that naturalized American citizens deserved the same legal protections enjoyed by native-born ones, and condemned the "personal liberty" laws enacted in many northern states to circumvent the 1850 Fugitive Slave Law. The crucial differences between them dealt with the extension and protection of slavery in the territories. The Breckinridge platform's first two resolutions unequivocally affirmed the *Dred Scott* decision. It maintained, first, that citizens had the right to "settle with their property," human or otherwise, in any federal territory. Furthermore, the platform affirmed that it was the federal government's legal responsibility to protect that right.

There was no mention of secession in the Breckinridge platform. The vice president, in fact, publicly stated that he was a Unionist and a constitutionalist. But fire-eaters such as Yancey and Rhett outspokenly supported his candidacy as part of their plan to split the Democrat vote, throw the election to the Republicans, and create the split in the Union they wanted. There's no evidence to suggest that Breckinridge ever fully appreciated just how cynically he was being used by Yancey and his fellow secessionists.

The Douglas platform, like Douglas himself ever since his debate with Lincoln at Freeport, tried to hedge its bets. It acknowledged that there were differences of opinion in the party "over the institution of slavery within the Territories," and it therefore resolved to "abide by the decision of the Supreme Court of the United States upon these questions of Constitutional law." This in effect was an acknowledgment of *Dred Scott*. But the platform also declared loyalty to the resolutions made at the party's 1856 national convention, and one of those resolutions was in favor of popular sovereignty. So in effect the Douglas platform went through the motions of upholding the *Dred Scott* decision, thereby hoping to satisfy southern voters, while implicitly retaining the doctrine of popular sovereignty that the decision had made irrelevant. Presumably the way around this impasse was Douglas's trademark insistence that there was no contradiction between the two. *Dred Scott* was the law of the land, but local will and law enforcement determined its applicability.

After the Democratic conventions had nominated their separate candidates, New York journalist and party boss Thurlow Weed wasn't the only Republican leader to marvel and exult at the implosion of what only months earlier had been the nation's dominant political party. Writing to Lincoln at the end of June, he noted that the "madness which precedes destruction has come at last upon our opponents." Even Lincoln, never one to rush to political judgment, admitted that the split within Democratic ranks made it seem "as if the success of the Republican ticket is inevitable."[21]

A NEW THIRD PARTY

Shortly after the battle for the House Speaker ended in February, some 30 disgusted Whigs and Know-Nothings, members of political parties that were all but moribund, met to form a political alliance they hoped would offer a salutary way out of the sectional crisis that the *New York Times* reporter prematurely thought resolved. Declaring a pox on both the Republicans and Democrats—neither could be "safely entrusted with the management of public affairs"—they formed the Constitutional Union Party as an alternative for those Americans who feared that the two mainstream parties were dangerously close to fragmenting the nation.

At their national convention, held in May in Baltimore, the Unionists nominated border state politician and slaveholder John Bell for president and Massachusetts native Edward Everett (who three years later would give a long-winded oration immediately preceding Lincoln's Gettysburg

Address) as his running mate. Their party platform was nearly nonexistent, consisting of but one pledge: "to recognize no political principle other than the Constitution of the Country, the Union of the States, and the Enforcement of the Laws."[22] The party remained silent about the morality of slavery and its extension into the territories. At first glance, given the heated times, this reticence seemed oddly out of touch. But there was method to the platform's minimalism. The Democrats had adjourned their first convention a month earlier without nominating a candidate, and everyone anticipated that the Republicans, whose convention hadn't yet been held, would nominate William Seward at theirs. The Unionist hope was to take advantage of the power vacuum created by the fragmentation of the Democrats and the radicalism of the presumptive Republican nominee. Under such circumstances, their thinking was that the best position for them to take was no position.

SECOND BECOMES FIRST

Months before his speech at Cooper Union, several of Lincoln's closest friends had begun to think of him as presidential material. Two in particular, David Davis and Norman Judd, were especially instrumental, both before and during the Republican convention, in making sure Lincoln got the party's nomination. In December 1859, at a meeting of the Republican National Committee in New York, Judd lobbied hard for Chicago to be the location of the party's national convention the following May. He stressed its geographical centrality and easy access by railway, but his underlying motive was to secure a Lincoln-friendly venue where he could pack the spectator stands with native son boosters. The choice came down to St. Louis or Chicago, and it was Judd's own vote that finally decided the issue in favor of the latter.

David Davis, an Illinois circuit judge and longtime Lincoln friend, took on the task of managing Lincoln's campaign. He was a shrewd dealmaker who skillfully worked behind the scenes to gather the necessary support for Lincoln's nomination.

Lincoln was also quietly active prior to the convention, smoothing over disagreements between the state's Republican leaders, courting ex-Whigs and Know-Nothings, and above all avoiding ruffling feathers. Lincoln remembered the take-away lesson from his 1858 loss to Douglas, when he failed to win the support of old Whigs: he couldn't hope to be endorsed by the state's Republican committee, be nominated as the party's candidate, or win in a general election unless he built bridges. As he realistically noted in March 1860, "My name is new in the field; and I suppose I am not the first choice of a very great many. Our policy, then, is to give no offence to others—leave them in a mood to come to us, if they shall be compelled to give up their first love."[23]

His diplomacy paid off. On May 9, 1860, just a week before the national convention was scheduled to convene in Chicago, 600 Illinois Republicans gathered for their state convention in Decatur. Despite the resistance of "Long John" Wentworth, influential editor of the *Chicago Tribune*, mayor of the city, and supporter of William Seward, the delegates enthusiastically and unanimously endorsed Lincoln as their choice for the presidential nomination and pledged to support him at the national convention. Lincoln, who attended the convention (it was his last major public appearance until after the national election; like most presidential candidates up to that time, he followed tradition by keeping a low profile during the campaign), was hoisted on shoulders and carried to the front stage. To the cheering of delegates, Lincoln's cousin John Hanks and another man paraded through the hall carrying two weathered fence rails and a banner sporting the words, ABRAHAM LINCOLN THE RAIL CANDIDATE. The two assured the delegates that "ol' Abe" had actually split the rails himself 30 years earlier—a patent falsehood, by the way—thereby bestowing on Lincoln his campaign persona as the "rail splitter," a self-made man who worked his way up from humble beginnings. Henceforth, Lincoln didn't simply advocate the merits of free labor. He embodied them.

Winning the endorsement of the Illinois state convention was one thing, but securing the national nomination was another. In most observers' eyes, Republican and non-Republican alike, Seward was still the man to beat. His status as front-runner for the nomination was dramatically confirmed on May 14, two days before the convention opened, when 13 rail cars loaded with 2,000 of his cheering supporters pulled into Chicago to be greeted with a warm welcome by Mayor Wentworth. Even Judd, who had done his best to pack the convention hall with Lincoln supporters, must have felt temporarily outgunned.

Partisan enthusiasm for particular candidates to one side, Republican leaders knew that the bottom line for deciding who the nominee would be was his electability. The Republican Party was clearly sectional—whether by choice or because southern opposition had made it so, as Lincoln rather implausibly claimed in his Cooper Union Address—and so could rely on no support from the South. That meant that in order to win the White House, the Republican candidate had to make a virtual clean sweep of the North. In addition to the states Frémont carried in the 1856 election, the candidate in this one would also have to take Pennsylvania and either Illinois or Indiana. Relying on the party faithful in these key states wasn't enough. Middle-of-the-road Democrats, cautious ex-Whigs, and suspicious ex-Know-Nothings who had gone with Fillmore four years earlier had to be courted. John Bell's entry into the election as the Constitutional Union candidate complicated matters even more. As a longtime and respected leader in the Whig party, he was likely to draw undecided ex-Whigs away from casting their votes for a Republican ticket.

When considered in light of what the Republicans had to do to win the November election, the leading candidates for the party's nomination brought definite strengths to the table. Seward, the front-runner, was the person most associated in the public mind with the Republican cause. Two-time governor of New York and a seated senator in his second term, he had made a national name for himself with his 1850 "higher law" speech and his 1858 "irrepressible conflict" one.

There were other less luminous but still serious contenders. The best situated after Seward was Salmon P. Chase, ex-governor of Ohio and one-time Free Soil Party leader. He had a solid reputation as an opponent of slavery and was coauthor of the 1854 *Appeal of the Independent Democrats in Congress to the American People*, which savaged the Kansas-Nebraska bill's proposed repeal of the Missouri Compromise. A third possibility was Edward Bates of Missouri, an old Henry Clay Whig turned Republican who was an opponent of slavery's extension but was also perceived as politically conservative. Simon Cameron, who started out as a Whig, then became a Democrat, and finally wound up as a Republican, was a fourth contender. His primary draw was the expectation that he could deliver his home state of Pennsylvania. Finally, there was John McLean, Supreme Court judge since 1829, who had been a contender for the 1856 Republican nomination and had written a strongly worded dissent to the 1857 *Dred Scott* decision.

The problem facing convention delegates was that each of these possibilities also carried liabilities that raised red flags about their electability.

The two speeches that had gained Seward a national reputation also painted him as a dangerous radical in the minds of many undecided ex-Whigs and even many Republicans. Additionally, he was unlikely to attract ex-Know-Nothings. As governor of New York, Seward had been clear in his opposition to nativism, and had even allocated state funds to Roman Catholic schools. Finally, his nomination was vigorously opposed by Horace Greeley, powerful editor of the *New York Tribune*, who nursed a personal grievance against him. Greeley's paper was the most influential in the nation, making him a bad enemy for any man with political aspirations to have.

The other contenders also carried undesirable baggage. Chase, like Seward, was perceived by many as too radical. As a member of the abolitionist Liberty Party before he threw in his lot with first the Free Soilers and then the Republicans, he'd pushed for a platform statement that urged the withdrawal of federal support of slavery. Moreover, he failed to gain unanimous support from Republicans in his own state for his bid for the presidential nomination. Cameron had an unsavory and well-deserved reputation for corruption. Bates was an ex-slaveholder and in the past had shown some sympathy for Know-Nothing nativism, a potential deal breaker when it came to the immigrant vote. And McLean was widely viewed as either too old or, less benignly, as a political opportunist who flip-flopped from party to party in his perennial quest for the presidency.

And then there was Lincoln, the "second choice." He was neither an unknown nor a dark horse. He had gained a national reputation from his debates with Douglas as well as the many speeches he'd since made. He was known as a moderate when it came to slavery, defending the constitutional property right of slaveholders but opposing extension. He disliked Know-Nothing nativism, but hadn't been as publicly critical of it as other Republicans. He hailed from a border state (Kentucky) and was the favorite son of an increasingly powerful economic and political one (Illinois). He personified the old Whig ideal of the self-made man and was a proponent of federally sponsored internal improvements, even though he advised his people to downplay protective tariffs at the convention. He combined the down-home authenticity of a frontiersman—his ill-fitting clothes, his twang, his funny stories—with the sharp mind of an experienced trial lawyer. He could allay fears about Republican radicalism, appeal to the wary Know-Nothing bloc, and potentially draw the Whigs who had been lost to Fillmore in 1856. As the convention progressed, these qualities steadily moved Lincoln from second to first choice.

Delegates to the convention, which convened on May 16 and lasted for three days, gathered in a building christened the Wigwam, presumably because it vaguely resembled the shape of Native American dwellings of the same name. Built especially for the convention at a cost of $5,000, the Wigwam's enormous size, 180 by 100 feet, could hold 10,000 delegates and spectators. Crowds at least three times that size hovered in the streets around the Wigwam to cheer on their favorite candidates and eagerly await news about the proceedings inside. At the height of the balloting, the din that arose from the thousands of people inside and outside the building was deafening. As one reporter described it, "Imagine all the hogs ever slaughtered in Cincinnati giving their death squeals together." Then, switching images: "A herd of buffaloes or lions could not have made a more tremendous roaring."[24]

David Wilmot, the Pennsylvania congressman whose 1846 proposal to ban slavery from lands acquired in the Mexican War stirred up a hornet's nest, opened the convention by rapping with a gavel of heavy oak carved from Commodore Oliver Hazard Perry's War of 1812 flagship. His opening speech was a firm but nonbelligerent statement of the issue on which the Republican Party had been built. Wilmot announced that Republicans opposed the extension of slavery into the territories, but that they posed no political threat to the continuation of slavery in the slave states. The official party platform stressed both of these policies, condemned the possibility of reopening the slave trade, affirmed the Republican conviction that under the Declaration of Independence all men were created equal, supported federal support of internal improvements, joined the Democrats in advocating a transcontinental railway, condemned the Buchanan administration for its opposition to a homestead act which would open up western territories to white settlers, championed protective tariffs, and concluded with a promise to close ranks with any and all citizens who agreed with the party's basic principles.

The first ballot, which took place on the convention's second day, made it clear that the race came down to Seward and Lincoln. As expected, Seward did well, gaining 173 and a half votes out of the 233 needed for the nomination. But Indiana joined Illinois to throw its first-ballot weight for Lincoln, who chalked up 102 votes, a respectable showing for someone who was "everyone's second choice." Cameron, Chase, and Bates received 50 or fewer votes each. On the second ballot, Seward picked up 10 more votes, but Simon Cameron released his Pennsylvania delegates, with all but two of them going for Lincoln. Before the convention met, Lincoln had cautioned Davis against making any deals with delegates that might bind him were he elected president. But before the second ballot was taken, Davis apparently insinuated to Cameron that a cabinet post in a Lincoln administration awaited him if he dropped out of the race and instructed his supporters to switch their votes to the Illinoisan. When reminded that Lincoln had forbidden such offers, Davis pithily replied, "Lincoln ain't here."[25]

Delegates from New Hampshire and Vermont as well as a few Ohio delegates who had supported Chase on the first ballot also switched to Lincoln on the second. This brought Lincoln's tally just one vote short of Seward's, giving him the three states—Indiana, Illinois, and Pennsylvania—that Republicans knew they had to carry in order to win the presidential election. A reporter on the spot later wrote that "it now dawned upon the multitude that the presumption entertained the night before, that the Seward men would have everything their own way, was a mistake."[26] When the third balloting got under way, delegates from Maryland, Kentucky, New Jersey, and other northeast states threw their support to Lincoln, bringing him up to a total of 231 and a half. Dramatically, the chairman of the Ohio delegation then announced that four more delegates from his state were switching their votes to Lincoln. "The Four Votes," as the newspapers called them, clinched the nomination for Lincoln, and the hall went wild. The same reporter who earlier had marveled at the Wigwam's din was now even more amazed at the "thousands cheering with the energy of insanity."[27] When a Lincoln supporter stationed atop the Wigwam got word of the nomination, he fired a small-bore cannon to announce the glad tidings to the hundreds of people gathered outside. The blast filled the auditorium below with choky black powder smoke, but none of the jubilant delegates seemed to mind.

Back in Springfield, Lincoln took the news of his nomination calmly. He was at a newspaper office when he got the word. "Well," he said, "I guess I will go and tell my wife about it; she cares more about it than I do." Later, addressing the huge and noisy gathering of well-wishers that assembled outside his house as word of his nomination spread through the town, he apologized for having a house too small to invite everyone in. "We will give you a larger house on the fourth of next March," someone shouted, and the crowd roared.[28]

When the news that Lincoln was the Republican candidate reached Stephen Douglas in Washington, one of his supporters expressed delight. "You have beaten him once," he told the Little Giant, "and will beat him again." But Douglas wasn't so optimistic. He knew he was in for a hard contest. Lincoln, he said, will put up "a devil of a fight."[29]

THE POLITICAL QUADRILLE

Harper's Weekly ran a political cartoon in the summer of 1860 that cleverly parodied the four presidential candidates. Captioned "The Political Quadrille" with "Music by Dred Scott," the cartoon featured a black man, presumably Scott, playing a fiddle as the candidates danced around him. Stephen Douglas high-stepped with a slovenly Irishman, symbolizing the Democrat's courtship of the immigrant vote, John Breckinridge with a satanic James Buchanan, the doughface president, and an aged John Bell, who once had served as chair of the House Committee on Indian Affairs, with a Native American. The fourth candidate, Lincoln, danced arm in arm with a woman of color whose gaze was somewhere between coquettish and salacious.

The cartoonist nicely captured popular negative impressions of the four candidates: Douglas as an opportunist, Breckinridge as Buchanan's puppet, Bell as an antique, and Lincoln as a race-mixer. But it was his broader insinuation, that slavery was the engine driving the presidential campaign, which was the cartoon's real and utterly accurate message. The slavery controversy transformed the election into two presidential contests separated by section: Lincoln against Douglas north of the Mason-Dixon Line and Breckinridge vying with Bell south of it. After Freeport and Lecompton, Douglas could expect little support in the South, and Republicans weren't even on the ticket in 10 southern states. Despite his self-identification as a Unionist, too many northerners associated Breckinridge with the Slave Power to give him much support. For moderate southerners who feared secession above all else, the only real alternative to Breckinridge was Bell.

In keeping with the tradition up to that time of presidential elections, neither Bell nor Breckinridge actively campaigned. Breckinridge wrote a

THE POLITICAL QUADRILLE
Music by Dred Scott

This cartoon, titled *The Political Quadrille, Music by Dred Scott*, is a parody of the 1860 presidential contest, highlighting the impact of the Dred Scott decision on the race. John Breckinridge is paired with incumbent James Buchanan, depicted as a devil; Abraham Lincoln dances with a black woman, a pejorative reference to his party's abolitionist stance; John Bell dances with an Indian; and Stephen A. Douglas dances with an Irishman. (Library of Congress)

rather tepid acceptance letter stating his support of slavery's extension and the Fugitive Slave Law while reaffirming his Unionism, and then left Washington for his Kentucky home. Along the way he made a few short speeches, but kept quiet for the rest of the election season except for one public appearance at Ashland, Henry Clay's old estate, where he gave an unbearably dull three-hour-long speech.

In the minds of his critics, Bell's inactivity during the campaign was of a piece with the Constitutional Union Party's minimalist platform. Northern Unionists and southern secessionists alike found the party's refusal to take a stand on slavery exasperating. A Massachusetts editor fulminated that Bell was the candidate of "the party of no idea and no purpose," and that its feeble platform should be "laid away in a box of musk, and kept there."[30] A Tennessee editor, making generous use of

exclamation points, complained that Bell "Stands on nobody's platform!!
Fights nobody!!! Loves nobody!!!!"[31] As the campaign wore on, it became
increasingly clear that a vote for the Constitutional Union ticket was more
an expression of dissatisfaction with the other candidates than a full-
bodied endorsement of Bell.

Unlike Breckinridge and Bell, Douglas energetically campaigned on his
own behalf, partly because he was a born scrapper who cared more for victory than tradition, partly because his campaign purse was perpetually near
empty, making it difficult to pay others to campaign for him, and partly
because he sensed that the momentum of the Republican Party required
him to personally roll up his sleeves in the struggle for the White House.
He started out in a coy way, swinging northward on the pretext of visiting
his mother in his native state of Vermont. But en route he made so many
political speeches that it was soon more than apparent what he was up
to. After speaking himself hoarse throughout New England, Douglas
headed south, stopping in Norfolk, Virginia, where he affirmed his commitment to the Union, and getting as far as Raleigh, North Carolina,
before he headed west to Ohio, Pennsylvania, and Indiana, the battle-
ground states of the Lower North.

Douglas and his Democratic supporters predictably highlighted the virtues of popular sovereignty and the dangers to the Union posed by both
Breckinridge and Lincoln. The Little Giant didn't hesitate to play the
same race card against Lincoln he'd used in the 1858 Senate race, and fellow Democrats followed suit. One of their wilder accusations was that the
swarthy Hannibal Hamlin of Maine, Lincoln's running mate, was a
mulatto. They also resurrected "Spotty" Lincoln's congressional challenge
of President Polk, accusing the Republican candidate of traitorous
opposition to the Mexican War and mocking him with an inane but
catchy campaign chant: "Mr. Speaker! Where's the spot? Is it in Spain or
is it not? Mr. Speaker! Spot! Spot! Spot!"[32]

For his part, Lincoln stayed in Springfield during the presidential campaign, bored and restless, occupying much of his time with responses to
written requests for his autograph. (He found the work so tedious that he
eventually had a form letter printed that he signed and returned to autograph seekers.) Republican strategists thought it best for him to keep out
of the public eye lest he slip and say anything that could be misconstrued
by the already edgy South or used against him by Douglas. Although he

chafed at the bit, Lincoln was willing to keep a low profile because of a misstep he'd made at the beginning of the campaign that could have proved harmful. In a private letter, he'd joked about worrying that the people of Kentucky would lynch him if he traveled there during the campaign. The letter was leaked and Lincoln, alarmed about alienating an Upper South state where he just might have some chance, made a swift public retraction. After that, except for an interview that resulted in a brief campaign biography, which sold an incredible 1 million copies prior to the election, and a single speech at a Springfield rally, he remained mostly quiet.

But his boosters didn't. The Republican National Committee, unlike Douglas, had an enormous budget and spent money lavishly campaigning across the country for their candidate. After his nomination, Lincoln went out of his way to mend fences with his rivals, especially Seward, and all of them wound up gladly making stump speeches for him in their native states and elsewhere. Republican rallies across the North seasoned the speeches with long and boisterous parades, often featuring full-scale replicas of log cabins hitched to wheels and drawn by teams of horses to remind voters of Lincoln's humble origins. Split rails carried by enthusiastic supporters showed up everywhere.

Adding to the general excitement were the Wide Awake Clubs, huge bands of young men eventually numbering upwards of half a million in dozens of chapters across the North. The organization reportedly got its name from an incident in which a young Republican punched an offending Democrat, thus proving that he was "wide awake" to the threat of the Slave Power. True or not, the story inspired a military-like comportment in club members, who frequently marched in torchlight parades, wore uniforms of black oilcloth capes, and lustily belted out campaign songs like "Ain't You Glad You Joined the Republicans?" Lincoln was less than enthusiastic about Wide Awake activities, usually finding them either tiresome or troublingly rowdy. But he couldn't deny that they drew attention to his candidacy. They were so effective, in fact, that they inspired the formation of similar although much smaller booster clubs for the other candidates. Breckinridge youth organized themselves into Hickory Clubs and Douglas supporters somewhat unimaginatively called themselves Little Giants. Most creatively, a Brooklyn-based group of Douglasites called themselves the Chloroformers, and vowed to put Wide Awakes to sleep.

Above all, Republican campaign strategy for selling candidate Lincoln emphasized moderation. Antislavery rhetoric that might frighten away ex-Fillmorite Whigs was toned down, and an effort was made to walk a fine line about nativist issues so as not to alienate either ex-Know-Nothings on the one hand or immigrants on the other. Republicans knew that the Democrats pretty much had the Irish Catholic vote sewed up, but they hoped they had a good chance of attracting German Protestants. (One particularly underhanded way in which Republicans sought Know-Nothing support was by spreading the rumor that Douglas was a secret Catholic—he wasn't—who had vowed submission to the "wicked woman of Babylon.") The campaign strategy of moderation didn't set well with abolitionists, even though many of them eventually voted for Lincoln on the grounds that he was better than the alternatives. Frederick Douglass was particularly hostile to the Republicans and wound up endorsing Gerrit Smith, the abolitionist candidate representing the remnants of the old Liberty Party.

As the weeks leading up to the election rolled by, it became increasingly apparent that the Republicans were going to take the White House. As early as mid-September, Douglas's running mate soberly told him that he considered the election lost. In some areas of the North, Constitutional Unionists and Douglas Democrats tried to fuse in an effort to stop the Republican momentum. But their efforts proved fruitless. State elections in September in Vermont and Maine brought in solid Republican victories, and the next month saw sweeping Republican wins in the crucial states of Pennsylvania, Indiana, and Ohio. Carl Schurz, a prominent German immigrant, dedicated Republican, and future Civil War general, said that when he got word of the October victories he felt as though he heard "cannon thunder all over the North." Stephen Douglas, campaigning in Iowa when he heard the news, was more sober. "Mr. Lincoln is the next President," he told his secretary. "We must try to save the Union. I will go South." He was as good as his word, embarking immediately on the second southern tour of his campaign. But this time he wasn't canvassing for votes. He was trying to persuade the people of the Lower South to accept Lincoln's inevitable victory. Although he planned to oppose a Republican administration, he told his listeners, he would do so legally and as a loyal son of the Union. Secessionists, he declared, should be hanged "higher than Haman."[33] It was a courageous and noble position for the Little Giant to take, but it was too little, too late.

"WE ARE ELECTED!"

Election Day finally arrived. At home in Springfield, Lincoln had resolved to stay away from the ballot box, thinking it unseemly for candidates to cast votes for themselves. But his law partner and friend William Herndon persuaded him that he owed it to the other Republican candidates running for state and local office to vote. As Lincoln walked to the polls, a Democrat good-naturedly shouted, "You ought to vote for Douglas, Uncle Abe, he has done all he could for you!"[34] When he received his ballot, Lincoln cut off the top part, which had his name on it, so that he wouldn't vote for himself.

That night he and friends awaited election returns at a telegraph office near the state capitol. The results came in quickly; state after state went for him and the Republican Party. The only disappointment that night was the sad news that even though he carried Springfield, Douglas took Sangamon, the county in which Springfield was located. When it became clear to Lincoln that he was the president-elect, he simply said to friends and supporters, "I guess there's a little lady at home who would like to hear this news," and made his way to his house. His outward calm masked an excitement that finally broke through as he stepped over his threshold. "Mary, Mary," he cried out. "We are elected!"[35] But the thrill of victory was laced through and through with a deep, almost foreboding sense of responsibility. As he later said, "I went home, but not to get much sleep, for I then felt as I never had before, the responsibility that was upon me." Late that night, after the enthusiastic crowds that thronged the streets to celebrate his election had gone to their beds, Lincoln's response to the day's events was a simple and poignant prayer. "God help me," he said. "God help me."[36]

In the 1860 presidential election, a candidate needed 152 electoral votes to win. Lincoln received 180. The total received by his three rivals was 123. Lincoln received 54 percent of the votes cast in the North for a total of 1,865,908 (half a million more than Frémont got in 1856), or 39.8 percent of the nation's total votes—not bad for a man who wasn't even on the ballot in the Lower South states. He captured all the northern states as well as the far western ones of Oregon and California, most of them by an outright majority. Douglas received the second highest popular vote at 1,380,201 for a total of 29.4 percent of all votes cast, but he wound up with the lowest number of electoral college votes, only 12, managing to win only Missouri and to split New Jersey with Lincoln. Breckinridge predictably swept 11 of the 15 slave states, finishing second in the electoral college with 72 votes. Bell took his (and Lincoln's) home state of Kentucky as well as Virginia and Tennessee, and missed winning Maryland by less than a thousand votes. But he finished second in every one of the other slave states, suggesting that at least in November 1860, many southerners, despite their perceived grievances against the North, still hoped to keep the Union together.

Douglas was in Mobile, Alabama, when he learned not only that Lincoln had bested him, but that he had finished dead last in the political quadrille. He was bone weary from his campaigning for the presidency and then the Union, and at least for a while, according to one of his aides, was "more hopeless than I had ever before seen him." But he soon took solace in the fact that he was the only one of the four candidates who'd managed to win votes in both free and slave states, and that he, despite Buchanan's enmity and the South's anger, was still a major force in the Democratic party. In New Orleans, where he and his wife retreated for a few days of well-deserved rest, a more confident Douglas told a crowd of well-wishers, "This is no time to despair or despond. The bright sun will soon chase away these clouds and the patriots of the country will rally as one man." Herschel Johnson, his running mate, wasn't so sure. "I think," he told Douglas, "the Union is gone."[37]

Johnson was despondent at the thought that the Union might be on the verge of collapse. But not everyone shared his sadness. Fire-eaters like William Lowndes Yancey and Robert Barnwell Rhett were overjoyed at the election results. Things had turned out just as they hoped when they schemed to split the Democrats at the two national conventions. Now they would work to stoke southern anxiety over Lincoln's victory. Two days after the election, a huge celebratory rally for secession supporters, complete with fireworks, was held in Charleston, South Carolina. Rhett addressed the excited, cheering crowd. "The long weary night of our dishonor and humiliation, is dispersed at last," he told them, "by the glorious day-spring of a southern Confederacy."[38]

When Carl Schurz imagined he heard cannon booming a month earlier when it became clear that Lincoln would win the White House, he was more prophetic than he could have possibly known.

NOTES

The Schurz chapter epigraph is from Michael S. Green, *Lincoln and the Election of 1860* (Carbondale: Southern Illinois University Press, 2011), 99. The Douglas chapter epigraph is from David M. Potter, *The Impending Crisis* (New York: Harper & Row, 1976), 441.

1. Potter, *The Impending Crisis*, 383.

2. Stephen Oates, *To Purge This Land with Blood* (Amherst: University of Massachusetts Press, 1984), 310.

3. Roy P. Basler (ed.), *The Collected Works of Abraham Lincoln* (New Brunswick, NJ: Rutgers University Press, 1953), 3:502. Hereafter cited as CW.

4. Allen C. Guelzo, *Lincoln and Douglas: The Debates That Defined America* (New York: Simon & Schuster, 2008), 301.

5. CW 3:337.

6. CW 3:339.

7. Henry Rankin, *Intimate Character Sketches of Abraham Lincoln* (Philadelphia: J. B. Lippincott, 1924), 118.

8. Henry Villard, *Memoirs* (Boston: Houghton Mifflin, 1904), 1:96.

9. CW 3:391.

10. CW 3:444.

11. CW 3:479.

12. CW 4:45.

13. CW 4:547, 550.

14. Douglas R. Edgerton, *Year of Meteors: Stephen Douglas, Abraham Lincoln, and the Election That Brought on the Civil War* (New York: Bloomsbury Press, 2010), 128.

15. CW 4:24.

16. CW 4:7.

17. *New York Times*, February 2, 1860.

18. William C. Davis, *Rhett: The Turbulent Life and Times of a Fire-Eater* (Columbia: University of South Carolina Press, 2001), 377.

19. Douglas R. Egerton, *Year of Meteors*, 74.

20. William B. Hesseltine (ed.), *Three Against Lincoln: Murat Halstead Reports the Caucuses of 1860* (Baton Rouge: Louisiana State University Press, 1960), 54.

21. Edgerton, *Year of Meteors*, 174.

22. *New York Herald*, May 9, 1860.

23. CW 4:34.

24. Hesseltine, *Three Against Lincoln*, 165, 158.

25. Doris Kearns Goodwin, *Team of Rivals: The Political Genius of Abraham Lincoln* (New York: Simon & Schuster, 2005), 246.

26. Ibid., 169.

27. Ibid., 171.

28. CW 4:50.

29. Edgerton, *Year of Meteors*, 146.

30. Roy Morris Jr., *The Long Pursuit: Abraham Lincoln's Thirty-Year Struggle with Stephen Douglas for the Heart and Soul of America* (New York: HarperCollins, 2008), 185.

31. Edgerton, *Year of Meteors*, 191.

32. Morris, *The Long Pursuit*, 183.

33. Potter, *The Impending Crisis*, 441.

34. Green, *Lincoln and the Election of 1860*, 102.

35. Jean Harvey Baker, *Mary Todd Lincoln: A Biography* (New York: W. W. Norton, 2008), 162.

36. Harold Holzer, *Lincoln President-Elect* (New York: Simon & Schuster, 2008), 48, 59.

37. All quotations from Morris, *The Long Pursuit*, 96.

38. William C. Davis (ed.), *A Fire-Eater Remembers: The Confederate Memoir of Robert Barnwell Rhett* (Columbia: University of South Carolina Press, 2000), 9.

Storm's Eve: "Think Calmly and Well"

The slavery agitation will soon make the North and the South two separate nations.

> —"The Indications of the Coming Storm"
> October 1860

We are not enemies, but friends. We must not be enemies.

> —Abraham Lincoln
> First Inaugural Address

L incoln had received the Republican nomination in part because he was viewed as more moderate, and therefore more electable, than his chief rivals William Seward and Salmon Chase. But despite his reputation for moderation, the prospect of a Lincoln presidency— which after the October elections in Pennsylvania and Ohio became a near certainty—alarmed everyone south of the Mason-Dixon Line who saw all Republicans as abolitionists at heart. So even before Election Day, Lincoln's friends and associates began urging him to issue a public statement that would reassure worried southern Unionists and put a damper on fire-eating secessionists. By late October, Lincoln evidently had had enough of their advice. "What is it I could say which would quiet alarm?" he irritably asked. "Is it that no interference by the government, with slaves or slavery within the states, is intended? I have said this so often already, that a repetition of it is but mockery, bearing an appearance of weakness, and cowardice."[1]

Lincoln's response revealed more than just pique. It also reflected an abiding conviction on the one hand and a pretty confident suspicion on the other. The conviction was that he had no constitutional right to inter-fere with slavery where it existed in states, a point he'd made again and again during his political career. The suspicion was that talk of secession was mere bluster on the part of a few hotheads that would soon fizzle out. Like many other northerners, Lincoln had heard so many southern threats to secede over the years that it was hard to take this latest round too seriously. So any conciliatory gesture, he believed, would be both poltroonish and unnecessary. Given time, cooler heads would prevail. As he wrote two months before the election, "The people of the South have too much of good sense, and good temper, to attempt the ruin of the government."[2] Nor was he alone in this judgment. The *New York Herald* dismissed southern threats as "the old game of scaring and bullying the North."[3] William Seward openly defied the fire-eaters. "Who's afraid?" he mocked. "Nobody's afraid."[4]

Lincoln's optimism was so naïve that it bordered on denial. Although he had indeed repeatedly said that his only goal in regards to slavery was to prevent its spread, his hope that containing it within southern states would lead to its eventual collapse was also part of the public record. Moreover, ever since the Kansas-Nebraska Act, Lincoln had been consistent in his moral condemnation of slavery and bold in his charge that the Slave Power was conspiring to control the federal government and national courts. Given all this, many southerners, and not just fire-eaters, viewed a Republican victory to be a virtual declaration of war on their way of life. As a broadside entitled "The Indications of the Coming Storm" that began circulating in Louisiana a week before the election insisted, "We can never submit to Lincoln's inauguration; the shades of Revolutionary sires will rise up to shame us if we shall do that."[5]

General-in-Chief of the Army Winfield Scott, perhaps because he was Virginia-born and bred and better understood the southern mind than Lincoln did, had no illusions about what would happen if Republicans took the White House. As early as October he warned President Buchanan that some states were likely to secede if Lincoln was elected, and recommended beefing up garrisons at southern federal forts in preparation for the event. Doughface Buchanan, who disliked Scott almost as much as he did Lincoln and "Black Republicans," ignored the advice.

The swiftness of the southern response to Lincoln's election proved Scott right. On November 9, the *Richmond Examiner* ominously proclaimed that a political party born solely from "hatred of African slavery" was now the "controlling power" in the nation.[6] That same day, John Winsmith, a member of South Carolina's General Assembly, introduced

"A Resolution to Call the Election of Abraham Lincoln as US President a Hostile Act." Over the next two days, both of South Carolina's senators, James Chesnut and James "Cotton is King" Hammond, resigned. Robert Toombs, senator from Georgia, announced he would leave in January. (He did, along with seven other southern-born members of Congress, including Mississippi's Jefferson Davis.) Six weeks later, on December 20, South Carolina seceded from the Union, justifying its decision in part by claiming that Lincoln aimed to emancipate southern slaves. In the first five weeks of 1861, six more Lower South states followed.

The southern clamor prompted by Lincoln's election generally focused on two perceived dangers. The first was that now that the South-despising North controlled the government, southern honor was affronted and southern freedom jeopardized. As the *New Orleans Bee* put it, "Lincoln's triumph" was but the "practical manifestation" of the North's rabid conviction that the South "is degraded and unworthy." For southerners to bow their heads and consent to be regarded as "inferior in every respect" to northerners was to "ignore the history of our revolutionary struggles."[7] The editorial's reference to the American Revolution was a clear message. Just as the patriots of 1776 fought for the right of self-determination, so too should southern patriots of 1861.

Rhetoric that invoked the spirit of 1776 appealed to the idealism, howsoever misplaced, of southerners as well as to their fierce sense of independence. But a second warning about a Republican administration's threat to the South was distinctly less high-minded, focusing as it did on the deep-seated racism of most southern poor whites. Dire and often lurid predictions that Lincoln would emancipate slaves, ignore the *Dred Scott* decision by bestowing legal rights on them, and encourage miscegenation flew left and right. Alabama congressman J. L. M. Curry was just one of the many proponents of this position. Now that Black Republicans were in power, he thundered in a turn of phrase both sexually discreet and racially coarse, they will "amalgamate the poor man's daughter and the rich man's buck-nigger."[8]

A SCRAMBLE FOR COMPROMISE

As Lincoln sat in Springfield selecting members of his cabinet (as tradition at the time dictated, he offered the position of secretary of state to his chief rival for the nomination, Seward) and refusing to publicly comment on the unfolding crisis, frantic efforts to appease the South and salvage the Union, or at least to keep the Upper South states from following the Lower South ones, were being made in Washington, D.C. Few Republican voters showed much stomach for the conciliation proposals because, like Horace Greeley, they were happy to see the slave states depart or, like Lincoln, they thought the crisis an artificial one stirred up by a fanatical minority. But the proponents of the various schemes for compromise and reconciliation thought otherwise, and viewed the departure of the South with anxiety bordering on panic.

Proposals for compromise were presented to Congress as soon as it reassembled in December 1860—so many, in fact, that both House and Senate created special committees to examine them. One of the more fanciful recommendations, reminiscent of the dual-executive model defended by John C. Calhoun years earlier, was that the office of the president be replaced by an executive committee comprised of statesmen from different regions of the country. Another proposal urged a ban on all future legislation in regards to slavery. In the middle of December, Kentucky senator John Crittenden proposed a legislative package that consisted of no fewer than six constitutional amendments and four congressional resolutions. Among its provisions was an extension of the Missouri Compromise line to the Pacific, an explicit constitutional guarantee that Congress would never abolish slavery in the states, federal forts, or the District of Columbia, and a toughening of slave fugitive laws. Moreover, the package contained a provision that forbade the possibility of its future repeal. Stephen Douglas threw his weight behind Crittenden's proposal, but added several provisions that prevented free blacks from voting, laid out criminal penalties for antislavery speech, and authorized federal monies to colonize freed slaves.

Lincoln saw more appeasement than compromise in Crittenden's proposal. To his mind, it was yet another series of costly concessions to the South that "would lose us everything we gained by the election." If the Republicans caved at this point, he warned, "[I]t is the end of us. They [the South] will repeat the experiment upon us ad libitum. A year will not pass, till we shall have to take Cuba as a condition upon which they will stay in the Union."[9] Crittendon's bill failed in both the House and Senate, prompting Mississippi senator Jefferson Davis to predict that, "No human power can save the union, all the cotton states will go."[10]

Crittenden's compromise was barely off the table before a delegation of New York merchants hand-carried a petition to President Buchanan, signed by 40,000 of their fellow businessmen, urging a compromised end to the crisis. Stocks had dropped sharply after Lincoln's election, largely because of fears about the prospect of war. The business community in New York, which had close commercial ties and joint financial interests with cotton and tobacco brokers in the South, wanted something done to infuse confidence back into the market.

Although he'd made his notorious "irrepressible conflict" speech just two years earlier, Seward, impressed by the worries of his fellow New Yorkers, joined the ranks of those who advocated a compromise. In mid-January he proposed a bill to the Senate that promised to call a national convention in two years to resolve the slavery issue. Charles Francis Adams backed the proposal, and sweetened the pot for the South by recommending that New Mexico be admitted as a slave state. Seward wrote to Lincoln, urging a conciliatory policy of forbearance and patience in the hopes of bringing the seceded states back into the Union. But he received a response that dashed cold water on his proposal. "On the territorial question—that is, the question of extending slavery under the national auspices—I am inflexible."[11]

Throughout February, a peace conference, attended by 100 politicians and chaired by ex-president John Tyler, met in Washington, D.C., in an effort to hammer out some sort of solution to the crisis that would at least keep the Upper South states in the Union. Horace Greeley sneeringly called it the "Old Gentlemen's Convention" because of the advanced age (and insinuated dotage) of most of its delegates. After three weeks of wrangling, the conference produced a package that nearly duplicated Crittenden's earlier one, despite the fact that the latter had proven unacceptable to Congress.

The only piece of legislature to actually emerge from the three-month-long whirlwind of compromise proposals prior to Lincoln's inauguration was a constitutional amendment drafted by Seward but named after Thomas Corwin, the Ohio congressman who proposed it. The amendment, which denied Congress the authority to abolish slavery in states, was passed by both House and Senate in the week leading up to Lincoln's swearing-in, but mooted by the coming of the Civil War. Had it been ratified by the states, it would've become the Thirteenth Amendment to the

Constitution. Ironically, the legislation ratified in December 1865 as the Thirteenth Amendment abolished slavery in the United States.

In early December 1860, Lincoln wrote that there could be no compromise on the "question of extending slavery" or "Pop.[ular] Sov.[ereignty]." "Stand firm," he advised. "The tug has to come, & better now, than any time hereafter."[12] But it's not clear that he then envisioned the tug as anything more than a battle of sectional wills that could be resolved, in the long run, peaceably and rationally. The domino-like secession of seven Lower South states and the spate of proposed and failed efforts at reconciliation in January and February brought Lincoln the sobering realization that southern rage at his election, coupled with the deep sectional divide over slavery that had been building for years, was less of an artificial and more of a real crisis than he'd thought. By the time he departed Springfield in mid-February to journey to Washington, D.C., he felt the full weight of what was happening to the nation. To those who gathered at the train station in Springfield to see him off, he offered a message heavy with foreboding. "Today I leave you," he said. "I go to assume a task more difficult than that which devolved upon General Washington . . . Let us all pray that the God of our fathers may not forsake us now."[13]

"THE ESSENCE OF ANARCHY"

Lincoln arrived in Washington, D.C., on February 23, deliberately 10 hours ahead of schedule to thwart a rumored assassination plot. When he stepped down from the train, only one person, Illinois congressman Elihu Washburne, was there to meet him. For a president-elect, it was a dismal entry into the nation's capital.

Lincoln's trip from Springfield to Washington had lasted 12 days, and he'd taken the opportunity to give more than 100 impromptu speeches at rail stops along the way. In most of them, he reassured some listeners and probably alarmed others with promises that he would never agree to any compromise with the South that led to the destruction of the Union.

Between the time of his arrival and his swearing-in on March 4, Lincoln resided at the Willard Hotel and used some of his time there to polish his inaugural address. He'd started writing it back in Springfield, closely consulting the Constitution as well as pertinent documents like Henry Clay's speeches defending the 1850 Compromise resolutions and Andrew

Jackson's 1832 denunciation of nullification. Lincoln knew that the secession crisis had to be the focus of his address, and he wanted his remarks to be thoughtful, lucid, and nonbelligerent but firm. To that end, he gladly asked several of his acquaintances to read and comment on drafts. William Seward gave him the most feedback, filling nine pages of closely written script with nearly 50 suggestions. Seward above all encouraged Lincoln to soften some of his language so as not to antagonize the Upper South or further alienate the states that had already seceded.

A strong gale hit Washington the evening before the inauguration, muddying the city's wide, unpaved streets and whistling through the unfinished Capitol dome and around the equally unfinished Washington Monument. But the next day, although cold and raw, was brilliantly sunny, and a crowd estimated at between 25,000 and 50,000 turned out for the inauguration. (Given that Washington's population was around 75,000 at the time, the smaller number is more likely.) Lincoln arose that morning before dawn, and President Buchanan arrived at Willard's just before noon to pick up the president-elect and ride with him in an open coach to the Capitol. Lincoln was so preoccupied that he neglected to pay his hotel bill.

Buchanan and Lincoln rode to the Capitol surrounded by marching soldiers and prancing cavalry. Gen. Winfield Scott intended them to serve as living walls between Lincoln and any would-be assassin. (Unfortunately for many of the citizens who came out either to cheer or jeer the procession, the soldiers also obstructed their view of the president-elect.) Scott also stationed sharpshooters on rooftops along Pennsylvania Avenue, surrounded the speaker's platform at the Capitol with riflemen, and even posted artillery batteries at the Treasury and Capitol. "Old Fuss and Feathers" was taking no chances.

After arriving at the Capitol without incident, Lincoln stepped up to the podium, faced the waiting crowd, and began reading his address. In just 3,600 words, he spelled out for his listeners and the nation as a whole his central reason for refusing to accept secession as a legitimate political option. It is the essence of democracy, he said, that the will of the majority be honored. Such a majority, "held in restraint by constitutional checks, and limitations, and always changing easily, with deliberate changes of popular opinions and sentiments, is the only true sovereign of a free people." Unanimity of opinion will never be possible, even under the best of circumstances, and the rule of a minority is "wholly inadmissible," reducing as it does "the majority principle" either to anarchy or despotism.[14]

Secession, Lincoln continued, "is the essence of anarchy" first and foremost because it defies the majority principle and sunders the body politic, but also because secessionists unknowingly plant the seeds of their own destruction. "If a minority, in such a case, will secede rather than acquiesce, they make a precedent which, in turn, will divide and ruin them; for a minority of their own will secede from them, whenever a majority refuses to be controlled by such minority."[15]

So secession is morally wrong (especially, although Lincoln didn't explicitly say so, when instigated in order to protect the immoral institution of slavery). But it's also impractical. Despite fire-eating dreams of building a separate nation, the North and the South can't physically separate or distance themselves from one another. "We cannot remove our respective sections from each other, nor build an impassable wall between them." Given this, it makes more sense for them to resolve their differences *before* rather than *after* separation. "Can aliens make treaties easier than friends can make laws?"[16]

But Lincoln didn't want his first presidential address to the nation to be exclusively one of accusations or warnings. Although he had repeatedly rejected any compromise on the extension of slavery into the territories, he once more assured the South that he had no intention of interfering with slavery in existing states. The same constitutional protection of slavery that had always existed continued to exist. That was the law of the land, and he had no intention as president of disregarding it. Moreover, he assured the breakaway states that if military action erupted down the road, it would be instigated by them, not the federal government. So there was no need for the South to fall into a panic. Ever the champion of reason, Lincoln advised "one and all," northerners as well as southerners, to "think calmly and well" instead of allowing longstanding resentment to erupt in rash destruction.[17]

The "only substantial dispute" between the two sections revolved around the question of the morality of slavery and whether it ought to be extended. But, Lincoln concluded, North and South were more strongly connected by a shared heritage preserved in "mystic chords of memory, stretching from every battlefield and patriot grave, to every living heart and hearthstone, all over this broad land." Given this common ground, surely "the better angels of our nature" will prevail.[18]

On concluding his address, Lincoln was sworn into office by Chief Justice Taney, author of the 1857 *Dred Scott* decision. One observer noted that the chief justice resembled "a galvanized corpse." Part of his wooden appearance was doubtlessly from age and infirmities—Taney was in his eighties and in ill health—and partly from the day's chilly temperature. But it's likely that his expressionless demeanor was also an attempt to mask his distaste of Lincoln and everything he and the Republicans represented.

After the oath of office was administered, Stephen Douglas, one of the dignitaries on the speaker's platform, rushed up to shake Lincoln's hand and congratulate him. It was a gracious gesture on the Little Giant's part, and it nicely symbolized the spirit of cooperation between adversaries so eloquently recommended by Lincoln in his address. But a symbol was all it turned out to be. Two days after the inauguration, the Confederate Congress called for the mustering of 100,000 volunteer troops to protect the breakaway nation's borders. Five weeks later, Fort Sumter in Charleston's harbor was bombarded by Confederate forces. This time it was Lincoln's turn to call up 75,000 state militiamen. In his inaugural address, Lincoln had expressed the hope that although "passion may have strained, it must not break our bonds of affection."[19] But those bonds had been stretched too far since at least the annexation of Texas. Fort Sumter finally snapped them.

THE REPUBLICAN REVOLUTION

When the editor of the *New Orleans Bee* warned its southern readers that acquiescing to a Lincoln presidency would be a betrayal of their forebears' "revolutionary struggles" against British rule, he invoked a comparison that both secessionists and Unionists frequently made in the months preceding and following the national election. Each side claimed that it was the true heir of the 1776 revolution, just as each accused the other of counterrevolutionary sentiments, policies, and actions. Appealing to the likes of George Washington or Thomas Jefferson lent moral credibility to each side's position. It added the weight of venerated tradition to a sectional dispute.

Charles Francis Adams, son and grandson of presidents and longtime foe of slavery, excitedly wrote the day after Lincoln's election that "the great revolution has actually taken place ... The country has once and for all thrown off the domination of the Slaveholders."[20] (But as noted earlier, Adams's initial enthusiasm was replaced in the wake of secession by an alarmed willingness to seek a very nonrevolutionary compromise.) On the same day, Salmon Chase exulted that "the first of the great wishes of my life is accomplished. The Slave Power is overthrown."[21] The implication, echoed in hundreds of victory proclamations throughout the North, was that the nation had finally liberated itself from the oppressive yoke of southern bullying. The Slave Power conspiracy that Lincoln had made so much of in his debates with Douglas was defeated by the revolutionary will of the people—or at least those in the North.

Defenders of slavery, on the other hand, insisted that they were the true revolutionaries, and justified secession by appealing to the Declaration of Independence–enshrined right to revolt from an oppressive government. In drawing up Mississippi's grievances against the North, the state convention that voted for secession stated: "For far less cause than this, our fathers separated from the Crown of England."[22] An Alabama editorial likewise explicitly compared the secessionists of 1861 with the revolutionaries of 1776. Weren't the latter likewise secessionists when they "withdrew their allegiance from George III and set up for themselves?" it asked.[23] For Jefferson Davis, it came down to this single question: "Will you be slaves or will you be independent?"[24]

To the minds of most secessionists, the North's election of a Black Republican was a negatively counterrevolutionary move because it betrayed the spirit of 1776 by demanding that the South relinquish property rights and endure despotic interference in her domestic affairs. Other secessionists used similar language but reversed its application. For them, it was *secession* that was positively "counterrevolutionary" in that it resisted an unjust revolutionary effort on the part of the North to emancipate slaves, wash southern whites in their own blood, and trample on the vision of the founding fathers. Unionists, on the other hand, argued that southern invocation of the founding fathers was absurd, a "libel," as William Cullen Bryant wrote, "upon the whole character and conduct of the men of '76." They had fought for the rights of human beings, while the secessionists were willing to fight for the alleged right to own other human beings.[25] Lincoln agreed. Revolution is a moral right, he argued, if it's "exercised for a morally justifiable cause." But if the cause is unworthy, then it's nothing more than "a wicked exercise of physical power."[26]

Putting to one side all the rhetorical claims and counterclaims of North and South to represent the spirit of 1776, most historians agree that the civil war that erupted from the sectional crisis really was revolutionary in two ways: it culminated in the abolition of slavery and it devastated the southern economy and way of life. But preceding the revolution of the Civil War—or perhaps constituting the first stage of it—was the Republican revolution.

The two decades leading up to the Civil War were politically cataclysmic. Sectional tension arising from the issue of slavery's expansion gradually overtook and submerged virtually all other political concerns and business. In the process, it shattered the Second American Party System by destroying one of the two mainstream political parties (Henry Clay's Whigs), so severely damaging the other (the Democrats) that it remained the minority for an entire generation, and spawning a number of alternative political parties which either failed to thrive (the Liberty Party and the Free Soil Party) or split on the slavery question (the Know-Nothings) just like the Whigs and Democrats did.

After the 1854 Kansas-Nebraska Act, politicians and citizens from a background of diverse political loyalties attempted to join forces to oppose it. The genius of the Republican Party—and Lincoln was unquestionably a leader in this regard—was its ability to coalesce or "fuse" members from these disparate groups—ex-Whigs, antislavery Democrats, Free Soilers and old Liberty Party adherents, and even a few hard-line abolitionists—into a cohesive and powerful political coalition that in only six years captured the White House. Just as remarkably, the Republicans pulled this off by remaining true to their core principles of free soil and free labor, refusing to back away from them in order to attract votes. The very fact that this principled strategy worked attests to the degree to which the North was morally repulsed by slavery and weary of what it perceived as the South's grandstanding. By 1860, a large percentage of northerners were ready to cast their votes for an overtly sectional political party that promised to stand firm against the Slave Power. Northern uneasiness with slavery, regardless of the motives behind it, had been growing for decades. But it's undeniable that Republican agitation throughout the second half of the 1850s encouraged and utilized that disgruntlement to bring about a political sea change unimaginable just a decade earlier. William Seward

was genuinely prescient when he proclaimed in his 1858 "irresistible conflict" speech: "I know, and you know, that a revolution has begun. I know,
and all the world knows, that revolutions never go backwards."[27]

NOTES

The first chapter epigraph is from William C. Davis, *Look Away! A History
of the Confederate States of America* (New York: The Free Press, 2002), 26. The
Lincoln chapter epigraph is in Roy P. Basler (ed.), *The Collected Works of Abraham
Lincoln* (New Brunswick, NJ: Rutgers University Press, 1953), 4:271. Hereafter
cited as CW.

1. CW 4:132–33.
2. CW 4:95.
3. *New York Herald*, October 18, 1860.
4. David M. Potter, *The Impending Crisis, 1848–1861* (New York: Harper &
Row, 1976), 431.
5. Davis, *Look Away!*, 26.
6. *Richmond Semi-Weekly Examiner*, November 9, 1860.
7. *New Orleans Bee*, December 10, 1860.
8. Davis, *Look Away!*, 30.
9. CW 4:172.
10. James McPherson, *Battle Cry of Freedom: The Civil War Era* (New York:
Oxford University Press, 1988), 254.
11. CW 4:183.
12. CW 4:149–50.
13. CW 4:191.
14. CW 4:268.
15. CW 4:267.
16. CW 4:269.
17. CW 4:270.
18. CW 4:271.
19. Ibid.
20. Eric Foner, *Free Soil, Free Labor, Free Men: The Ideology of the Republican
Party Before the Civil War* (New York: Vintage, 1995), 223.
21. Eric Foner, *The Fiery Trial: Abraham Lincoln and American Slavery* (New
York: W. W. Norton, 2010), 144.
22. James Oakes, *The Ruling Race: A History of American Slaveholders* (New
York: Alfred A. Knopf, 1982), 239.
23. Ibid., 240.

24. William L. Barney, *The Secessionist Impulse: Alabama and Mississippi* (Princeton, NJ: Princeton University Press, 1974), 192.

25. *New York Evening Post*, February 18, 1861.

26. CW 4:434, n. 83.

27. William H. Seward, "The Irrepressible Conflict," in George E. Baker (ed.), *The Works of William H. Seward* (Boston: Houghton, Mifflin, 1853–84), 4:302.

BIOGRAPHIES: PERSONALITIES IN THE ANTEBELLUM SLAVERY DEBATE

DAVID RICE ATCHISON (1807–1886)

One of the more unsavory characters in the run-up to the Civil War, Democratic senator David Atchison from Missouri was instrumental in fomenting violence in the Kansas Territory after the passage of the Kansas-Nebraska Act in 1854.

Born, educated, and admitted to the bar in Kentucky, Atchison migrated while in his early twenties to Missouri, where he practiced law and served in a number of local and state offices such as county commissioner, state legislator, and circuit court judge. He was also an officer in the state militia.

Sent to the U.S. Senate in 1843 to fill a vacated term, Atchison was subsequently elected to a full term and served until 1855. While in the Senate, he gained a reputation as a fiery defender of slavery and territorial expansion. He supported the Texas annexation, the Mexican War, and the Kansas-Nebraska Act.

The act mandated popular sovereignty on the issue of slavery in Kansas. Atchison saw this as both opportunity and danger, the former because it meant that slavery could be expanded, but the latter because there was a chance that Kansas residents might decide to ban slavery. If that happened, Atchison worried, slaves in western Missouri would be tempted to flee to Kansas. In order to ensure that Kansas became a slave state, Atchison began organizing bands of men to cross the Missouri border into Kansas, fraudulently claim residence, and cast proslavery votes in local and territorial elections. Atchison also encouraged these men to intimidate free soil settlers in order to either run them out of the territory or prevent them from voting. The strong-arm tactics of Atchison's thugs became so egregious that the bands soon became known as "Border Ruffians." They were responsible for the massive election frauds that seated the proslavery Lecompton legislature, whose petition for statehood sparked the feud between Sen. Stephen Douglas and President James Buchanan, further splintering an already divided Democratic Party. Atchison personally participated in some Border Ruffian raids, including the burning of Lawrence, Kansas, in 1856. By that time, Missourians, in part disgusted by Atchison's hand in stirring up trouble in "Bleeding Kansas," had declined to elect him to another Senate term.

When the Civil War began, Atchison served for a few months in Missouri under Confederate general Sterling Price, who was decisively defeated by Union forces in March 1862 at the Battle of Pea Ridge. Atchison relocated to Texas for the duration of the war.

JOHN BELL (1796–1869)

The Tennessee congressman who ran for president on the Constitutional Union Party ticket in 1860, John Bell was a man of independent thought whose convictions trumped his political loyalties, first to the Democrats and then to the Whigs. During his first three terms in the U.S. House of Representatives (1827–1833), he was a loyal Jacksonian Democrat. He supported Jackson's forced removal of southeastern Cherokees to an Indian Territory (now Oklahoma) reservation as well as the president's response to South Carolina's nullification resolution. But in his fourth term, he disagreed with Jackson's opposition to a national bank and began to nurse a personal grudge against Jackson because of the president's favoritism to James Polk, Bell's chief rival for prominence in the party. During the presidential election of 1836, Bell threw his weight behind one of the candidates running from the newly formed Whig Party instead of Martin Van Buren, Jackson's designated successor.

In the election of 1840, Bell campaigned in Tennessee for the Whig candidate, William Henry Harrison. After the election, Harrison appointed Bell secretary of war. But when Harrison died soon after taking office and it became apparent that his successor, John Tyler, was out of sympathy with the Whig ticket on which he had been elected, Bell, along with most of

Tyler's cabinet, resigned in protest. He practiced law for the next six years, but in 1847 he was elected to the U.S. Senate, where he remained until 1859.

As a senator, Bell once more proved himself something of a maverick. Like most of his fellow Whigs, he opposed the Mexican War, seeing it as an unjustifiable grab for additional slave territory. Although a slave owner himself, Bell objected to the geographical extension of slavery, arguing that a violation of the Missouri Compromise agreement would fragment the Union. During the 1850 congressional debate over the Mexican cession, he proposed that California enter as a free state and the rest of the newly acquired territory be split into an additional free state and two slave ones, thus maintaining senatorial balance. But he voted for most of Henry Clay's resolutions when his proposal was rejected. Four years later, he was one of only two southern senators—Sam Houston was the other—to vote against the Kansas-Nebraska bill. Toward the end of his senate career, he joined northern Whigs in speaking against proposals to annex Cuba, but broke ranks with them by voting against a homestead bill.

Increasingly alarmed by the sectional polarization that cut across traditional political lines, Bell met in 1860 with other concerned ex-Whigs and a handful of Democrats to form the Constitutional Union Party. The party's only real goal was preservation of the Union, and it nominated Bell as its presidential candidate. Given that he could expect little if any support from the Lower South states as well as the fact that the 1860 election had devolved into a four-candidate race, Bell hoped that the election would ultimately go to the House, where he expected his moderate position would win the day. This didn't happen, but Bell did better than he expected, winning nearly 600,000 popular votes, carrying three Upper South border states, and only narrowing losing four other southern ones. That he did so well suggested how alarmed the nation was over the possibility of secession.

Bell initially resolved to remain loyal to the Union, but like so many other border state southerners changed his mind after Fort Sumter. Throughout the war years and afterwards, he chose to remain out of the public eye.

JOHN BRECKINRIDGE (1821–1875)

Breckinridge, the youngest vice president in U.S. history, was one of the four presidential candidates in the election of 1860. Although he disapproved of slavery, he was a staunch defender of states' rights. He carried most of the South but lost to Abraham Lincoln.

Born into a politically distinguished Kentucky family, Breckinridge studied law at Princeton University and Kentucky's Transylvania College before being admitted to the bar when he was 20. After serving a stint in Mexico during the war, he was elected to the Kentucky state legislature and then two terms in the U.S. House of Representatives (1851–1855), where he actively supported Stephen Douglas's Kansas-Nebraska bill in 1854.

A year after leaving the House, Breckinridge was elected as Democrat James Buchanan's vice president. Buchanan almost totally ignored him throughout his term of office, but supported his bid for the presidency in 1860. Disagreements over slavery split the Democrats into northern and southern factions, with the former running Stephen Douglas as their candidate and the latter endorsing Breckinridge. Given the split, it was almost inevitable that Lincoln would take the White House, carrying as he did nearly every northern state as well as California and Oregon.

Before the presidential race, Breckinridge had been appointed U.S. senator from Kentucky. After the election, as Lower South states seceded, he hoped he could use his influence in the Senate to avoid war and to keep his home state of Kentucky neutral if a conflict erupted. Failing in both, he returned to the South, joined the Confederate Army, and was immediately expelled from the Senate as a traitor. He is the only vice president to be so designated.

First as a brigadier and then a major general, Breckinridge saw action at several engagements, including Shiloh (in which he was wounded), Chickamauga, New Market, and Cold Harbor. Confederate president Jefferson Davis named him secretary of war in February 1865. By this time it was obvious to Breckinridge that the war was lost, and he spent the few weeks before the government abandoned Richmond making sure that the official records of the Confederacy were preserved. At the end of the war, he went into exile for four years, living at various times in Cuba, England, Europe, and Canada, and returning to the United States only after President Andrew Johnson declared a general amnesty on Christmas Day, 1868. As a private citizen, he practiced law and invested in railroads. He refused to return to politics, but didn't shy away from occasional public stands. In 1870, for example, he condemned the Ku Klux Klan, and two years later supported a Kentucky bill that permitted blacks to testify in court against whites.

PRESTON BROOKS (1819–1857)

As the congressional wrangle over slavery grew increasingly acrimonious, insults and sometimes fists flew on the floors of both the House and Senate. After the 1854 passage of the furiously debated Kansas-Nebraska Act, many congressmen began carrying firearms and knives when they went to the Capitol. But the most outrageous act of violence committed in Congress during the turbulent 1850s was the caning of Massachusetts senator Charles Sumner, a Republican, by South Carolina representative Preston Brooks, a Democrat.

Brooks was known for his hair-trigger temper and propensity for physical violence whenever he felt slighted. He was expelled from South Carolina College (present-day University of South Carolina) for threatening officers of the law. At the age of 21, he fought a duel in which he suffered a hip wound that obliged him to use a cane for the rest of his life. Despite his disability, he served in the Mexican War with a South Carolina regiment. In 1853, he was elected to the U.S. House of Representatives.

Like so many of his fellow South Carolinians, Brooks was a zealous defender of slavery's expansion into the western territories. Along with Missouri senator David Rice Atchison, he was a supporter of Border Ruffian activity in the Kansas Territory. The resulting violence prompted Sumner, an equally zealous opponent of slavery, to deliver a two-day harangue on the Senate floor, entitled "The Crime against Kansas," in which he savaged slaveholders in general and South Carolina senator Andrew Butler in particular. His denunciation may have been motivated by noble intentions, but the language he used was needlessly harsh.

On May 22, 1856, two days after Sumner's speech, Brooks entered the Senate chamber, accompanied by Laurence Keitt, another representative from South Carolina. Striding over to Sumner, who was seated at his desk collecting papers, Brooks beat him about the head and shoulders with his cane until it shattered. When other senators attempted to intervene, Keitt pulled a pistol and warned them to stand back. Sumner was seriously injured, and unable to return to his senatorial duties for three years.

Brooks later explained that he had decided to beat Sumner because his "Crime against Kansas" speech proved he was no gentlemen and hence not worthy of challenging to a duel. The South responded jubilantly to the beating, and dozens of admirers sent Brooks new canes. He and Keitt both resigned their seats in the House, immediately stood for reelection, and were overwhelmingly returned, thus vindicating their claims that their constituents approved of their violent actions. The North generally condemned the attack, pointing to it as an example of the brutality practiced by slaveholders.

In the wake of his attack, Brooks was roundly condemned in a speech on the floor of the House by Sumner's friend and fellow Bostonian Anson Burlingame. Brooks heatedly challenged Burlingame to a duel, and apparently to Brooks's surprise, Burlingame immediately accepted. The duel was arranged to take place on the Canadian side of Niagara Falls, but Brooks, perhaps because he'd learned that Burlingame was a crack shot, failed to show up.

Brooks died in January 1857, reviled by the North and adored by the South. Laurence Keitt was slain in the Battle of Cold Harbor seven years later.

JOHN BROWN (1800–1859)

An abolitionist who came to the conclusion that only armed resistance would end slavery, John Brown is most notorious for his 1859 raid on the federal arsenal at Harpers Ferry, in what is now the state of West Virginia. But his violent campaign against slavery began years earlier. Some historians see Brown as a hero, while others view him as a possibly insane zealot. But all concur that his raid and execution in the closing months of 1859 were flashpoints in the 1860 presidential election, with many northerners applauding him as a martyr and most southerners branding him a traitor.

Brown's first four decades were characterized by personal and professional failures. Intending to become a Congregationalist minister, he dropped out of school when unable to pay tuition. A tanner by training, he never managed to keep any of the tanneries he started financially afloat. Drowning in debt from his failed business ventures, he was eventually declared a bankrupt in federal court in 1842. But by that time, he had discovered his true calling. Always opposed to slavery, he was so shocked by the 1837 murder of abolitionist editor Elijah Lovejoy that he publicly vowed before God to consecrate himself to destroying it.

Living in Springfield, Massachusetts, when the Fugitive Slave Act of 1850 became law, Brown immediately organized a vigilante group called the League of Gileadites to resist slave catchers in search of runaways. Five years later, hearing from sons who had settled in Kansas that Border Ruffians were using intimidation, ballot-box stuffing, and even violence to get Kansas admitted to the Union as a slave state, Brown headed west to join free soil forces. Serving as captain of a band of marauders, Brown and several of his men massacred five proslavers on the night of May 24, 1856, along the Pottawatomie Creek. The assault was in retaliation for the earlier Border Ruffian assault on the free soil town of Lawrence. Following several skirmishes with both federal forces and Ruffian bands, Brown and his sons headed back east to raise funds to finance his next scheme. Brown had been an early supporter of the Underground Railroad, the series of secret routes and safe houses set up in the northern states to assist runaway slaves. He dreamed of establishing a "subterranean passage" in the Appalachian Mountains for escaping slaves, but one that encouraged armed revolt rather than flight. His hope in raiding the federal arsenal at Harpers Ferry was to motivate slaves to join him in mountain retreats from which they would descend to burn plantations and free their brothers and sisters. But the raid was a blundering failure from beginning to end. Brown was quickly captured, tried for treason, and hanged on November 2, 1859.

After his capture, Republicans, including Lincoln, worried about being associated in the public mind with Brown, quickly repudiated his actions. But many northerners extolled him as a courageous crusader, which alarmed many southerners more than Republican condemnations of Brown soothed them. During the Civil War, a song written in Brown's honor, popularly known as "John Brown's Body," became a favorite marching tune of Union troops.

JAMES BUCHANAN (1791–1868)

Before he became the 15th president, James Buchanan had held so many public offices that he was known among his detractors and even some allies as "Old Public Functionary." By the time he reached the White House at age 65, he had been a legislator in his home state of Pennsylvania (he's the only president from the Commonwealth), a five-term representative in the U.S. House, envoy to Russia, U.S. senator, secretary of state, and minister to Great Britain. Buchanan had high aspirations. He tried for the presidency four times, in 1844, 1848, 1852, and 1856, but failed to receive the Democratic nomination until his final attempt. Unfortunately, his performance as chief executive didn't match his ambition. He is generally reckoned by historians to be one of the weakest presidents in a succession of mediocre presidents (Polk being the exception) throughout the 1840s and 1850s.

The son of an Irish immigrant who settled in Pennsylvania and succeeded in business, Buchanan graduated from Dickinson College in 1809, was admitted to the bar four years later, practiced law in Lancaster, and amassed a small fortune by the time he was 30. But his ambition extended beyond making money, and beginning in 1814 he served five years in the state legislature as a member of the Federalist Party. He ran for the U.S. Congress in 1820, won despite local resentment sparked by a tragic and scandalous love affair, and served for five terms.

While a member of the House, Buchanan left the dying Federalist Party to join the Jacksonian Democrats. He canvassed for Jackson in the 1828 presidential election, and four years later, when Jackson was elected to a second term, was rewarded with an appointment as U.S. envoy to Russia. Two years later, he won a seat in the U.S. Senate, served there until 1845, and fought hard for the Democratic presidential nomination in 1844. He lost to James Polk, who went on to become president, but was appointed Polk's secretary of state. Trying for the Democratic nomination again in 1848, Buchanan lost to Michigan senator Lewis Cass, who in turn was beaten by Mexican War hero and Whig candidate Zachary Taylor in the general election.

Buchanan retired to his Lancaster law practice in 1849 to await the Democratic national convention three years later, confident that he would be his party's nominee. But in the meantime, Illinois senator Stephen Douglas made a name for himself by reorganizing and pushing through Congress Henry Clay's compromise resolutions for ending the crisis over the Mexican War cession. Douglas's eye was also on the White House in 1852, and the two men fought bitterly for the nomination at the Democratic convention. Finally, on the 48th ballot, dark horse Franklin Pierce won the nomination and went on to win the election. As a consolation prize, the new president appointed Buchanan to the prestigious position of minister to England.

Although Buchanan may have accepted the appointment with mixed feelings, it was actually a lucky break for a man with political aspirations.

It got him out of the United States for the next two-and-a-half turbulent years when Congress furiously debated the Kansas-Nebraska Act, the Whig Party imploded, and "Bleeding Kansas" was fought over by pro- and antislavery rivals. As a consequence, Buchanan, although a member of the same party that sponsored the Kansas Act, was relatively untainted by its fallout when he finally received the Democratic nomination in 1856.

Although northern-born, Buchanan's sympathies were southern. He personally disapproved of slavery, but held that it should be allowed to follow the geographical growth of the nation. While minister to England, he had been involved in the writing of the subsequently leaked Ostend Manifesto, a recommendation that the United States forcibly seize Cuba from Spain. The manifesto was widely seen as a ploy on the part of the Slave Power to add Cuba to the Union as a slave state.

In the 1856 election, Buchanan defeated John C. Frémont, the first Republican presidential candidate, and ex-president Millard Fillmore, who ran on the Know-Nothing ticket. But 11 northern states went with Frémont while Buchanan carried only 4, barely managing a victory in his own home state. Seeing that the slavery issue was dangerously dividing the nation and convinced that abolitionists (a group into which Buchanan indiscriminately threw all slavery opponents) were deliberately seeking a violent showdown, Buchanan exerted pressure on the Supreme Court before his inauguration to settle the slavery issue once and for all. Two days after he took the oath of office, the Court handed down the *Dred Scott* decision, which denied that blacks, free or enslaved, were rights-bearing citizens of the United States and declared that the Missouri Compromise's geographical limitation of slavery was unconstitutional. Buchanan rather naïvely proclaimed the slavery matter settled once and for all. Republicans and other slavery foes declared that they would not recognize the new law. Stephen Douglas, whose championship of popular sovereignty seemed mooted by the Court's decision, argued that in fact there was no incompatibility between the doctrine and the *Dred Scott* ruling.

Buchanan's endorsement of *Dred Scott* was followed closely by his attempt to ramrod through Congress the admission of Kansas as a slave state. His rival for the 1852 presidential nomination, Stephen Douglas, challenged the move, correctly arguing that the Kansas proslave constitution submitted for congressional approval didn't reflect the majority will of Kansans. The resulting feud between the two leading Democrats of the day further splintered their party. Buchanan did everything he could to see to it that Douglas was defeated in his 1858 bid for reelection to the U.S. Senate. Despite his efforts, Douglas managed to best his rival, Abraham Lincoln. But Democrats did badly throughout the North in that midterm election, signaling widespread disapproval of Buchanan's prosouthern policies.

Buchanan reacted in part by continuously warning that the up-and-coming Republican Party, which did quite well in both the 1858 and 1859 elections, was composed of miscegenation-favoring abolitionists whose hatred of slavery would drive the South out of the Union. Buchanan's dire pronouncements only pushed an already jittery South closer to a decision to secede if a Republican took the White House in the 1860 presidential election. John Brown's 1859 raid on Harpers Ferry did nothing to quell their alarm.

The rivalry between Douglasites and Buchananites as well as the entry of a fourth candidate, John Bell, into the 1860 election, ensured Lincoln's victory. Afterwards, thanks in some part to Buchanan's presidential scaremongering, southern states began pulling out of the Union. In the few months remaining in his term, Buchanan, confronted with the secession crisis, seemed paralyzed by indecision—so much so that his secretary of state, Lewis Cass, resigned in disgust. Buchanan's official position was that although the departing states had no legal grounds for their actions, the federal government had no legal right to prevent their going. So he marked time until he could turn the White House, and the impending crisis, over to his successor.

Buchanan retired to his Lancaster estate, Wheatland, where he spent some of his seven remaining years writing his memoirs, which he hoped would salvage his reputation. But the public put much of the blame for the Civil War on his shoulders, and his book, when published, was largely ignored.

JOHN C. CALHOUN (1782–1850)

One of the most powerful intellects to serve in government, South Carolinian John Calhoun was, along with Henry Clay and Daniel Webster, a member of the "Great Triumvirate" of American statesmen in the antebellum years. A Democrat, he became known in the final two decades of his career as the nation's most vocal champion of southern states' rights against the authority of the federal government and of the thesis that slavery is a positive good, for both whites and blacks, rather than a necessary evil.

Calhoun, like many other young southerners, was sent north for his education, graduating from Yale College and going on to study law in Litchfield, Connecticut. Returning to South Carolina in 1807, he was elected to the U.S. House of Representatives three years later. He was one of the most vocal hawks in Congress at the outbreak of the War of 1812, and worked hard to supply U.S. troops with necessary weapons and supplies. Discouraged by the unpreparedness of the army, one of his primary goals when he was appointed secretary of war by James Monroe a few years later was to strengthen the nation's military. He served ably in that office for the duration of Monroe's two terms.

In 1824, Calhoun ran for the vice presidency. Because no candidate that year received a majority of Electoral College votes, the final decision was made by the House of Representatives. Calhoun was elected to be John Quincy Adams's vice president, but the fact that a national election had been decided by the federal government reinforced his growing suspicion of centralized authority. During the next presidential election, when Andrew Jackson defeated Adams, Calhoun was retained as vice president.

As part of Jackson's campaign strategy, his supporters had pushed through a tariff that they hoped would reflect badly on President Adams and cost him reelection. The strategy worked, but imposed high duties on imported goods, which southerners, with some justification, believed unfairly penalized them and benefited the North. Calhoun's state of South Carolina, suffering an economic decline, was especially vociferous in its objections, and in the late 1820s and early 1830s agitated for its right to nullify federal law within its borders. The nullification movement, which Calhoun encouraged, eventually created a crisis in 1832 in which South Carolina threatened to secede if the tariff was enforced. Jackson condemned the move and in turn threatened to invade South Carolina. Calhoun resigned as his vice president, formed the short-lived Nullifier Party, and entered the Senate. From then until the end of his life, he was the great champion of the southern way of life and the proponent of the right of a minority—in this case, southern whites—to set aside majority decisions that had negative impacts on it. This position served in 1860 as a justification for the secession of slave states from the Union. He served in the Senate, with a break in 1844–1845 to serve as secretary of state, until his death.

During his years in the Senate, Calhoun vigorously defended the institution of slavery, arguing from the chamber floor on several occasions that civilization depended on the enforced labor of inferior humans, that slaves were better cared for than free laborers, and that therefore slavery was a positive good to be encouraged rather than a shameful but necessary evil to be tolerated. During the crisis of 1850, he gave a speech (through a proxy; he was dying at the time, and too weak to deliver it himself) in which he declared that the only way for the Union to be preserved was for the North to allow the expansion of slavery into the western territories. In taking this stand, he aligned himself against his fellow members of the triumvirate, Clay and Webster. His *Disquisition on Government*, written in the last months of his life and published posthumously, set forth his views on states' rights and what he called the "concurrent majority," the claim that a minority had the right to nullify offensive majority decisions.

LEWIS CASS (1782–1866)

In December 1847, Lewis Cass, then a Democratic senator from Michigan, made the earliest defense of the doctrine of popular sovereignty, the claim that inhabitants of western territories had the right to decide for themselves whether or not to permit slavery. The doctrine was offered as an alternative to both the Wilmot Proviso, which sought to ban slavery in all territory won in the Mexican War of 1846–1848, and the plan favored by President Polk and others to extend the Missouri Compromise line straight through to the Pacific Ocean. Popular sovereignty was eventually incorporated in the Compromise of 1850 and became the centerpiece of Stephen Douglas's Kansas-Nebraska bill four years later, and the doctrine is most closely associated with Douglas. But it was Cass who first formulated it.

A native of New Hampshire, Cass relocated to Ohio in his late teens, was admitted to the bar there in 1802, and served a term in the state house of representatives before being appointed U.S. marshal for the district of Ohio. Following the War of 1812, President Madison appointed him governor of the Michigan Territory, a region much larger than the present-day state. Although frequently absent from the territory, Cass served there until 1831 and eventually settled in Detroit. As governor, he was responsible for surveying and building roads and, less admirably, dispossessing

Native Americans of their land. He was called by Andrew Jackson to serve as secretary of war between 1831 and 1836, during which time he directed the Black Hawk War in Illinois and Wisconsin and the Seminole War in Florida. In the final year of Jackson's administration, Cass was appointed the U.S. ambassador to France. Returning to the United States in 1842, he was elected to the Senate, where he served, with one hiatus of six months, until 1857.

Although he sided with Jackson during the Nullification Crisis of 1833, Cass became known as a senator with southern sympathies. Political enemies accused him of being a pawn of the Slave Power. He supported the annexation of Texas and the Mexican War, opposed the Wilmot Proviso, and endorsed the Kansas-Nebraska Act. His tolerant attitude to slavery became so apparent that his state, then Republican-controlled, declined to return him to the Senate in the 1857 elections. Yet Cass was no secessionist. Appointed secretary of state by James Buchanan, he resigned in 1860 over the president's refusal to reinforce Fort Sumter in Charleston Harbor.

Cass was a player in the presidential elections of 1844, 1848, and 1852. In 1844 and 1852, he was a strong although ultimately unsuccessful contender for the Democratic nomination. Winning the nomination in 1848, he resigned his Senate seat in May of that year to run. But the slavery issue split the Democratic Party, ending his chance of victory. The party platform remained silent on slavery in the hope of not stirring up controversy. But this silence as well as Cass's defense of popular sovereignty infuriated antislavery Democrats, who broke away, founded the Free Soil Party, and nominated Martin Van Buren, Cass's main competitor for the Democratic nomination, as their candidate. The Whig candidate, Mexican War hero Zachary Taylor, beat Cass handily when it came to electoral votes, but just managed to squeeze past him in popular ones. Van Buren and the Free Soil Party took 10 percent of the total vote, badly damaging Cass. After his defeat in the presidential race, Cass was reelected to his old Senate seat.

SALMON P. CHASE (1808–1873)

Antislavery statesman Salmon Chase was a leader in the Republican Party from its earliest days. Along with William Henry Seward, he was a leading contender for the Republican presidential nomination in 1860. But as was also the case with Seward, his perceived radicalism when it came to the issue of slavery prompted delegates to go with the more moderate Abraham Lincoln.

Born in New Hampshire, Chase spent his teen years after his father's death with his uncle, Episcopal bishop Philander Chase, founder of Kenyon College in Ohio. He attended Cincinnati College (now the University of Cincinnati) and Dartmouth, read law in the District of Columbia, and was admitted to the bar in 1829. He returned to Cincinnati the following year to practice law.

Once back in Cincinnati, he became acquainted with some of the city's leading abolitionists, including Harriet Beecher Stowe, future author of *Uncle Tom's Cabin*, and her husband Calvin Stowe. The Cincinnati race riots during the summer of 1836, in which blacks were assaulted and fled the city in large numbers and the offices of abolitionist newspaperman James Birney were ransacked by an angry mob, shocked Chase to his core. He began identifying himself with the antislavery movement and acquired a reputation for legally defending fugitive slaves and whites who aided them in their escape from bondage. Because Cincinnati was right across the Ohio River from the slave state of Kentucky, it was a favorite stop on the Underground Railroad, the loosely organized network of safe houses and routes for runaway slaves.

In defending fugitive slaves from rendition to their masters, Chase consistently advocated taking the slave states at their word when they insisted that the decision of whether or not to permit slavery was exclusively a state matter. It followed, argued Chase, that when a slave escaped to a free state, he or she automatically became free under the laws of that state. In making this case, Chase directly challenged the constitutionality of the 1793 Fugitive Slave Law, which contended that the federal government had a responsibility to guarantee the return of runaway slaves to their masters. Chase's best-known case was his defense of fellow Ohioan John van Zandt, who was sued for damages by a man whose fugitive slave van Zandt had aided. Chase argued the case all the way to the Supreme Court, which upheld the Fugitive Slave Law and found against van Zandt.

In 1840, Chase joined the newly formed Liberty Party, the platform of which demanded that the federal government "divorce" itself completely from slavery, thereby nullifying the 1793 Fugitive Slave Law. The Liberty Party was the first abolitionist political organization. Up to its formation, most abolitionists, under the influence of William Lloyd Garrison, eschewed political activism on the grounds that the U.S. Constitution's acknowledgement of slavery corrupted the entire government. Chase and other members of the Liberty Party argued that the Constitution was a living document that could be modified to reflect changes in the nation's moral sensibilities.

The Liberty Party participated in presidential elections in 1840 and 1844, both times running James Birney as its candidate. But the controversy over the Wilmot Proviso led to most party members fusing with other antislavery groups such as New York "Barnburner" Democrats to form the Free Soil Party. Chase actively campaigned for the Free Soil candidate, former president Martin Van Buren, who lost to Mexican War hero and Whig candidate Zachary Taylor.

Despite the defeat of the Free Soil presidential candidate, Chase was elected as a Free Soiler to the U.S. Senate, where he served during the stormy years between 1849 and 1855. As an opponent of the extension of slavery, he voted against both Henry Clay's resolutions of 1850 and Stephen Douglas's Kansas-Nebraska bill four years later. Even more, he coauthored with Ohio congressman Joshua Giddings a public protest, *Appeal of the Independent Democrats in Congress to the People of the United States*, that savaged the bill as part of an "atrocious plot" on the part of the Slave Power to "convert" western territories into a "dreary region of despotism."

While a senator, Chase joined a new anti-Kansas fusion whose members called themselves Republicans. Leaving the Senate after a single term, Chase ran as a Republican and won the governorship of Ohio, which he held until 1860. Although denied the presidential nomination in that year, he was reelected to the Senate, resigning shortly thereafter to become Lincoln's secretary of the Treasury. During his three years in that office, he established a national banking system that both stabilized currency and raised half a billion dollars in much-needed war funds by issuing government bonds.

Chase and Lincoln never got along particularly well, owing largely to the secretary's presidential ambitions. So when Chase offered his resignation for the third time in as many years, Lincoln, somewhat to Chase's surprise, accepted it. When Chief Justice Roger Taney, author of the *Dred Scott* decision, died soon afterwards, Lincoln nominated Chase as his successor, a position that Chase held until his death. As chief justice, Chase presided at the 1868 impeachment trial of President Andrew Johnson. He unsuccessfully tried for a presidential nomination in 1868 and again in 1872, the first time on the Democratic ticket and the second on the Liberal Republican's, a protest splinter party that vanished after the election.

HENRY CLAY (1777–1852)

One of the so-called Great Triumvirate of politicians (the other two were South Carolina's John C. Calhoun and Massachusetts's Daniel Webster), Kentuckian Clay was one of the most powerful government leaders in the United States during his lifetime, serving at both the state and federal levels. As Speaker of the House, he transformed the position into one of the most powerful in government, and in the Senate, where he brokered deals to resolve the Nullification Crisis and the 1850 crisis, he helped to postpone southern secession. He also served as John Quincy Adams's secretary of state. He was Abraham Lincoln's "beau ideal" of a statesman, and to this day is reckoned by historians to be one of the best congressmen the country has ever produced.

Clay read law and was admitted to the bar in Virginia, the state where he was born. He relocated to Lexington, Kentucky, where he practiced law, married, and began purchasing land that would eventually grow into a 600-acre estate called "Ashland," worked by a number of slaves. Clay owned slaves his entire life, inheriting his first two at the age of four when his father died.

Clay entered politics in 1807 with his election to the Kentucky General Assembly. He was chosen on two occasions to fill vacated U.S. Senate seats before being elected to the U.S. House of Representatives in 1811. He served there for the next 14 years, and was elected Speaker three different times. During his tenure, he was a strong supporter of the War of 1812, helped found the American Colonization Society in 1816, an organization founded to colonize freed slaves in Africa, and began advocating a platform, known as the "American System," which defended tariffs on imports to protect American industry, federal appropriations for improvement of transportation systems, and a national bank. These policies later became identified with the Whig Party, and they were ones that Abraham Lincoln would endorse. In 1820, Clay acquired the nickname "the Great

Compromiser" by helping to broker the Missouri Compromise, an agreement to maintain senatorial parity between slave and free states and to limit slavery to territory below the 36-30 latitude. It was the first of three significant compromises between North and South that Clay would help arrange.

Clay ran for president in 1824. Because no candidate vying for the office received a majority, the decision went to the House of Representatives. In a tie between Andrew Jackson and John Quincy Adams, Clay threw his weight behind the latter. Although the two men never enjoyed cordial relations, they both agreed on the policies of the American System. After Adams was sworn in, he promptly named Clay his secretary of state. Jackson and his supporters cried foul, charging that a deal had been struck between Adams and Clay. There's no conclusive evidence to support the accusation, but it damaged Clay's reputation.

Senate Democrats engineered the passage of the so-called Tariff of Abominations in 1828 to swing public support away from Adams's bid for reelection and in the direction of Andrew Jackson, who was trying once more for the White House. The maneuver succeeded in getting Jackson elected, but the heavy duty on imported goods that the tariff mandated enraged the South, especially South Carolina, a state already in an economic downturn. Tension built until 1832, when South Carolina's legislature, encouraged by John C. Calhoun, declared that the federal government had no right to impose its will upon the states, proclaimed the tariff null and void within its borders, and threatened to secede if pushed too far by Washington, D.C. President Jackson responded by threatening to personally lead federal troops into the state. Clay, who by then was serving in the U.S. Senate, collaborated with Calhoun to resolve the Nullification Crisis by writing legislation that progressively lessened tariff rates over a period of 10 years.

In 1832, prior to his successful Tariff Compromise bill, Clay had run a second time against Jackson, and had been severely beaten at the polls. Convinced that Jackson's policies called for strong resistance from a new organization, Clay formed the Whigs, a political party that would be a major player in national politics for a generation. Even though Clay remained the undisputed leader of the Whigs for the rest of his life, he failed to secure the party's nomination in the 1840 election year. Having been defeated by Martin Van Buren, Jackson's heir apparent, in the 1836 race, Whigs wanted a candidate they thought had a chance of winning. Considering Clay was too tainted by his previous failures, the Whigs nominated William Henry Harrison, who became the first of two elected Whig presidents. When Harrison died, he was succeeded by Vice President John Tyler, whose policies quickly alienated the Whig Party. The closing months of Tyler's administration were consumed by a congressional battle over the annexation of Texas. Free soil advocates resisted it, believing that it was a ploy of the Slave Power to expand slavery. Clay joined the opposition, although he tried to hedge his bets by declaring that he would favor annexation if it were done "properly." But his opposition probably cost him the presidential election of 1844, his final attempt at attaining the White House. He lost to Democrat James Polk, an ardent expansionist whose goal of stretching the United States' borders from coast to coast led to the Mexican War of 1846–1848.

At the beginning of the war, Pennsylvania congressman David Wilmot proposed a prohibition of slavery in all land that might be ceded to the United States from Mexico. The Wilmot Proviso, as it came to be called, splintered old political loyalties and drove the nation deeper into sectional animosity. In early 1850, Clay proposed eight resolutions to quell the uproar, some favoring the free states and others the slave states. After months of debate, during which John C. Calhoun spoke against them (his final address before dying) and Daniel Webster spoke for them, the Senate voted them down. But they were resurrected and pushed through Congress by Stephen Douglas. The resulting Compromise of 1850 admitted California as a free state but left open the possibility of slavery in future states carved from the Mexican cession. It also ended the slave trade in the District of Columbia while mandating a strong Fugitive Slave Law. The compromise was Clay's swan song as a public servant. He died in 1852 of the tuberculosis from which he was already suffering when he proposed his resolutions two years earlier.

STEPHEN DOUGLAS (1813–1861)

Few congressmen were as powerful in the 1850s as Stephen Douglas, Democratic senator from Illinois. Known as the "Little Giant" because of his small stature but boundless energy (some less charitably said because of his disproportionately sized head), Douglas was the popularizer, although not originator, of the doctrine of popular sovereignty. A rival of Abraham Lincoln's in a senatorial race in 1858 and a presidential one in 1860, he won the first but lost the second, and probably for the same reason: his defense of popular sovereignty.

A native of Vermont, Douglas moved to Illinois when he was 20. Once there he read law, was admitted to the bar, and soon became a leader of the state's Democrats. In quick succession he served as a state legislator, Illinois secretary of state, and associate justice of the Illinois Supreme Court, all before his 30th birthday. Even though he held the last position for only about a year, he was often referred to as "Judge Douglas" for the rest of his life.

Douglas resigned his judgeship to enter the U.S. House of Representatives, where he represented Illinois between 1842 and 1846. As a loyal Democrat who championed westward expansion, he supported President Polk's Mexican War, which erupted shortly before Douglas left the House for the Senate, where he would serve for the rest of his life. Shortly after his election to the Senate, he married a North Carolina planter's daughter. When his father-in-law died the following year, Douglas's wife inherited a Mississippi plantation worked by at least 100 slaves. She died in childbirth four years later, leaving him with two sons and a substantial income.

The territorial cessions won at the end of the Mexican War created a crisis in government in 1850, first because they threatened to upset the senatorial balance between slave and free states, second because of the sectional disagreement over whether slavery should be expanded into them. Henry Clay proposed eight compromise resolutions to end the crisis, subsequently lumped together into an omnibus package, but at the last minute a dispute over territorial boundaries scuttled the bill. Douglas took it upon himself to salvage Clay's compromise. He separated the motions and by intensive lobbying was able to gather enough votes to pass each of them through the Senate. Although Clay was hailed as the author of the Compromise of 1850, it was really Douglas who deserves the credit for turning it into law.

Still, the 1850 Compromise was only a stopgap, and sectional disagreement over slavery expansion flared up again four years later. The immediate cause was discussion of the construction of a transcontinental railroad, a project favored by both entrepreneurs and politicians of all political persuasions. Two routes were envisioned for the railroad: a southern route, extending from New Orleans to California, and a central one that would begin in Chicago, now Douglas's hometown and a city in which he owned real estate. The central route would necessarily run through the vast Nebraska Territory, the northern remnant of the Louisiana Purchase. But southern congressmen promised to block that possibility unless the territory was opened up to slavery, an impossibility given that the Missouri Compromise prohibited slavery north of the 36-30 latitude.

As chair of the powerful Senate Committee on Territories, Douglas was the obvious senator to break the impasse. After a great deal of behind-the-scenes negotiations with powerful southern colleagues, he proposed what came to be called the Kansas-Nebraska bill, which moved that the Nebraska Territory be divided into two, with the southernmost region called Kansas, and that the provisions of the Missouri Compromise be repealed in favor of a policy of popular sovereignty when it came to slavery in the territories. Dividing the territory in two was to maintain senatorial balance and mollify the North, since presumably Kansas would opt for slavery and Nebraska, the northernmost region, would not. The repeal of the 36-30 boundary was to please the South in order to win its approval for a Chicago–San Francisco rail track.

Douglas anticipated that his bill would, as he said, raise a "hell of a storm," and it did. Northern legislators and citizens alike were shocked at its repudiation of the Missouri Compromise, which many of them held as a sacred pledge binding for all time. But Douglas responded vigorously to criticisms, taking the high ground justification that popular sovereignty was the perfect expression of the American democratic ideal of local self-determination. Eventually Douglas's bill was approved by both the Senate and the House and signed into law by President Franklin Pierce, who had already thrown his weight behind it by declaring that Democrats' support of it was a measure of their party loyalty.

Free soilers, or people (generally northerners) opposed to the extension of slavery into the territories, were outraged. One of them was Abraham Lincoln, who had all but retired from electoral politics but was agitated enough by the Kansas-Nebraska Act to give a series of speeches in Illinois against it.

Douglas, who had presidential aspirations, toured the country to gain popular support for the Kansas Act. But the Democrats thought he was too hot to handle for the 1856 nomination, and instead selected James Buchanan, who had been safely out of the country during the 1854 debate. Shortly after Buchanan's nomination, the Supreme Court's *Dred Scott* decision mooted both Douglas's doctrine of popular sovereignty and the newly formed Republican Party's resistance to it by declaring that the Missouri Compromise was unconstitutional and that slavery couldn't be prohibited anywhere in the territories, either by federal mandate or local decision. Douglas, recognizing that the decision was welcomed by the South but not by the North, scrambled to find a way to satisfy both sections, and ultimately arrived at an argument, made famous in his later debates with Lincoln as the "Freeport Doctrine," that even though *Dred Scott* legalized slavery everywhere, popular sovereignty still determined whether local enforcement of it would or would not be a reality. It was a clumsy attempt to wed two essentially incompatible positions, but Douglas clung to it for the rest of his life.

Buchanan and Douglas had never gotten along, and the Little Giant's loss of the nomination to Buchanan strained their relationship even more. But the breaking point came in the first year of Buchanan's administration when he embraced the obviously rigged proslavery constitution submitted by Kansas legislators as a condition for admission to statehood. Because many of the legislators were fraudulently elected, and because it was clear that a majority of Kansas residents in fact were free soilers, Douglas correctly saw the constitution as a violation of popular sovereignty and publicly condemned the president's endorsement. Buchanan, understandably furious that a fellow Democrat would break ranks with him, vowed to destroy Douglas.

His opportunity came the following year, when Douglas was up for reelection to the Senate. In effect, Douglas ran against two opponents: Abraham Lincoln, a Republican free soiler, and James Buchanan, who exerted all of his presidential authority in an effort to end Douglas's career, even if it meant that a Republican took his senate seat. In the end, Douglas prevailed, largely because many of the state's ex-Whigs joined Democrats to reelect him. But his victory was costly, because in a series of nationally reported debates with Lincoln, Douglas's defense of popular sovereignty alienated the South. A common sentiment among southerners was that Douglas had betrayed them.

In 1860, Douglas's 1858 senate campaign came back to haunt him when the Democrats, manipulated by fire-eaters such as William Lowndes

Yancey and Robert Barnwell Rhett, split into northern and southern factions. The northern faction nominated Douglas, and the southern faction nominated Kentuckian John Breckinridge, Buchanan's vice president. Given the failure of the Democrats to create a united front as well as the entry into the race of a fourth candidate, John Bell of the newly formed Constitutional Union Party, Lincoln's victory was virtually guaranteed. In the general election, Douglas came in a distant last in electoral votes.

To his great credit, Douglas, who accepted his inevitable defeat even before Election Day, spent the end of his campaign touring the South trying to quell secessionist threats. After the election, when slave states began to leave the Union, he publicly condemned their actions as treasonous and fully supported Lincoln. He was a guest on the grandstand at Lincoln's inauguration, and was the first person to congratulate Lincoln after the oath of office was taken. Afterwards, at Lincoln's request, he toured the border states in an effort to keep them in the Union. But his premature death in June 1861 put an end to the career of a politician who would have been an invaluable member of the loyal opposition during Lincoln's administration.

MILLARD FILLMORE (1800–1874)

Lacking formal schooling but capable of great industry, Millard Fillmore was a perfect example of a self-made man, rising from humble beginnings in western New York to become the 13th president of the United States. He was instrumental in pushing the hotly debated Compromise of 1850 through Congress.

Apprenticed to cloth makers as a youth, Fillmore eventually clerked himself to a local judge, read law under him, and was admitted to the bar in 1823. He was a well-regarded and successful lawyer.

Fillmore spent three years in the New York Assembly before moving on to the U.S. House in 1832, where he served for the next decade. While there, he declared his allegiance to the newly formed Whigs and tended to vote strictly along party lines, supporting appropriations for internal improvements and opposing the annexation of Texas and the spread of slavery. Upon leaving Congress, Fillmore unsuccessfully ran for governor of New York, but shortly afterwards was elected New York state comptroller. His defeat of his Democratic rival was so crushing that he was tagged to be Zachary Taylor's running mate in the presidential election of 1848. The two of them offered bisectional representation—Taylor from the South, Fillmore from the North—but they didn't actually meet one another until after the election, at which point Taylor, taking a dislike to his vice president, proceeded to shut him out.

As vice president, Fillmore presided over the Senate and by virtue of his office cast tie-breaking votes. Although President Taylor disliked Henry Clay's proposed resolutions to resolve the crisis over slavery in the Mexican War cessions, Fillmore let it be known that he both approved of them and would swing in their favor if the Senate vote was tied. After Taylor unexpectedly died in July 1850, Fillmore went even further by replacing Taylor's cabinet with men in favor of Clay's resolutions and threw the weight of his administration behind their passage.

Fillmore somewhat reluctantly sought a second term. But by 1852, the Whig Party was imploding over the slavery issue, and the three contenders for the nomination—Fillmore, Daniel Webster, and Gen. Winfield Scott—were all handicapped by the sectional discord. Fillmore and Webster, who had served as Fillmore's secretary of state, were disliked by northern Whigs because of their enforcement of the Fugitive Slave Law. Additionally, Webster was old and obviously on his last legs. Scott was disliked by southern Whigs because he had backed Andrew Jackson's threat to intervene militarily during the 1832 Nullification Crisis. But in the end, Scott proved the least offensive candidate, finally receiving his party's nomination on the 53rd ballot. He was crushed in the national election by Democrat Franklin Pierce, ending for all practical purposes the run of the Whig Party as a player in national politics.

Tragedy struck Fillmore upon leaving the White House: his wife and daughter both died unexpectedly within a few months of his retirement. Grief-stricken, Fillmore left for a grand tour of Europe. Returning to the United States in time for the presidential election of 1856, he accepted the nomination of the Know-Nothings. He carried only the state of Maryland, coming in third after Republican John C. Frémont and Democratic victor James Buchanan. But he took enough popular votes away from Buchanan to make his margin of victory over Frémont slimmer than it otherwise would have been.

Remarrying in 1858, Fillmore retired to private life in Buffalo, New York.

JOHN C. FRÉMONT (1813–1890)

Perhaps nothing better illustrates the disarray of American politics in 1856 than the fact that all the major contending parties courted John C. Frémont, popularly known as the Pathfinder, to be their presidential nominee. Frémont eventually went with the Republicans, becoming the party's first presidential candidate and doing remarkably well in the election. But he was an unlikely choice and would have been an unqualified president.

Born in Georgia, the illegitimate son of a wealthy Virginian's wife who ran off with a French tutor, Frémont joined the Army Corps of Topographical Engineers as a young man. The corps was a relatively small branch of the military whose members, all officers, were charged with surveying and mapping western routes. Throughout the 1840s, Frémont led three expeditionary parties into the Sierra Nevadas, tracing the source of the Arkansas River and exploring the Sacramento Valley. The frontiersman and scout Kit Carson accompanied Frémont each time. The maps the corps drew on each trip proved invaluable to westward-bound migrants, especially the prospectors who headed for the California goldfields in 1848 and 1849, and earned Frémont his popular nickname.

During the Mexican War, Frémont was appointed commander of a California battalion of volunteers, and in late 1846 succeeded in capturing both Santa Barbara and Los Angeles. In January 1847, Commodore Robert Stockton, the U.S. military governor of California, appointed Frémont to succeed him. But in the meantime, President Polk had given the same assignment to Gen. Stephen Kearney. When word of Kearney's appointment finally reached California, he conveyed the news to Frémont and asked him to step down. Frémont's initial refusal brought a court martial and a dishonorable discharge from the army, a sentence that Polk quietly commuted.

Frémont settled in California with his wife, Jessie, daughter of Missouri senator Thomas Hart Benton and persistent promoter of her husband's political and military career, buying large sections of land. Following an unsuccessful expedition in 1848 to find a suitable railroad route through the mountains to the Pacific Coast, he served a few months as one of the first two senators from the newly admitted state of California. His selection as the Republican presidential candidate five years later was based more on the force of his celebrity than his political experience. Although he lost the election to James Buchanan, he and other Republican candidates did exceptionally well in the northern states, establishing the Republican Party as the Democrats' leading rival.

When war erupted between the North and the South, Frémont was commissioned a major general and made head of the Army's Department of the West, a geographical area that included the slave state of Missouri. Lincoln had negotiated with the Missouri state government to ensure its neutrality in the war. But upon taking the command, Frémont unseated the state governor, provoked a couple of military showdowns with proslavery forces, and issued a decree emancipating the state's slaves. Lincoln was outraged, fearful that Frémont's unilateral actions would push other border states in the Upper South to join the Confederacy. He ordered Frémont to rescind the emancipation proclamation. Frémont stalled, sending his strong-willed wife to Washington to speak with Lincoln.

Angered even more than he already was by this move, Lincoln removed Frémont from his command in late 1861. But the Pathfinder's popularity was so great that Lincoln couldn't completely dismiss him. So he appointed him commander of the Mountain Department of Virginia, Tennessee, and Kentucky. For part of the summer of 1862, Frémont unsuccessfully pursued "Stonewall" Jackson's army. When the department was reorganized and Frémont became the subordinate of Gen. John Pope, he refused his new position and retired to New York. Although still officially in the army, he was for all practical purposes a civilian for the rest of the war. Still seething in 1864 over what he considered Lincoln's ill treatment of him, Frémont ran against him in that year's presidential election, but eventually dropped out of the race.

Frémont's star sank after the war. By 1867, he was bankrupt, having made rash railroad investments, and was forced to sell his large Hudson Valley estate. President Rutherford B. Hayes, who had briefly served under Frémont in the Civil War, helped his old commander in 1878 by appointing him governor of the Arizona Territory. But Frémont so neglected his duties and antagonized his constituents that he resigned in 1881 rather than face a recall. Just a few months before his death, Congress granted him an annual military pension.

JAMES HAMMOND (1807–1864)

South Carolinian fire-eater James Hammond entered national politics as a member of the Nullifier Party, dedicated to the proposition that states have the right to reject displeasing federal legislation. Founded by John

Calhoun, the party lasted only a decade. But one of the southerners it sent to the U.S. House of Representatives in 1835 was Hammond.

An ardent proponent of states' rights and slavery, Hammond practiced law, taught school, and edited a newspaper before entering Congress. While there, he became notorious for his arguing that abolitionists deserved to be executed on the grounds that they encouraged sedition and insurrection. Resigning his seat after slightly less than a year because of ill health, Hammond and his wife toured Europe before settling on his plantation on Beech Island, South Carolina. He served as his state's governor between 1842 and 1844, but left public life for a while because of personal scandal. He returned in 1857 when he was appointed to take the place of U.S. senator Andrew Butler, who had died in office. Hammond resigned three years later when South Carolina seceded from the Union.

On March 4, 1858, Hammond delivered a speech on the floor of the Senate that delighted the South and enraged the North, and also contributed two new expressions to the era's lexicon. Noting that southern-grown cotton was by far the nation's leading export, he defiantly proclaimed that "Cotton is King." Were the South to withhold its cotton for three years, the whole civilized world would "topple." Consequently, he concluded, the South was unassailable by the North, and if she seceded, the North would be economically crippled.

Besides "King Cotton," Hammond also used the architectural word "mudsill" to refer to the lowest "inferior" class in society that performed the unpleasant work no one with higher social standing was willing to take on. Hammond argued that even though the North criticized slave states for relegating such tasks to slaves, it too employed a mudsill class, common laborers, to perform its own dirty work. Moreover, Hammond contended, slaves were better cared for than northern laborers, who worked totally at the whim of employers. Abraham Lincoln, among others, objected to this characterization of northern laborers, arguing that they, unlike slaves, had opportunity for upward mobility.

WILLIAM HENRY HARRISON (1773–1841)

The first of two elected Whig presidents, and the first chief executive to die in office (after only 32 days), Harrison was born into a distinguished Virginia family, was well educated (including, for a while, the study of medicine), and joined the army in 1791 on the death of his father. He was assigned to frontier duty in the Northwest Territory, a vast geographical region including all or parts of the modern states of Ohio, Indiana, Illinois, Michigan, Wisconsin, and Minnesota, where he served for the next seven years helping to quell Indian rebellions. Elected as a nonvoting territorial delegate to the U.S. Senate in 1799, he was appointed governor of the Indiana Territory, a region cut from the Northwest holdings, the following year.

Harrison served there for the next 12 years, arranging treaties with the region's Indian leaders and buying upwards of 60 million acres from them. In 1811, a Shawnee chief, Tecumseh, objected to Harrison's land-grabbing policy and declared war. His confederacy was decisively defeated in what came to be known as the Battle of Tippecanoe. The clash later provided the famous campaign slogan for Harrison's 1840 run for the presidency, despite the fact that Harrison, away on a recruiting trip, wasn't actually in the battle. Harrison also served in the War of 1812, capturing Detroit from the British and defeating them in Ontario in the Battle of the Thames, a fight in which his old rival Tecumseh was slain.

Following the war, Harrison served for a three-year period in the U.S. House of Representatives and another year and a half as minister to Columbia before retiring to private life in his adopted state of Ohio. By then he was one of the nation's military heroes, and the Whigs recruited him as their presidential candidate for the northern states in 1836. The Whig strategy that year was to run two regional presidential candidates, one in the North and one in the South, in the hope of so fragmenting the national vote as to throw the decision into the U.S. House, which the Whigs anticipated controlling after the elections. (They didn't.) The strategy didn't work; Democrat Martin Van Buren easily beat both of his Whig rivals, and Harrison returned to private life.

The Whigs ran him again four years later, choosing John Tyler from Virginia as his running mate and coining the famous campaign slogan "Tippecanoe and Tyler Too!" Although both candidates came from aristocratic Virginian families, their supporters presented them as simple, log cabin–born men of the people up against the out-of-touch patrician Van Buren. The strategy worked, bringing Harrison a landslide victory.

Henry Clay and the Whig Party had high hopes that Harrison's presidency would promote the party's "American System" of higher tariffs and federally financed infrastructural improvements. But the 68-year-old Harrison died a month into office, and his successor, John Tyler, soon made it clear that his own political loyalties were more Democrat than Whig.

Although born into a slave-owning family, Harrison's own views on slavery were ambivalent. He believed, along with most of his contemporaries, that the government had no right to interfere with the institution in slave states or the District of Columbia, and he owned several slaves himself. Moreover, as governor of the Indiana Territory, he lobbied in 1802 for legislation that would repeal the territory's ban on slavery for 10 years. Unsuccessful, he later pushed through legislation that allowed slave owners in the territory to redefine their human property as indentured servants, thus legalizing slavery in all but name. But when the legislation was repealed in 1810, he willingly signed the new law, and in 1833 even announced that he had been an abolitionist-minded "Friend of Liberty" from the age of 18. Had he lived, it's not clear what position he would have taken on the annexation of Texas as a slave state, a goal that his successor, John Tyler, eagerly pursued.

FRANKLIN PIERCE (1804–1869)

The 14th president of the United States, Franklin Pierce signed into law the Kansas-Nebraska Act, a piece of legislation which virtually destroyed the Whig Party, so damaged the Democratic Party that it remained a minority player in national politics for a generation afterwards, and gave rise to a number of anti-Kansas fusion groups which eventually coalesced into the Republican Party. Pierce, a northern Democrat with southern sympathies, wanted above all to reunite the bickering southern and northern wings of his party. But his presidency only widened the rift.

The only president from New Hampshire, Pierce was a student at Bowdoin College (where he met his lifelong friend, the author Nathaniel Hawthorne), studied law in Massachusetts, and was admitted to the New Hampshire bar in 1827. He was a Democrat in the state legislature for four years before going to Washington, serving first as a member of the House (1833–1837) and then in the Senate (1837–1842). When the Mexican War erupted, Pierce enlisted as a colonel of volunteers and fought courageously in several battles, suffering wounds in one of them. He took part in the capture of Mexico City, and was mustered out after his one-year enlistment expired.

By the 1852 presidential election, none of the major political parties wanted the troublesome issue of slavery to be part of their campaigns. Major contenders for the Democratic nomination such as Lewis Cass or Stephen Douglas were too closely associated with the Compromise of 1850 to be serious candidates, and former president Martin Van Buren broke with the Democrats to run on the antislavery Free Soil ticket. So ballot after ballot ended with no contender receiving the requisite number of votes for a nomination. Finally, on the 49th ballot, dark horse Franklin Pierce was unanimously elected by the weary delegates. Because the Democratic platform was deliberately noncommittal on slavery, the Democrats based their campaign on the force of Pierce's personal appeal. He was handsome, a war veteran, affable, and best of all had virtually no political enemies. Running with the campaign slogan of "We Poked you in '44, we shall Pierce you in '52!", the Democrats handily defeated Whig candidate Winfield Scott.

Two months after Pierce's election, tragedy struck his family. He, his wife, and their only child, a son, were in a train accident that took the boy's life in a particularly gruesome way. Pierce's wife never recovered from the blow, and Pierce, already suffering from a tendency to depression and alcohol abuse, found the first months of his administration especially trying.

Hopeful of healing the sectional conflicts over slavery that had simmered for years and reemerged in the crisis of 1850, Pierce selected men from both slave and free states for his cabinet positions. But his efforts at reconciliation crashed when Jefferson Davis and other powerful southern congressmen pressured him into backing Stephen Douglas's Kansas-Nebraska Act. They convinced him to make support of the bill a measure of party loyalty, thereby alienating many northern Democrats. He further antagonized the North by ordering federal troops to Boston to assist in the rendition of runaway Anthony Burns to his Virginia master. Finally, Pierce, who became vilified throughout the North as a "doughface" president in the grip of the Slave Power, supported the illegally elected proslavery government and used federal troops to break up a shadow antislavery government in the Kansas Territory. His presidency was so disastrous that the Democrats declined to nominate him for a second term.

After leaving the White House, Pierce and his wife went on a grand tour of Europe. Returning to the United States, he was sounded out by Democrats as a possible nominee in the 1860 presidential election, but Pierce had had enough of national politics. During the Civil War, he criticized Lincoln's administration on several occasions, especially when habeas corpus was suspended, and in private letters expressed his sympathy for the South and his opposition to the war. Several of these letters were discovered when Gen. Ulysses Grant captured the Mississippi city of Vicksburg, and when they were publicized, Pierce was denounced in the North as a traitor. On the night of Lincoln's assassination, angry citizens gathered in front of his Concord, New Hampshire, home.

Pierce's wife died in the second year of the Civil War. He survived her by six years, eventually dying from the effects of alcoholism. Before his death, his reputation was partially rehabilitated. But he is still judged as one of the nation's worst presidents.

JAMES K. POLK (1795–1849)

A Tennessean who became the 11th president of the United States (1844–1849), Polk was the strongest chief executive between Andrew Jackson and Abraham Lincoln. An expansionist who increased the size of the United States by a full one-third, Polk stretched the nation all the way to the Pacific coast. In the process, he also helped divide the nation on the slavery issue.

Born in North Carolina, Polk moved with his family to Tennessee in 1806. He graduated from the University of North Carolina in 1818, was admitted to the bar two years later, and became an ardent Jacksonian Democrat. In 1825, he won election to the U.S. House of Representatives, serving a term as Speaker (the only president to do so). He left Congress in 1839 to make a successful bid for the governorship of Tennessee.

Polk was a slaveholder throughout his adult life. He inherited a number of slaves from his father and acquired additional ones to work on a Mississippi cotton plantation he owned. As a defender of slavery, he also advocated its expansion and was an enthusiastic proponent of the annexation of Texas. In 1844, Polk's commitment to adding new territory to the United States in which to expand slavery earned him the Democratic nomination for president, beating out Martin Van Buren, who opposed slavery expansion.

Polk ran against Whig Henry Clay, whose lukewarm response to Texas annexation helped cost him the election. Sensing that his rivalry with Van Buren and northern Democrats in general risked splintering his own party, Polk promised to step down after a single term of office.

As a Jacksonian Democrat, Polk had three major goals while president: to reduce tariffs, establish a Treasury independent of private banks, and expand the nation's borders. He achieved all three, but his success in the third was the signature accomplishment of his administration.

John Tyler, Polk's predecessor, had secured the annexation of Texas in the final days of his presidency, and Polk oversaw its admission as a slave state at the end of 1845. But he also set his sights on the Oregon Territory in the Pacific Northwest as well as California.

Since 1818, the Oregon Territory had been claimed by both Great Britain and the United States. It was an immense area, stretching as far north as Russian Alaska and including all or parts of the present states of Oregon, Washington, Idaho, Wyoming, and Montana. In 1846, Polk negotiated a treaty that granted to the United States all of the territory south of the 49th parallel, the present border separating Canada and the United States.

At around the same time, Polk sent an emissary to Mexico to negotiate for the purchase of California and New Mexico. When the Mexican government refused even to meet the man, Polk decided that the rebuff was sufficient for a declaration of war. But his case was strengthened when U.S. troops under the command of Zachary Taylor were attacked by Mexican forces on land claimed by both nations. In May 1846, Polk used the incident as an occasion for asking Congress to declare war.

Whigs and other opponents of slavery saw Polk's decision to go to war as a ruse to acquire additional territory for the expansion of slavery. Abraham Lincoln, a junior congressman from Illinois, attacked Polk on the House floor, demanding to know the "exact spot" where the clash with Mexican troops occurred. But even Whigs felt it politically expedient to support troops once the war began, and the general population greeted news of battlefield victories with enthusiasm. The war was over in less than two years, and the geographical cessions made by Mexico in the 1848 Treaty of Guadalupe Hidalgo halved Mexico's territory and increased the United States' by over 1 million square miles. The entire future states of California, Utah, and Nevada, most of Arizona, and parts of New Mexico,

Wyoming, and Colorado were added to the nation's borders. Moreover, Mexico gave up all claims to Texas.

Only three months into the war, when it became obvious that the United States, if victorious, would win large geographical holdings, a Democratic junior congressman from Pennsylvania, David Wilmot, proposed a resolution, subsequently called the Wilmot Proviso, banning slavery from any territory that might be ceded by Mexico. The resolution was in large part a reaction on the part of northern congressmen to what they saw as the disproportionate influence of the Slave Power in affairs of state. The proviso, which sought to contain slavery within states where it already existed, was introduced and hotly debated on several occasions in the following years. The acrimony with which it was attacked or defended helped to fragment political parties along a North-South sectional line. Polk himself favored a simple extension of the Missouri Compromise line to the Pacific Ocean. The way to deal with slavery extension in the ceded territory remained unsettled when he left the White House. Also unaccomplished was his hope of buying Cuba, further slave territory, from Spain.

True to his word, Polk refused a second term as president. Worn out by his efforts, he died scarcely three months after leaving office.

ROBERT BARNWELL RHETT (1800–1876)

Sometimes called the Father of Secession, South Carolinian Robert Barnwell Rhett (whose birth surname was "Smith"; he changed it as an adult to honor a distinguished ancestor) collaborated with fellow fire-eater William Lowndes Yancey to split the Democratic Party in 1860, thereby swinging the election in favor of Lincoln in the hope of provoking southern secession.

Active in state as well as federal politics, Rhett supported John Calhoun in the Nullification Crisis and was a prominent player in the 1850 Nashville Convention, a gathering of delegates from nine slave states. The convention—called by Calhoun, who died three months before it met—was intended to frame a South-friendly policy for dealing with the issue of slavery expansion in the western territories acquired by the United States at the end of the Mexican War. Rhett and his supporters called for the convention to endorse an ultimatum: untrammeled spread of slavery throughout the cession or secession from the Union. More moderate voices, led by Jefferson Davis, carried the day with a recommendation for the extension of the Missouri Compromise latitude all the way to the Pacific. Henry Clay's resolutions for resolving the crisis ultimately adopted neither of these possibilities, only fueling Rhett's conviction that the South's rights were in jeopardy.

A U.S. senator at the time of the congressional debates over Clay's resolutions, Rhett resigned from Congress two years later and devoted himself to secession agitation. When Lincoln became the Republican presidential candidate in 1860, Rhett drafted South Carolina's Ordinance of Secession in anticipation of the breakup of the Union for which he longed. A few months later he helped write the Confederate Constitution. He was considered by many to be a strong contender for the presidency of the Confederacy, but in the end lost to the more moderate Jefferson Davis. During the war, the *Charleston Mercury* under his editorship became noted for its vigorous criticisms of Davis, whom Rhett blasted for not extending the Confederacy southwards to incorporate Cuba, as well as its belligerent defiance of the North. After Union victory, Rhett left South Carolina for Louisiana. Unreconstructed to the end, he refused to seek a federal pardon.

WILLIAM HENRY SEWARD (1801–1872)

New York native William Henry Seward was one of the ablest politicians of his generation. As a Whig and, later, a nationally known Republican, his outspoken opposition to slavery cost him the presidential nomination in 1860, even though he was considered the front-runner prior to the Republican convention. Bitterly disappointed, Seward nonetheless loyally supported Lincoln's candidacy and served as Lincoln's as well as President Johnson's secretary of state.

Admitted to the New York bar in 1821, Seward was a successful litigator before entering politics a decade later as a Whig. He served for four years in the New York State Senate and then two terms (1839–1842) as New York governor. Despite the prevalence of strong anti-immigration sentiments in his state, Seward supported state financial support of parochial schools, including Roman Catholic ones.

Although Seward grew up in a slave-owning family, he condemned the institution from an early age. His marriage to Frances Miller in 1824 only strengthened his antislavery beliefs. She was an early abolitionist who later convinced her husband to open their Auburn, New York, home as a refuge for runaway slaves making their way to Canada on the Underground Railroad.

In 1846, after returning to the practice of law following his two terms as governor, Seward gained notoriety for defending William Freeman, a black man accused of stabbing four white people to death. Seward's defense was that Freeman was insane—he had suffered a head wound some years earlier that impaired his ability to reason or to control his emotions—and argued that he should be sent to an asylum rather than the gallows. Seward lost the case, but the decision against Freeman was reversed on appeal. Seward's determined legal defense of a black man accused of a horrendous, violent act against whites shocked conservatives in and out of his own political party.

Seward returned to politics in the late 1840s, winning election to the U.S. Senate just in time to participate in the congressional debate over Henry Clay's resolutions to resolve the Mexican cession crisis. A member of the so-called Conscience Whigs, northerners opposed to slavery, Seward rejected all provisions of Clay's compromise except the admission of California as a free state. Slavery was immoral, he declared in 1850 on the Senate floor, and compromise with wickedness could never be right. Even though the U.S. Constitution affirmed the legal right to own slaves, Seward declared, human-made law is subordinate to a "higher law" that condemns one person owning another. This "higher law" speech, as well as one Seward gave in 1858 that claimed an "irrepressible conflict" between defenders and opponents of slavery, added to the public perception of him as an uncompromising abolitionist.

Four years after his opposition to Clay's compromise, Seward also voted against Stephen Douglas's Kansas-Nebraska Act. Leaving the Whigs after the congressional debate over the bill splintered the party, Seward threw in his lot with other anti-Kansans who called themselves "Republicans." He shied away from the 1856 Republican presidential nomination, believing that the party was too young to win the election and fearing that a national defeat would diminish his political prospects. Still a member of the Senate, Seward left the country in 1859 for a nearly yearlong tour abroad. By the time he returned, he discovered that Abraham Lincoln, whose moderation appealed to Republicans worried by Seward's past, had become a strong contender for the party's presidential nomination.

After his election, Lincoln appointed Seward his secretary of state. Seward, a man with years of political experience, initially sought to dominate the relatively inexperienced Lincoln. But the president soon established his authority, and thereafter the two men collaborated fruitfully. On the night of Lincoln's assassination, April 14, 1865, Seward was also attacked by one of the conspirators while he lay in bed at his home recovering from a carriage accident. The only thing that saved his life was a neck brace he was wearing, which deflected the dagger blows launched at him. Even so, his convalescence lasted for months, and his face remained scarred for the rest of his life. One of his sons was wounded in the attack, and both his frail wife and only daughter, traumatized by the attack, died soon afterwards.

Seward stayed on as secretary of state during Andrew Johnson's troubled administration and worked behind the scenes for Johnson's acquittal when radical Republicans in Congress began impeachment proceedings against him. In 1867, Seward succeeded in purchasing the huge Alaska Territory from Russia for two cents per acre, mocked at the time as a waste of money and referred to by the press as "Seward's Folly" or "Seward's Icebox."

ALEXANDER STEPHENS (1812–1883)

The future U.S. congressman, vice president of the Confederacy, and postwar governor of Georgia was orphaned at the age of 14 and educated through the largesse of surviving relatives and family friends. As a college student he was brilliant, graduating at the top of his class. He read law afterwards, was admitted to the bar in 1834, and despite never enjoying robust health, he became one of the most successful attorneys in Georgia.

Stephens began his political career with a six-year stint as a Georgia state legislator. In 1843 he was elected to the U.S. House of Representatives as a Whig. By the time he finished his congressional career in 1859, he had declared himself a Democrat. Although he supported the annexation of Texas, breaking ranks with many of his fellow Whigs, he joined with them in opposing President Polk's Mexican War. As a southern legislator, he also strongly opposed the Wilmot Proviso.

Although Stephens was a man of slight stature, reedy voice, and fragile health, he was, in keeping with the convention of politics during his day, ready to assault critics verbally and, at least once, physically as well. In 1848 he was insulted by one Judge Cone, a political rival, in an Atlanta hotel. Stephens apparently struck Cone with his cane, whereupon the burly judge pulled out a knife and stabbed Stephens at least six times, nearly killing him.

In the 1850 congressional debate over the expansion of slavery into the Mexican cessions, Stephens ultimately although somewhat reluctantly supported Henry Clay's compromise resolutions. But the debate made him wary of what he took to be the antisouthern sensibility of northern Whigs, and he left the party, first for the Constitutional Union Party (not to be confused with the party of the same name formed in 1860) and then for the Democrats. During the 1854 debate over the Kansas-Nebraska bill, Stephens became its primary proponent in the House. He afterwards considered his work in getting the bill ratified the greatest achievement of his congressional career.

Refusing to run for reelection in 1858 because of the growing sectional tension, Stephens left Congress when his term expired the following year. Although he initially opposed secession, he sided with the Confederacy when his state left the Union. After his election to the Confederate Congress in 1861, he was selected later that same year as the new nation's vice president. His reputation as a congressional defender of southern rights, as well as his so-called Cornerstone Speech, delivered in March 1861, in which he declared that the enslavement of "inferior" humans was the cornerstone of the new Confederacy, doubtlessly contributed to his election.

Stephens served as vice president throughout the entire war. He was arrested by federal authorities in 1865 and imprisoned for half a year before being released. Overwhelmingly elected to the U.S. Senate the following year but forbidden to take his seat, he was elected to the House in 1873 and served there for nine years until being elected governor of Georgia. Stephens died only four months into his term.

CHARLES SUMNER (1811–1874)

Charles Sumner, the man who succeeded to the Senate seat held for years by Daniel Webster, was one of the period's most vocal opponents of slavery. Webster had supported the Compromise of 1850, and as secretary of state under Millard Fillmore had vigorously enforced the controversial Fugitive Slave Law. Sumner, by contrast, was a committed abolitionist who came to Congress on the Free Soil Party ticket.

Born into a genteel but not terribly well-off family, Sumner was taught from an early age to dislike slavery. His father, an attorney, was one of Boston's earliest advocates of desegregated public schools, and instilled in his son the conviction that blacks deserved a full share of civic and political rights.

Educated at Harvard and following in his father's legal footsteps, Sumner was more interested in jurisprudence than trial work. He practiced law in a desultory fashion for a couple of years, occupied with writing scholarly articles and editing court decisions, before sailing to Europe in 1837. He studied a variety of subjects at the Sorbonne and learned several languages, returning home in 1840 as one of the most learned legal minds in the United States.

While teaching at Harvard Law School in the 1840s, Sumner delivered several well-received speeches advocating penal and educational reform. He became active in abolitionist circles after the annexation of Texas, and spoke out against the Mexican War the following year. His public denunciation of slavery led to his being courted by the Conscience Whigs, the antislavery faction of the party in Massachusetts, but they appeared too lukewarm for the zealous Sumner, who instead cast his lot with the new Free Soil Party. Standing as a candidate for the U.S. Senate, he was elected by a margin of one vote in the spring of 1851. He remained in Congress until his death nearly 23 years later.

Sumner lost no time in defending abolitionism on the floor of the Senate, quickly denouncing the Compromise of 1850 as unconstitutional and ungodly. Known for his florid and often unrestrained rhetorical style, particularly when speaking on slavery, Sumner pulled out the stops in May 1856 with his "Crime against Kansas" speech, a two-day marathon that condemned the Slave Power and the ongoing violence in "Bleeding Kansas." In the process, he went out of his way to personally insult several of his fellow legislators, including South Carolina senator Andrew Butler and Illinois senator Stephen Douglas, the author of the Kansas-Nebraska Act. Two days later, South Carolina representative Preston Brooks, a nephew of Butler's, beat Sumner senseless on the Senate floor. Sumner was unable to return to his duties for three years, and the assault on him helped inflame the already divisive sectional clash over slavery. When Sumner finally returned to the Senate, his first speech before the chamber, "The Barbarism of Slavery," resumed his defiant challenge to slavery.

Sumner welcomed the outbreak of war and opposed all talk of compromise in the weeks immediately leading up to it. He was known as one of the Radical Republican congressmen who viewed the war as a crusade to end slavery, and he caused much consternation in the Lincoln administration when he said as much in October 1861. During the war, Sumner was a member of the Joint Committee on the Conduct of the War, a group that ostensibly examined battlefield performance but in actuality also evaluated the loyalty, usually determined by the extent of their antislavery sentiments, of Union officers.

After the war, Sumner championed draconian treatment of the southern states, arguing that in seceding from the Union they had relinquished both legal and moral claims to be treated as anything other than a conquered nation. He subsequently softened his position, until by the end of his life he advocated conciliatory measures such as an end to military occupation of the South. He tried unsuccessfully on several occasions to pass legislation granting full civil rights to freed blacks, and in 1872, dismayed by the corruption in President Grant's administration, supported the Liberal Republican Party candidate Horace Greeley. After Greeley's defeat, Sumner's political star sank within the Republican Party, whose leaders felt betrayed by his support of Greeley.

ZACHARY TAYLOR (1784–1850)

The 12th president of the United States, the second of two elected Whigs to hold the office, and the second chief executive to die in office, most of Taylor's short term (1848–1850) was taken up with the debate over whether or not to allow slavery in the Mexican War cessions. The only other elected Whig president, William Henry Harrison, also died in office.

Taylor was born into a respected Virginia family whose intensive farming depleted the soil and forced them to migrate westward to Louisville, Kentucky. Although the family lived roughly for a few years, by the turn of the century Taylor's father had acquired over 10,000 acres of rich Kentucky land and nearly 30 slaves.

Taylor, a poor scholar in school, joined the army in 1808. Sent to frontier posts in present-day Wisconsin, Minnesota, Mississippi, Oklahoma, Kansas, Louisiana, Arkansas, Florida, and Texas, he earned a reputation as a competent and courageous officer who was willing to share the hardships of camp life with his men—hence his affectionately bestowed nickname "Old Rough and Ready." Taylor distinguished himself in the Illinois Black Hawk and the Florida Seminole wars. He also began buying up slaves and farmland in Louisiana, Mississippi, and Kentucky. By the time of his death, he was worth an estimated $6 million dollars in today's money.

Taylor gained a national reputation during the Mexican War. The conflict was sparked when he was ordered by President Polk into territory claimed by both the United States and Mexico, provoking a Mexican attack upon him and his men. Later he won crushing victories against the Mexicans at the battles of Monterrey, Veracruz, and Buena Vista. Overnight he became a popular hero by virtue of his courage under fire as well as his apparent disdain for military regalia and dapper uniforms. (In this, he differed greatly from another hero of the Mexican War, Gen. Winfield Scott, who had the revealing nickname of "Old Fuss and Feathers.")

Although Taylor had no obvious loyalty to any political party—he claimed that he had never even voted—he was courted by both the Whigs and Democrats as a potential candidate in the 1852 presidential election. Taylor's personal political views seemed to be an amalgamation of principles held by the two major parties. He was viewed favorably by many southerners because he was born in the South and was a slave owner. But many northerners applauded his publicly stated conviction that expanding slavery into the Mexican cession was pointless because neither climate nor soil favored the cotton and rice crops that required slave labor. Additionally, Taylor let it be known that as president he would veto neither the Wilmot Proviso nor any other legislation concerning slavery expansion passed by Congress. Finally, Taylor was a strong Unionist who had no patience with threats of secession by disgruntled southerners.

Taylor won the Whig nomination, even though there was a certain awkwardness in selecting as a presidential candidate a man associated in the public mind with a war that the Whigs had opposed. He ran without a platform, relying instead on his reputation as a war hero. Taylor beat

Democratic rival Lewis Cass and Free Soil Party candidate Martin Van Buren, although his margin of victory wasn't wide. Voting was largely on the basis of party rather than sectional loyalty.

As president, Taylor disliked Henry Clay's proposed resolution of the 1850 debate over the Mexican cessions, proposing instead that both California and New Mexico be admitted into the Union immediately as free states. In promoting his plan, Taylor publicly criticized Clay's more complicated proposal. Clay privately expressed relief when Taylor suddenly died after only 16 months in office to be succeeded by his vice president Millard Fillmore. As president pro tem of the Senate before Taylor's death, Fillmore had let it be known that he supported Clay's proposals. After he became president, he actively lobbied for them.

Fillmore was the last Whig president. Before the 1850s had run its course, the party disintegrated in the sectional dispute over slavery extension.

JOHN TYLER (1790–1862)

The first vice president to become chief executive (the 10th) on the death of an incumbent and the only former president to ally with the Confederacy during the Civil War, John Tyler's administration is most noted for the annexation of Texas in 1845, a move that helped spark war with Mexico one year later and the 1850 crisis over the expansion of slavery in Mexican cessions.

Born into an aristocratic and slave-owning Virginia family, Tyler was educated at the College of William and Mary and admitted to the Virginia bar when he was only 19. Elected to the Virginia State Assembly two years later, he served there until sent to the U.S. House in 1816. In Congress during the debate over the Missouri Compromise, Tyler strongly opposed it, arguing rather bizarrely that expanding slavery into new territories would actually weaken rather than strengthen the institution, presumably because "diffusing" slaves over large geographical areas would lessen reliance upon their labor. Tyler maintained this position to the end of his life. After the Missouri Compromise was struck, Tyler refused to stand for renomination to the House. He returned to Virginia, served a couple more terms in the assembly, and then two years as the Commonwealth's governor, a relatively powerless position. In 1827 he returned to the District of Columbia as a newly elected member of the U.S. Senate.

Although a Democrat, Tyler soon became disenchanted with the party's leader, Andrew Jackson, disapproving of the blatant cronyism practiced by the president in the allocation of federal jobs. But the final rupture came during the Nullification Crisis of 1832. As a strict constitutional constructionist, Tyler did not believe that states had the right to nullify offensive federal legislation such as overly burdensome tariffs. But his sympathies during the crisis were with the Calhounites who defended South Carolina's nullification resolution. When President Jackson responded by threatening military action against the state, Tyler publicly condemned the move, effectively breaking his ties with the Democratic Party and throwing in his lot with Henry Clay's newly formed Whig Party. Although Tyler was narrowly reelected to a second term in 1833, the Virginia Assembly was captured by Democrats within the space of two years. Rather than follow their instructions to him and thereby violate his own convictions, Tyler resigned from Congress in 1836, having served for a brief period as president pro tem of the Senate.

Tyler was chosen in 1849 as the running mate of William Henry Harrison, the first of two Whigs to be elected president of the United States. Although nominally a member of the party, what attracted Tyler to the Whigs was more a matter of his disagreement with Jackson than his agreement with Whig principles. He was a foe of strong federal government and consequently resisted the idea of a national bank, protective tariffs, and federally financed internal improvements, all essential features of the Whig "American System" program. But for the sake of getting a Whig in the White House, all this was downplayed during the campaign.

When Harrison died and Tyler ascended to the presidency, his Democratic tendencies quickly came to the fore and he stalled or actively blocked the Whig legislative agenda. As a consequence, most of the cabinet he had inherited from Harrison resigned in protest, he was formally drummed out of the party and threatened with impeachment, and Whigs joined others in disdainfully referring to Tyler as "His Accidency" rather than "His Excellency." Tyler quickly found himself a man without a party, and consequently unable to rally enough support to achieve much on the domestic front.

To compensate, he turned his attention to foreign affairs, and in this he was more successful. An enthusiastic expansionist—another way in which he differed from the Whigs—Tyler opened markets with China and the Sandwich Islands (Hawaii), settled the Canadian-Maine border in a treaty with Great Britain, and most importantly entered into secret negotiations for the annexation of the Republic of Texas—a move that, because it risked going beyond his presidential prerogatives, should have but didn't give a strict constitutionalist such as Tyler pause for thought.

Texas had been interested in joining the United States since it declared itself an independent republic in 1836. But neither Andrew Jackson nor his successor Martin Van Buren felt prepared to agree for several reasons. First, Texas would enter the Union as a slave state, thus antagonizing northerners. Second, annexing Texas risked war with Mexico, which refused to recognize Texas independence. Finally, the financial panic of 1837 convinced Van Buren that the assumption of Texas debts was too much of a responsibility for the United States to take on.

Tyler had no such qualms, however, and instructed his secretary of state, fellow Virginian Abel Upshur, to begin secret negotiations with Texas officials, and at the same time to begin courting senators to ensure congressional approval. Upshur performed both tasks well, and a treaty of annexation had been written when Upshur was killed in a freak accident in late February 1844. In a colossal misstep, Tyler appointed John C. Calhoun to replace him. In the South Carolinian's hands, the annexation of Texas predictably became identified with the Slave Power's eagerness to acquire more slave states. Accordingly, Congress initially rejected Tyler's annexation request. The president finally succeeded in getting congressional approval three days before he was replaced by Democrat James Polk.

After leaving the White House, Tyler returned to his slave-worked plantation in Virginia. He came out of retirement in February 1861 to chair a peace conference in Washington, D.C., put together at the last minute to work out a nonviolent solution to the secession crisis. When the conference's proposals, which tended to favor the South, were rejected by Congress, Tyler returned to Virginia and was soon elected to the Confederacy's House of Representatives. He died the following year, reviled in the North as a traitor.

DANIEL WEBSTER (1782–1852)

A strong Unionist who opposed South Carolina's attempted nullification in 1832 and supported Henry Clay's Compromise of 1850, Daniel Webster represented the North in the "Great Triumvirate" of antebellum legislators which also included John C. Calhoun from the South and Henry Clay from the West. Reckoned the greatest constitutional scholar of his day and one of the nation's most eloquent orators, Webster was a powerful voice in American politics for over three decades.

Born in New Hampshire, educated at Dartmouth College, and admitted to the bar in 1805, Webster aligned early on with the Federalist Party. He first made a name for himself at the outbreak of the War of 1812, when he both denounced the Embargo Act of 1807 that forbade commerce with Britain, thereby damaging New England financially and helping to spark the conflict, and condemned the war itself. Elected to the U.S. House as a New Hampshire representative the same year, he served two terms before leaving to return to a lucrative law practice. Over the next few years he argued several landmark cases before the U.S. Supreme Court. Relocating to Massachusetts during the interval, he was returned to the U.S. House in 1822, where he remained until elected to the Senate in 1827. He would serve there, with a brief hiatus as secretary of state under President John Tyler, until 1850.

As a senator, Webster drew closer to the "American System" advocated by Kentucky senator Henry Clay. Although he had opposed earlier tariff legislation, he voted for the Tariff of 1828, which imposed high duties on imported goods and angered southerners because of what they saw as a benefit to the New England states and a burden to themselves. South Carolina, already in an economic downturn, especially objected, and over the next five years formulated, under the guidance of John Calhoun, a defense of nullification and secession. In a famous and fiery debate held in 1830, Webster squared off on the floor of the Senate with South Carolina's Robert Young Hayne. Hayne, looking for an opportunity to build the case for nullification, accused northern supporters of the tariff of discouraging migration into the western territories out of fear that labor would become scarce in the northeast, thereby driving up wages. Webster responded in what many described as one of the most eloquent speeches ever delivered in Congress. In it, his repugnance at the possibility of secession and his ardent commitment to the Union came through clearly in a line that became famous overnight: "Liberty and union, one and inseparable, now and forever!" When the crisis came to a head in 1832 with South Carolina passing a nullification resolution and President Andrew Jackson promising military retaliation, Webster supported the president's hard-line approach rather than the compromise hammered out by Henry Clay and John Calhoun. But finding himself increasingly sympathetic to Clay's politics, Webster joined the newly formed Whigs and in 1836 ran as one of the Whig candidates for president. It was the first of three tries for the White House. Like Henry Clay, Webster craved but never achieved the presidency.

The next presidential election took a Whig, William Henry Harrison, to the White House, and Webster accepted the cabinet post of secretary of state. When Harrison died and John Tyler succeeded him, most of the cabinet, disgruntled with Tyler's obvious anti-Whig sentiments, resigned. Webster stayed on for a few more months, eventually negotiating the important Webster-Asburton Treaty, which helped finalize the Canadian-U.S. border and established cordial relations between Great Britain and the United States. Resigning his position in 1842, Webster was reelected to the Senate in 1845, where he opposed both the annexation of Texas and the Mexican War. He tried for the Whig presidential nomination in 1848, but was beaten by Zachary Taylor. Although he was offered the vice presidential nomination, he declined, just as he had declined a similar offer in 1840. The irony is that in turning down the two offers, Webster, who longed to be the nation's chief executive, refused to serve under the two presidents who died in office during his lifetime.

Webster had opposed the Mexican War because he feared that the territory won from it would upset the senatorial balance between slave and free states. The conflict he anticipated arrived in 1849 and 1850 with the congressional battle over the expansion of slavery into the vast regions acquired through the Treaty of Guadalupe Hidalgo. Henry Clay proposed eight resolutions to defuse the crisis and asked Webster to speak in favor of them. In early 1850, Webster complied by giving his famous "Seventh of March" speech in which he began by making clear that his allegiance was to the Union rather than any particular section of it. In it, he identified himself "not as a Massachusetts man nor as a northern man, but as an American." His support for Clay's resolutions helped push them through to eventual success, but also put an end to Webster's senate career.

Northern opponents of slavery believed he had betrayed them, because in defending Clay's bill Webster agreed to draconian federal regulations concerning the capture and return of runaway slaves. Resigning from the Senate soon after the bill passed, Webster became Millard Fillmore's secretary of state and enraged abolitionists even more by vigorously enforcing the Fugitive Slave Law.

Despite the fact that he had fallen out of favor with the northern public, Webster made one last try for the presidency in 1852. But the Whig nomination went instead to Gen. Winfield Scott, subsequently trounced in the election by Democrat Franklin Pierce. Webster died shortly before the election, the last of the triumvirate to go. Calhoun had died in 1850, and Clay preceded Webster in death by just three months.

DAVID WILMOT (1814–1868)

As a fledgling Democrat in the U.S. House of Representatives, Pennsylvanian David Wilmot defied fellow Democrat President Polk and other powerbrokers in his party by proposing an amendment to an appropriations bill that forever banned slavery from any territory acquired from the Mexican War. Although he loyally supported the declaration of war against Mexico that Polk requested of Congress, Wilmot drew the line at extending slavery. The appropriations bill sent to Congress by the president in early August 1846 was in anticipation of funds needed to negotiate Mexican cession of land when the war ended. Wilmot, acting on behalf of other northern Democratic congressmen who suspected the Slave Power of planning to expand slavery into the new territory, offered the amendment, loosely based on the 1787 ban of slavery in the old Northwest Territory, to forestall that possibility. Wilmot's objection to extending slavery was based exclusively on a concern for white interests, not on moral objections to slavery. He believed that the presence of blacks, freed or enslaved, would unfairly compete with free labor, and that whites were debased by association with blacks.

Wilmot's amendment, which came to be known as the Wilmot Proviso, was debated strenuously in Congress for the next six years, helping to splinter both the Whigs and the Democrats along sectional lines. In the 1848 presidential election, when the Democrats officially rejected the proviso in favor of a popular sovereignty position, Wilmot supported Free Soil

Party candidate Martin Van Buren. His growing opposition to his party's position on slavery led to his being dropped as the Democratic House nominee in 1850. He served as a judge in Pennsylvania until the outbreak of the Civil War and switched political allegiance to the Republicans. Campaigning vigorously for both Frémont in 1856 and Lincoln in 1860, he filled the Senate seat of Simon Cameron, the Pennsylvanian named secretary of war by Lincoln, from 1861 to 1863. In recognition of his sponsorship of the proviso as well as his loyalty to the Republican Party, Lincoln offered Wilmot a cabinet post in his administration. Wilmot asked instead for an appointment as a federal judge, a position he held until his death.

WILLIAM LOWNDES YANCEY (1814–1863)

Ironically, William Lowndes Yancey, the man who engineered the 1860 split in the Democratic Party to throw the presidential race to the Republicans and ensure southern secession from the Union, was reared and educated in the North. After his father died, his widowed mother married a New Yorker and moved north with her children, one of whom was nine-year-old Yancey. He attended Williams College in western Massachusetts (but left without taking a degree) and became such a convinced Unionist that even after he returned to the South in 1833 he spoke out against the nullifiers and publicly attacked their champion John C. Calhoun.

Within a decade, Yancey's political views changed dramatically. He moved from being a Unionist to an ardent advocate of states' rights and slavery expansion, at least in part because he married into a wealthy slave-owning family, relocated to Alabama, and began to speculate in land. He was never very successful as a planter, however, and supplemented his income with journalism and, eventually, the practice of law. His personal life was disruptive, owing largely to an impetuously fiery temper. As a student at Williams, he had been disciplined repeatedly for drunkenness, swearing, and other infractions. As a young planter, he argued with his wife's uncle and, in a blind rage, killed him, an offense for which he went to prison for a short while.

After serving a couple of terms in the Alabama state legislature, Yancey was then elected to two more in the U.S. Congress, during which he defended Texas annexation with such intemperate language that a colleague challenged him to a duel. Returning to Alabama after leaving the House, he resumed his law practice and unsuccessfully tried to convince the 1848 Democratic National Convention to adopt the so-called Alabama Platform, a binding agreement to neither nominate nor support any presidential candidate who refused to disown the Wilmot Proviso and popular sovereignty, both of which interfered with the geographical expansion of slavery.

In the years between 1848 and 1860, Yancey became one of the South's most notorious fire-eaters, helping to found the Southern Rights Party and writing articles and speaking all across the South in favor of secession. At the April 1860 Democratic Convention in Baltimore, he reintroduced the Alabama Platform that had failed in 1848. He knew that it had little chance of passing, but his plan was to create a debate in the convention that would justify a walkout on the part of southern delegates. In January of the same year, he had also persuaded the Alabama legislature to approve an act of secession in the event that Lincoln was elected president. He succeeded in both these aims. The Democratic convention split, in April and again in June after delegates convened for a second time, with Yancey leading the breakaway delegates. The consequence was that northern Democrats nominated Stephen Douglas and southern ones ran John Breckinridge, thereby guaranteeing a Lincoln victory. Just as Yancey planned, Alabama became the fourth state, following South Carolina, Mississippi, and Florida, to secede.

After the Confederacy was formed, President Jefferson Davis sent Yancey to Europe as head of a diplomatic effort to win recognition from England and France. Given Yancey's acerbic personality, it was a poor choice on Davis's part, and the mission predictably failed. Yancey returned to the South, and represented Alabama in the Confederate Congress until his death in 1863, shortly after the Union victories at Gettysburg and Vicksburg.

APPENDIX: PRIMARY DOCUMENTS IN THE ANTEBELLUM SLAVERY DEBATE

FREE SOIL PARTY PLATFORM
1848

A coalition of breakaway Democrats and Whigs who opposed the extension of slavery, the Free Soil Party ran its first presidential campaign in 1848, with former president Martin Van Buren as its candidate. By the mid-1850s, it had fused with the Republican Party, which would adopt its banner slogan of "Free Soil, Free Speech, Free Labor, and Free Men."

> *Whereas*, We have assembled in convention, as a union of free men, for the sake of freedom, forgetting all past political differences, in common resolve to maintain the rights of free labor against the aggression of the slave power, and to secure free soil to a free people ...
>
> *Resolved*, Therefore, that we, the people here assembled, remembering the example of our fathers in the days of the first Declaration of Independence, putting our trust in God for the triumph of our cause, and invoking his guidance in our endeavors to advance it, do now plant ourselves upon the national platform of freedom, in opposition to the sectional platform of slavery.
>
> *Resolved*, That slavery in the several States of this Union which recognize its existence depends upon the State laws alone, which cannot be repealed or modified by the federal government, and for which laws that government is not responsible. We therefore propose no interference by Congress with slavery within the limits of any State.

Resolved, That the proviso of Jefferson, to prohibit the existence of slavery after 1800 in all the territories of the United States, southern and northern; the votes of six States and sixteen delegates in the Congress of 1784 for the proviso, to three States and seven delegates against it; the actual exclusion of slavery from the Northwestern Territory, by the Ordinance of 1787, unanimously adopted by the States in Congress, and the entire history of that period, clearly show that it was the settled policy of the nation not to extend, nationalize, or encourage, but to limit, localize, and discourage slavery; and to this policy, which should never have been departed from, the government ought to return.

Resolved, That our fathers ordained the Constitution of the United States in order, among other great national objects, to establish justice, promote the general welfare, secure the blessings of liberty; but expressly denied to the federal government, which they created, a constitutional power to deprive any person of life, liberty, or property, without due legal process.

Resolved, That, in the judgment of this convention, Congress has no more power to make a slave than to make a king; no more power to institute or establish slavery than to institute or establish a monarchy. No such power can be found among those specifically conferred by the Constitution, or derived by just implication from them.

Resolved, That it is the duty of the federal government to relieve itself from all responsibility for the existence or continuance of slavery wherever the government possesses constitutional power to legislate on that subject, and is thus responsible for its existence.

Resolved, That the true and, in the judgment of this convention, the only safe means of preventing the extension of slavery into territory now free is to prohibit its extension in all such territory by an act of Congress.

Resolved, That we accept the issue which the slave power has forced upon us; and to their demand for more slave States and more slave territory, our calm but final answer is, no more slave States and no more slave territory. Let the soil of our extensive domain be kept free for the hardy pioneers of our own land and the oppressed and banished of other lands seeking homes of comfort and fields of enterprise in the New World ...

Resolved, That we demand freedom and established institutions for our brethren in Oregon now exposed to hardships, peril, and massacre, by the reckless hostility of the slave power to the establishment

of free government for free territories; and not only for them, but for
our brethren in California and New Mexico . . .

Resolved, That we inscribe on our banner, "Free Soil, Free Speech,
Free Labor, and Free Men," and under it we will fight on, and fight
ever, until a triumphant victory shall reward our exertions.

Source: Edward Stanhope, *A History of Presidential Elections* (Boston:
Houghton, Mifflin, 1896), 172–75.

JOHN C. CALHOUN'S RESPONSE TO HENRY CLAY'S COMPROMISE RESOLUTIONS MARCH 4, 1850

In his final Senate speech, South Carolinian Calhoun blames the North
for sectional discord over slavery, opposes Clay's resolutions, and threatens
secession unless the Mexican cession territories are opened to slavery and
fugitive slave laws enforced.

What is it that has endangered the Union? To this question there can
be but one answer—that the immediate cause is the almost universal
discontent which pervades all the States composing the Southern section of the Union . . . What has caused this widely diffused and almost
universal discontent? . . . It will be found in the belief of the people of
the Southern States, as prevalent as the discontent itself, that they
cannot remain, as things now are, consistently with honor and safety,
in the Union . . .

The great and primary cause [of the discontent] is found in the fact
that the equilibrium between the two sections, in the Government as
it stood when the constitution was ratified and the Government put
in action, has been destroyed . . . As it now stands, one section has the
exclusive power of controlling the Government, which leaves the other
without any adequate means of protecting itself against its encroachment and oppression . . .

How can the Union be saved? There is but one way by which it
can with any certainty; and that is, by a full and final settlement, on
the principle of justice, of all the questions at issue between the two
sections. The South asks for justice, simple justice, and less she ought
not to take. She has no compromise to offer, but the constitution; and
no concession or surrender to make. She has already surrendered so
much that she has little left to surrender. Such a settlement would

go to the root of the evil, and remove all cause of discontent, by sat-
isfying the South, she could remain honorably and safely in the
Union, and thereby restore the harmony and fraternal feelings
between the sections . . .

The North has only to will it to accomplish it—to do justice by con-
ceding to the South an equal right in the acquired territory, and to do
her duty by causing the stipulations relative to fugitive slaves to be faithfully fulfilled—to cease the agitation of the slave question.

Source: Richard K. Cralle (ed.), *Speeches of John C. Calhoun* (New
York: D. Appleton, 1883), 4:542–43, 544, 571–72.

DANIEL WEBSTER'S SEVENTH OF MARCH SPEECH
1850

In this selection from Webster's Senate defense of Henry Clay's 1850 compromise resolutions, the Massachusetts senator offers a firm condemnation
of the secession Calhoun threatened three days earlier.

Mr. President, I wish to speak today, not as a Massachusetts man, nor
as a Northern man, but as an American, and a member of the Senate
of the United States . . . I speak today for the preservation of the
Union. "Hear me for my cause." I speak today, out of a solicitous
and anxious heart for the restoration to the country of that quiet
and harmonious harmony which make the blessings of this Union so
rich, and so dear to us all . . .

Mr. President, I should much prefer to have heard from every
member on this floor declarations of opinion that this Union could
never be dissolved, than the declaration of opinion by anybody, that,
in any case, under the pressure of any circumstances, such a dissolution was possible. I hear with distress and anguish the word
"secession," especially when it falls from the lips of those who are
patriotic, and known to the country, and known all over the world,
for their political services. Secession! Peaceable secession! Sir, your
eyes and mine are never destined to see that miracle. The dismember-
ment of this vast country without convulsion! The breaking up of the
fountains of the great deep without ruffling the surface! Who is so
foolish, I beg every body's pardon, as to expect to see any such thing?
Sir, he who sees these States, now revolving in harmony around a
common center, and expects to see them quit their places and fly off

without convulsion, may look the next hour to see heavenly bodies rush from their spheres, and jostle against each other in the realms of space, without causing the wreck of the universe. There can be no such thing as peaceable secession. Peaceable secession is an utter impossibility . . .

Peaceable secession! Peaceable secession! The concurrent agreement of all the members of this great republic to separate! A voluntary separation, with alimony on one side and on the other. Why, what would be the result? Where is the line to be drawn? What States are to secede? What is to remain American? What am I to be? An American no longer? Am I to become a sectional man, a local man, a separatist, with no country in common with the gentlemen who sit around me here, or who fill the other house of Congress? Heaven forbid! Where is the flag of the republic to remain? Where is the eagle still to tower? Or is he to cower, and shrink, and fall to the ground? Why, Sir, our ancestors, our fathers and our grandfathers, those of them that are yet living amongst us with prolonged lives, would rebuke and reproach us; and our children and our grandchildren would cry out shame upon us, if we of this generation should dishonor these ensigns of the power of the government and the harmony of that Union which is every day felt among us with so much joy and gratitude . . .

Sir, I am ashamed to pursue this line of remark. I dislike it, I have an utter disgust for it. I would rather hear of natural blasts and mildews, war, pestilence, and famine, than to hear gentlemen talk of secession. To break up this great government! to dismember this glorious country! to astonish Europe with an act of folly such as Europe for two centuries has never beheld in any government or any people! No, Sir! No, Sir! There will be no secession! Gentlemen are not serious when they talk of secession . . .

Source: Edward Everett (ed.), *The Works of Daniel Webster* (Boston: Charles C. Little and James Brown, 1851), 325, 326, 330–31, 360–62, 363.

HENRY CLAY'S DEFENSE OF THE 1850 COMPROMISE JULY 22, 1850

In this celebrated speech to the Senate, Clay makes a final plea for his compromise resolutions, now packaged together in an "omnibus" bill. He was unsuccessful, and it was up to Sen. Stephen Douglas to rescue Clay's compromise.

It has been objected against this measure that it is a compromise. It has been said that it is a compromise of principle, or of a principle. Mr. President, what is a compromise? It is a work of mutual concession—an agreement in which there are reciprocal stipulations—a work in which, for the sake of peace and concord, one party abates his extreme demands in consideration of an abatement of extreme demands by the other party: it is a measure of mutual concession—a measure of mutual sacrifice. Undoubtedly, Mr. President, in all such measures of compromise, one party would be very glad to get what he wants, and reject what he does not desire but which the other party wants. But when he comes to reflect that, from the nature of the government and its operations, and from those with whom he is dealing, it is necessary upon his part, in order to secure what he wants, to grant something to the other side, he should be reconciled to the concession which he has made in consequence of the concession which he is to receive, if there is no great principle involved, such as a violation of the Constitution of the United States. I admit that such a compromise as that ought never to be sanctioned or adopted. But I now call upon any senator in his place to point out from the beginning to the end, from California to New Mexico, a solitary provision in this bill which is violative of the Constitution of the United States . . .

I believe from the bottom of my soul that the measure is the reunion of this Union. I believe it is the dove of peace, which, taking its aerial flight from the dome of the Capitol, carries the glad tidings of assured peace and restored harmony to all the remotest extremities of this distracted land. I believe that it will be attended with all these beneficent effects. And now let us discard all resentment, all passions, all petty jealousies, all personal desires, all love of place, all hankerings after the gilded crumbs which fall from the table of power. Let us forget popular fears, from whatever quarter they may spring. Let us go to the limpid fountain of unadulterated patriotism, and, performing a solemn lustration, return divested of all selfish, sinister, and sordid impurities, and think alone of our God, our country, our consciences, and our glorious Union, that Union without which we shall be torn into hostile fragments, and sooner or later become the victims of military despotism or foreign domination.

Mr. President, what is an individual man? An atom, almost invisible without a magnifying glass—a mere speck upon the surface of the immense universe—not a second in time, compared to immeasurable, never-beginning and never-ending eternity; a drop of water in the great deep, which evaporates and is borne off by the winds; a grain of sand, which is soon gathered to the dust from which it sprung. Shall a being so small, so petty, so fleeting, so evanescent, oppose itself to the onward march of a great nation, to subsist for ages and ages to come—oppose itself to that long line of posterity which, issuing from our loins, will endure during the existence of the world? Forbid it God! Let us look to our country and our cause, elevate ourselves to the dignity of pure and disinterested patriots, and save our country from all impending dangers. What if, in the march of this nation to greatness and power, we should be buried beneath the wheels that propel it onward? What are we—what is any man worth who is not ready and willing to sacrifice himself for the benefit of his country when it is necessary? . . .

I call upon all the South. Sir, we have had hard words, bitter words, bitter thoughts, unpleasant feelings toward each other in the progress of this great measure. Let us forget them. Let us sacrifice these feelings. Let us go to the altar of our country and swear, as the oath was taken of old, that we will stand by her; that we will support her; that we will uphold her Constitution; that we will preserve her union; and that we will pass this great, comprehensive, and healing system of measures, which will hush all the jarring elements and bring peace and tranquility to our homes.

Let me, Mr. President, in conclusion, say that the most disastrous consequences would occur, in my opinion, were we to go home, doing nothing to satisfy and tranquillize the country upon these great questions. What will be the judgment of mankind, what the judgment of that portion of mankind who are looking upon the progress of this scheme of self-government as being that which holds the highest hopes and expectations of ameliorating the condition of mankind—what will their judgment be? Will not all the monarchs of the Old World pronounce our glorious republic a disgraceful failure? What will be the judgment of our constituents, when we return to them and they ask us, How have you left your country? Is all quiet—all happy—are all the seeds of distraction or division crushed and dissipated? Will you go home and leave all in disorder and confusion—all unsettled—all open? . . . Sir, we shall stand condemned by all human judgment below, and of that above it is not for me to speak. We shall stand condemned in own consciences, by our own constituents, and by our own country.

The measure may be defeated. I have been aware that its passage for many days was not absolutely certain. . . . But, if defeated, it will be a triumph of ultraism and impracticability—a triumph of a most extraordinary conjunction of extremes; a victory won by abolition-ism; a victory achieved by freesoilism; a victory of discord and agita-tion over peace and tranquility; and I pray to Almighty God that it may not, in consequence of the inauspicious result, lead to the most unhappy and disastrous consequences to our beloved country.

Source: *Congressional Globe*, 31st Congress, 1st session, 1407, 1413–14.

LINCOLN'S PEORIA SPEECH
OCTOBER 16, 1854

In this selection from his first great speech, Lincoln asks and answers whether the Kansas-Nebraska Act's repeal of the Missouri Compromise is morally right or wrong.

I think, and shall try to show, that it is wrong; wrong in its direct effect, letting slavery into Kansas and Nebraska—and wrong in its prospective principle, allowing it to spread to every other part of the wide world, where men can be found inclined to take it.

This *declared* indifference, but as I must think, covert *real* zeal for the spread of slavery, I cannot but hate. I hate it because of the mon-strous injustice of slavery itself. I hate it because it deprives our republican example of its just influence in the world—enables the enemies of free institutions, with plausibility, to taunt us as hypo-crites—causes the real friends of freedom to doubt our sincerity, and especially because it forces so many really good men amongst our-selves into an open war with the very fundamental principles of civil liberty—criticizing the Declaration of Independence, and insisting that there is no right principle of action but *self-interest*.

Before proceeding, let me say I think I have no prejudice against the Southern people. They are just what we would be in their situa-tion. If slavery did not now exist amongst them, they would not intro-duce it. If it did now exist amongst us, we should not instantly give it up. This I believe of the masses north and south. Doubtless there are individuals, on both sides, who would not hold slaves under any circumstances; and others who would gladly introduce slavery anew, if it were out of existence. We know that some southern men do free their slaves, go north, and become tip-top abolitionists; while some northern ones go south, and become most cruel slave-masters.

When southern people tell us they are no more responsible for the origin of slavery, than we; I acknowledge the fact. When it is said that the institution exists; and that it is very difficult to get rid of it, in any satisfactory way, I can understand and appreciate the saying. I surely will not blame them for not doing what I should not know how to do myself. If all earthly power were given me, I should not know what to do, as to the existing institution. My first impulse would be to free all the slaves, and send them to Liberia—to their own native land. But a moment's reflection would convince me, that whatever of high hope (as I think there is) there may be in this, in the long run, its sudden execution is impossible. If they were all landed there in a day, they would all perish in the next ten days; and there are not surplus shipping and surplus money enough in the world to carry them there in many times ten days. What then? Free them all, and keep them among us as underlings? Is it quite certain that this betters their condition? I think I would not hold one in slavery, at any rate; yet the point is not clear enough for me to denounce people upon. What next? Free them, and make them politically and socially, our equals? My own feelings will not admit of this; and if mine would, we well know that those of the great mass of white people will not. Whether this feeling accords with justice and sound judgment, is not the sole question, if indeed, it is any part of it. A universal feeling, whether well or ill-founded, cannot be safely disregarded. We cannot, then, make them equals. It does seem to me that systems of gradual emancipation might be adopted; but for their tardiness in this, I will not undertake to judge our brethren of the south.

When they remind us of their constitutional rights, I acknowledge them, not grudgingly, but fully, and fairly; and I would give them any legislation for the reclaiming of their fugitives, which should not, in its stringency, be more likely to carry a free man into slavery, than our ordinary criminal laws are to hang an innocent one.

But all this, to my judgment, furnishes no more excuse for permitting slavery to go into our own free territory, than it would for reviving the African slave trade by law. The law which forbids the bringing of slaves *from* Africa, and that which has so long forbid the taking them *to* Nebraska, can hardly be distinguished on any moral principle; and the repeal of the former could find quite as plausible excuses as that of the latter . . .

But one great argument in the support of the repeal of the Missouri Compromise, is still to come. That argument is "the sacred right of self-government." . . .

I trust I understand, and truly estimate the right of self-government. My faith in the proposition that each man should do precisely as he pleases with all which is exclusively his own, lies at the foundation of the sense of justice there is in me. I extend the principles to communities of men, as well as to individuals. I so extend it, because it is politically wise, in saving us from broils about matters which do not concern us. Here, or at Washington, I would not trouble myself with the oyster laws of Virginia, or the cranberry laws of Indiana.

The doctrine of self-government is right—absolutely and eternally right—but it has no just application, as here attempted. Or perhaps I should rather say that whether it has such just application depends upon whether a negro is *not* or *is* a man. If he is *not* a man, why in that case, he who *is* a man may, as a matter of self-government, do just as he pleases with him. But if the negro *is* a man, is it not to that extent, a total destruction of self-government, to say that he too shall not govern *himself*? When the white man governs himself that is self-government; but when he governs himself, and also governs *another* man, that is *more* than self-government—that is despotism. If the negro is a *man*, why then my ancient faith teaches me that "all men are created equal"; and that there can be no moral right in connection with one man's making a slave of another.

Judge Douglas frequently, with bitter irony and sarcasm, paraphrases our argument by saying "The white people of Nebraska are good enough to govern themselves, *but they are not good enough to govern a few miserable negroes!!*"

Well I doubt not that the people of Nebraska are, and will continue to be as good as the average of people elsewhere. I do not say the contrary. What I do say is, that no man is good enough to govern another man, without that other's consent. I say this is the leading principle—the sheet anchor of American republicanism. Our Declaration of Independence says:

> We hold these truths to be self-evident: that all men are created equal; that they are endowed by their Creator with certain inalienable rights; that among these are life, liberty and the pursuit of happiness. That to secure these rights, governments are instituted among men, DERIVING THEIR JUST POWERS FROM THE CONSENT OF THE GOVERNED.

I have quoted so much at this time merely to show that according to our ancient faith, the just powers of governments are derived from the consent of the governed. Now the relation of masters and slaves is, PRO TANTO, a total violation of this principle. The master not only governs the slave without his consent; but he governs him by a set of rules altogether different from those which he prescribes for himself. Allow ALL the governed an equal voice in the government, and that, and that only is self-government.

Let it not be said I am contending for the establishment of political and social equality between the whites and blacks. I have already said the contrary. I am not now combating the argument of NECESSITY, arising from the fact that blacks are already amongst us; but I am combating what is set up as MORAL argument for allowing them to be taken where they have never yet been—arguing against the EXTENSION of a bad thing, which where it already exists, we must of necessity, manage as we best can . . .

Let no one be deceived. The spirit of seventy-six and the spirit of Nebraska, are utter antagonisms; and the former is being rapidly displaced by the latter.

Fellow countrymen—Americans south, as well as north, shall we make no effort to arrest this? Already the liberal party throughout the world, express the apprehension "that the one retrograde institution in America, is undermining the principles of progress, and fatally violating the noblest political system the world ever saw." This is not the taunt of enemies, but the warning of friends. Is it quite safe to disregard it—to despise it? Is there no danger to liberty itself, in discarding the earliest practice, and first precept of our ancient faith? In our greedy chase to make profit of the negro, let us beware, lest we "cancel and tear to pieces" even the white man's charter of freedom.

Our republican robe is soiled, and trailed in the dust. Let us purify it. Let us turn and wash it white, in the spirit, if not the blood, of the Revolution. Let us turn slavery from its claims of "moral right," back upon its existing legal rights, and its arguments of "necessity." Let us return it to the position our fathers gave it; and there let it rest in peace. Let us re-adopt the Declaration of Independence, and with it, the practices, and policy, which harmonize with it. Let north and south—let all Americans—let us all lovers of liberty everywhere— join in the great and good work. If we do this, we shall not only have saved the Union; but we shall have so saved it, as to make, and to keep it, forever worthy of the saving. We shall have so saved it, that the succeeding millions of free happy people, the world over, shall rise up, and call us blessed, to the latest generations.

Source: John G. Nicolay and John Hay (eds.), *Complete Works of Abraham Lincoln*, vol. 1 (New York: Century Company, 1907), 186–87, 195–96, 203–4.

KNOW-NOTHING PARTY PLATFORM 1856

The nativist and anti-Catholic Know-Nothing or American Party adopted this platform in the presidential campaign of 1856. The party's candidate was former president Millard Fillmore.

1. An humble acknowledgement to the Supreme Being, for his protecting care vouchsafed to our fathers in their successful Revolutionary struggle, and hitherto manifested to us, their descendants, in the preservation of the liberties, the independence and the union of these States.

2. The perpetuation of the Federal Union and Constitution, as the palladium of our civil and religious liberties, and the only sure bulwarks of American Independence.

3. Americans must rule America, and to this end native-born citizens should be selected for all State, Federal, and municipal offices of government employment, in preference to all others. Nevertheless,

4. Persons born of American parents residing temporarily abroad, should be entitled to all the rights of native-born citizens.

5. No person should be selected for political station (whether of native or foreign birth), who recognizes any allegiance or obligation of any description to any foreign prince, potentate or power, or who refuses to recognize the Federal and State Constitution (each within its sphere) as paramount to all other laws, as rules of political action. . . .

8. An enforcement of the principles that no State or Territory ought to admit others than citizens to the right of suffrage, or of holding political offices of the United States.

9. A change in the laws of naturalization, making a continued residence of twenty-one years, of all not heretofore provided for, an indispensable requisite for citizenship hereafter, and excluding all

paupers, and persons convicted of crime, from landing upon our shores; but no interference with the vested rights of foreigners.

10. Opposition to any union between Church and State; no interference with religious faith or worship, and no test oaths for office ...

Source: Edward Stanwood, *A History of Presidential Elections* (Boston: Houghton, Mifflin, 1896), 195–96.

CHARLES SUMNER'S "THE CRIME AGAINST KANSAS" SPEECH
MAY 1856

In this selection from the speech that incurred Preston Brooks's wrath, Sumner compares slavery to harlotry and slave owners to adulterers. He especially targets South Carolina senator Andrew Butler and Illinois senator Stephen Douglas.

The wickedness which I now begin to expose is immeasurably aggravated by the motive which prompted it. Not in any common lust for power did this uncommon tragedy have its origin. It is the rape of a virgin Territory, compelling it to the hateful embrace of Slavery; and it may be clearly traced to a depraved longing for a new slave State, the hideous offspring of such a crime, in the hope of adding to the power of slavery in the National Government. Yes, sir, when the whole world, alike Christian and Turk, is rising up to condemn this wrong, and to make it a hissing to the nations, here in our Republic, force—aye, Sir, FORCE—has been openly employed in compelling Kansas to this pollution, and all for the sake of political power. There is the simple fact, which you will vainly attempt to deny, but which in itself presents an essential wickedness that makes other public crimes seem like public virtues.

But this enormity, vast beyond comparison, swells to dimensions of wickedness which the imagination toils in vain to grasp, when it is understood, that for this purpose are hazarded the horrors of intestine feud, not only in this distant Territory, but everywhere throughout the country. Already the muster has begun. The strife is no longer local, but national. Even now, while I speak, portents hang on all the arches of the horizon, threatening to darken the broad land, which already yawns with the musterings of civil war. The fury of the propagandists of slavery, and the calm determination of their opponents, are now diffused from the distant Territory over wide-spread communities, and the whole country, in all its extent—marshaling hostile divisions, and foreshadowing a strife, which, unless happily averted by the triumph of Freedom, will become war—fratricidal, parricidal war—with an accumulated wickedness beyond the wickedness of any war in human annals; justly provoking the avenging judgment of Providence and the avenging pen of history . . .

Such is the crime which you are to judge. But the criminal also must be dragged into day, that you may see and measure the power by which all this wrong is sustained . . . I mean the senator from South Carolina, (Mr. BUTLER,) and the senator from Illinois, (Mr. DOUGLAS,) who, though unlike as Don Quixote and Sancho Panza, yet, like this couple, sally forth together in the same adventure . . . The senator from South Carolina has . . . chosen a mistress to whom he has made his vows, and who, though ugly to others, is always lovely to him; though polluted in the sight of the world, is chaste in his sight—I mean the harlot, slavery . . . The frenzy of Don Quixote in behalf of his wench Dulcinea del Toboso is all surpassed . . .

As the senator from South Carolina is the Don Quixote, the senator from Illinois (Mr. DOUGLAS) is the squire of slavery, its very Sancho Panza, ready to do all its humiliating offices . . . The senator dreams that he can subdue the North. He disclaims the open threat, but his conduct still implies it. How little that senator knows himself, or the strength of the cause which he persecutes! He is but a mortal man; against him is an immortal principle. With finite power he wrestles with the infinite, and he must fall. Against him are stronger battalions than any marshaled by mortal man—the inborn, ineradicable, invincible sentiments of the human heart; against him is nature in all her subtle forces; against him is God. Let him try to subdue these.

Source: Charles Sumner, *The Crime against Kansas* (Boston: John P. Jewett, 1856), 5–6, 9–10, 13–14.

JOHN FRÉMONT'S ACCEPTANCE OF THE REPUBLICAN NOMINATION
1856

Part of Frémont's letter to the Republican Convention accepting its delegates' nomination of him as the first Republican candidate for the presidency.

Nothing is clearer in the history of our institutions than the design of the nation in asserting its own independence and freedom to avoid giving countenance to the extension of slavery. The influence of the small, but compact and powerful class of men interested in slavery, who command one section of the country, and wield a vast political control as a consequence, in the other, is now directed to turn back this impulse of the revolution, and reverse its principles. The extension of slavery across the continent is the object of the power which now rules the government, and from this spirit has sprung those kindred wrongs in Kansas, so truly portrayed in one of your resolutions, which prove that the elements of the most arbitrary governments have been vanquished by the just theory of our own.

It would be out of place here to pledge myself to any particular policy that may be suggested to terminate the sectional controversy engendered by political animosities operating on a powerful class, banded together by a common interest. A practical remedy is the admission of Kansas into the Union as a free State. The South should, in my judgment, earnestly desire such a consummation. It would vindicate its good faith; it would correct the mistake of the repeal, and the North, having practically the benefit of the agreement between the two sections, would be satisfied, and good feeling be restored. The measure is perfectly consistent with the honor of the South, and vital to its interests.

That fatal act which gave birth to this purely sectional strife, originating in the scheme to take from free labor the country secured to it by a solemn covenant, cannot be too soon disarmed of its pernicious force. The only genial region of the middle latitudes left to the emigrants of the Northern States for homes, cannot be conquered from the free laborers who have long considered it as set apart for them in our inheritance, without provoking a desperate struggle. Whatever may be the persistence of the particular class which seems ready to hazard everything for the success of the unjust scheme it has partially effected, I firmly believe that the great heart of the nation, which throbs with the patriotism of the free men of both sections, will have power to overcome it . . .

If the people entrust to me the administration of the Government, the laws of Congress in relation to the Territories will be faithfully executed. All its authority will be exerted in aid of the National will to re-establish the peace of the country, on the just principles which have heretofore received the sanction of the Federal Government, of the States, and of the people of both sections. Such a policy would leave no aliment to that sectional party which seeks its aggrandizement by appropriating the new territories to capital in the form of slavery, but would inevitably result in the triumph of free labor, the natural capital which constitutes the real wealth of this great country, and creates that intelligent power in the masses alone to be relied on as the bulwark of free institutions.

Source: *Republican Campaign Edition for the Million. Containing the Republican Platform, the Lives of Frémont and Dayton, with Beautiful Steel Portraits of Each* (Boston: John P. Jewitt, 1856), 29–34.

PLATFORM OF THE REPUBLICAN PARTY 1856

The national platform of the Republican Party's first presidential campaign.

... *Resolved:* That, with our Republican fathers, we hold it to be a self-evident truth, that all men are endowed with the inalienable right to life, liberty, and the pursuit of happiness, and that the primary object and ulterior design of our Federal Government were to secure these rights to all persons under its exclusive jurisdiction; that, as our Republican fathers, when they had abolished Slavery in all our National Territory, ordained that no person shall be deprived of life, liberty, or property, without due process of law, it becomes our duty to maintain this provision of the Constitution against all attempts to violate it for the purpose of establishing Slavery in the Territories of the United States by positive legislation, prohibiting its existence or extension therein. That we deny the authority of Congress, of a Territorial Legislation, of any individual, or association of individuals, to give legal existence to Slavery in any Territory of the United States, while the present Constitution shall be maintained.

Resolved: That the Constitution confers upon Congress sovereign powers over the Territories of the United States for their government; and that in the exercise of this power, it is both the right and the imperative duty of Congress to prohibit in the Territories those twin relics of barbarism—Polygamy, and Slavery.

Resolved: That while the Constitution of the United States was ordained and established by the people, in order to "form a more perfect union, establish justice, insure domestic tranquility, provide for the common defense, promote the general welfare, and secure the blessings of liberty," and contain ample provision for the protection of the life, liberty, and property of every citizen, the dearest Constitutional rights of the people of Kansas have been fraudulently and violently taken from them.

Their Territory has been invaded by an armed force;

Spurious and pretended legislative, judicial, and executive officers have been set over them, by whose usurped authority, sustained by the military power of the government, tyrannical and unconstitutional laws have been enacted and enforced;

The right of the people to keep and bear arms has been infringed;

Test oaths of an extraordinary and entangling nature have been imposed as a condition of exercising the right of suffrage and holding office;

The right of an accused person to a speedy and public trial by an impartial jury has been denied;

The right of the people to be secure in their persons, houses, papers, and effects, against unreasonable searches and seizures, has been violated;

They have been deprived of life, liberty, and property without due process of law;

That the freedom of speech and of the press has been abridged;

The right to choose their representatives has been made of no effect;

Murders, robberies, and arsons have been instigated and encouraged, and the offenders have been allowed to go unpunished;

That all these things have been done with the knowledge, sanction, and procurement of the present National Administration; and that for this high crime against the Constitution, the Union, and humanity, we arraign that Administration, the President, his advisers, agents, supporters, apologists, and accessories, either before or after the fact, before the country and before the world; and that it is our fixed purpose to bring the actual perpetrators of these atrocious outrages and their accomplices to a sure and condign punishment thereafter.

Resolved, That Kansas should be immediately admitted as a state of this Union, with her present Free Constitution, as at once the most effectual way of securing to her citizens the enjoyment of the rights and privileges to which they are entitled, and of ending the civil strife now raging in her territory.

Resolved, That the highwayman's plea, that "might makes right," embodied in the Ostend Circular, was in every respect unworthy of American diplomacy, and would bring shame and dishonor upon any Government or people that gave it their sanction . . .

Source: Edward Stanwood, *A History of Presidential Elections* (Boston: Houghton, Mifflin, 1896), 205–7.

JAMES HENRY HAMMOND'S KING COTTON SPEECH MARCH 4, 1858

Selections from South Carolina senator James Henry Hammond's notorious speech in which he proclaims the South an economic world power and defends "mud sill" labor, whether performed by slaves in the South or free workers in the North.

Would any sane nation make war on cotton? Without firing a gun, without drawing a sword, should they make war on us we could bring the whole world to our feet. The South is perfectly competent to go on, one, two, or three years without planting a seed of cotton. I believe that if she was to plant but half her cotton, for three years to come, it would be an immense advantage to her. I am not so sure but that after three years' entire abstinence she would come out stronger than ever she was before, and better prepared to enter afresh upon her great career of enterprise. What would happen if no cotton was furnished for three years? I will not stop to depict what every one can imagine, but this is certain: England would topple headlong and carry the whole civilized world with her, save the South. No, you dare not make war on cotton. No power on earth dares to make war upon it. Cotton *is* king . . .

But, sir, the greatest strength of the South arises from the harmony of her political and social institutions. This harmony gives her a frame of society, the best in the world, and an extent of political freedom, combined with entire security, such as no other people ever enjoyed upon the face of the earth. Society precedes government; creates it, and ought to control it; but as far as we can look back in historic times we find the case different; for government is no sooner created than it becomes too strong for society, and shapes and molds, as well as controls it. In later centuries the progress of civilization and of intelligence has made the divergence so great as to produce civil wars and revolutions; and it is nothing now but the want of harmony between governments and societies which occasions all the uneasiness and trouble and terror that we see abroad. It was this that brought on the American Revolution. We threw off a Government not adapted to our social system, and made one for ourselves. The question is, how far have we succeeded? The South, so far as that is concerned, is satisfied, harmonious, and prosperous, but demands to be let alone.

In all social systems there must be a class to do the menial duties, to perform the drudgery of life. That is, a class requiring but a low order of intellect and but little skill. Its requisites are vigor, docility, fidelity. Such a class you must have, or you would not have that other class which leads progress, civilization, and refinement. It constitutes the very mud-sill of society and of political government; and you might as well attempt to build a house in the air, as to build either the one or the other, except on this mud-sill. Fortunately for the South, she found a race adapted to that purpose to her hand. A race inferior to her own, but eminently qualified in temper, in vigor, in docility, in capacity to stand the climate, to answer all her purposes. We use them for our purpose, and call them slaves. We found them slaves by the common "consent of mankind," the highest proof of what is Nature's law. We are old-fashioned at the South yet; slave is a word discarded now by "ears polite"; I will not characterize that class at the North by that term; but you have it; it is there; it is everywhere; it is eternal.

The Senator from New York [William Seward] said yesterday that the whole world had abolished slavery. Aye, the name, but not the thing; all the powers of the earth cannot abolish that. God only can do it when he repeals the fiat, "the poor ye always have with you"; for the man who lives by daily labor, and scarcely lives at that, and who has to put out his labor in the market, and take the best he can get for it; in short, your whole hireling class of manual laborers and "operatives," as you call them, are essentially slaves. The difference between us is, that our slaves are hired for life and well compensated; there is no starvation, no begging, no want of employment among our people, and not too much employment either. Yours are hired by the day, not cared for, and scantily compensated, which may be proved in the most painful manner, at any hour in any street of your large towns. Why, you meet more beggars in one day, in any single street of the city of New York, than you would meet in a lifetime in the whole South. We do not think that whites should be slaves either by law or necessity. Our slaves are black, of another and inferior race.

The status in which we have placed them is an elevation. They are elevated from the condition in which God first created them, by being made our slaves. None of that race on the whole face of the globe can be compared with the slaves of the South. They are happy, content, unaspiring, and utterly incapable, from intellectual weakness, ever to give us any trouble by their aspirations. Yours are white, of your own race; you are brothers of one blood. They are your equals in natural endowment of intellect, and they feel galled by their degradation. Our slaves do not vote. We give them no political power. Yours do vote, and, being the majority, they are the depositories of all your political power. If they knew the tremendous secret, that the ballot-box is stronger than "an army with banners," and could combine, where would you be? Your society would be reconstructed, your government overthrown, your property divided, not as they have mistakenly attempted to initiate such proceedings by meeting in parks, with arms in their hands, but by the quiet process of the ballot-box. You have been making war upon us to our very hearthstones. How would you like for us to send lecturers and agitators North, to teach these people this, to aid in combining, and to lead them? . . .

Transient and temporary causes have thus far been your preservation. The great West has been open to your surplus population, and your hordes of semi-barbarian immigrants, who are crowding in year by year. They make a great movement, and you call it progress. Whither? It is progress; but it is progress toward Vigilance Committees. The South has sustained you in great measure. You are our factors. You fetch and carry for us. One hundred and fifty million dollars of our money passes annually through your hands. Much of it sticks; all of it assists to keep your machinery together and in motion. Suppose we were to discharge you; suppose we were to take our business out of your hands; we should consign you to anarchy and poverty. You complain of the rule of the South; that has been another cause that has preserved you. We have kept the Government conservative to the great purposes of the Constitution. We have placed it, and kept it, upon the Constitution; and that has been the cause of your peace and prosperity.

Source: *Selections from the Letters and Speeches of the Hon. James H. Hammond, of South Carolina* (New York: John F. Trow & Co., 1866), 316–20, 321–22.

LINCOLN-DOUGLAS DEBATES, 1858

First Debate
Ottawa, August 21

Douglas objects to Lincoln's claim, made in his 1857 Springfield speech, that "a house divided against itself cannot stand." The "house" was the Union, and the division was slavery.

Douglas: Mr. Lincoln says that this Government cannot endure permanently in the same condition in which it was made by its framers— divided into free and slave states. He says that it has existed for about seventy years thus divided, and yet he tells you that it cannot endure permanently on the same principles and in the same relative condition in which our fathers made it. Why can it not exist divided into free and slave states? Washington, Jefferson, Franklin, Madison, Hamilton, Jay, and the great men of that day, made this Government divided into free states and slave states, and left each state perfectly free to do as it pleased on the subject of slavery. Why can it not exist on the same principles on which our fathers made it? . . .

We are told by Lincoln that he is utterly opposed to the Dred Scott decision, and will not submit to it, for the reason that he says it deprives the negro of the rights and privileges of citizenship. This is the first and main reason which he assigns for his warfare on the Supreme Court of the United States and its decision. I ask you, are you in favor of conferring upon the negro the rights and privileges of citizenship? Do you desire to strike out of our State Constitution that clause which keeps slaves and free negroes out of the state, and allow the free negroes to flow in, and cover your prairies with black settlements? Do you desire to turn this beautiful state into a free negro colony, in order that when Missouri abolishes slavery she can send one hundred thousand emancipated slaves into Illinois, to become citizens and voters, on an equality with yourselves? If you desire negro citizenship, if you desire to allow them to come into the State and settle with the white man, if you desire them to vote on an equality with yourselves, and to make them eligible to office, to serve on juries, and to adjudge your rights, then support Mr. Lincoln and the Black Republican party, who are in favor of the citizenship of the negro. For one, I am opposed to negro citizenship in any and every form. I believe this government was made on the white basis.

I believe it was made by white men, for the benefit of white men and their posterity forever, and I am in favor of confining citizenship to white men, men of European birth and descent, instead of conferring it upon negroes, Indians and other inferior races.

Second Debate
Freeport, August 27

In what became known as the Freeport Doctrine, Stephen Douglas defends his assertion that popular sovereignty and the Dred Scott decision are compatible.

> **Douglas:** The next question propounded to me by Mr. Lincoln is, Can the people of a Territory in any lawful way, against the wishes of any citizen of the United States, exclude slavery from their limits prior to the formation of a State Constitution? I answer emphatically, as Mr. Lincoln has heard me answer a hundred times from every stump in Illinois, that in my opinion the people of a Territory can, by lawful means, exclude slavery from their limits prior to the formation of a State constitution. Mr. Lincoln knew that I had answered that question over and over again. He heard me argue the Nebraska Bill on that principle all over the State in 1854, in 1855, and in 1856, and he has no excuse for pretending to be in doubt as to my position on that question. It matters not what way the Supreme Court may hereafter decide as to the abstract question whether slavery may or may not go into a Territory under the Constitution, the people have the lawful means to introduce it or exclude it as they please, for the reason that slavery cannot exist a day or an hour anywhere, unless it is supported by local police regulations. Those police regulations can only be established by the local legislature; and if the people are opposed to slavery, they will elect representatives to that body who will by unfriendly legislation effectually prevent the introduction of it into their midst. If, on the contrary, they are for it, their legislation will favor its extension. Hence, no matter what the decision of the Supreme Court may be on that abstract question, still the right of the people to make a slave Territory or a free Territory is perfect and complete under the Nebraska Bill. I hope Mr. Lincoln deems my answer satisfactory on that point.

Seventh Debate
Alton, October 15

In perhaps his greatest moment during the debates, Lincoln enunciates the difference between his and Douglas's positions on slavery.

Lincoln: I have stated upon former occasions, and I may as well state again, what I understand to be the real issue in this controversy between Judge Douglas and myself. On the point of my wanting to make war between the free and the slave states, there has been no issue between us. So, too, when he assumes that I am in favor of introducing a perfect social and political equality between the white and black races. There are false issues, upon which Judge Douglas has tried to force the controversy. There is no foundation in truth for the charge that I maintain either of these propositions. The real issue in this controversy—the one pressing upon every mind—is the sentiment on the part of one class that looks upon the institution of slavery *as a wrong*, and of another class that *does not* look upon it as a wrong. The sentiment that contemplates the institution of slavery in this country as a wrong is the sentiment of the Republican party. It is the sentiment around which all their actions—all their arguments circle—from which all their propositions radiate. They look upon it as being a moral, social and political wrong; and while they contemplate it as such, they nevertheless have due regard for its actual existence among us, and the difficulties of getting rid of it in any satisfactory way and to all the constitutional obligations thrown about it. Yet having a due regard for these, they desire a policy in regard to it that looks to its not creating any more danger. They insist that it should as far as may be, be treated as a wrong, and one of the methods of treating it as a wrong is to make provision that it shall grow no larger. They also desire a policy that looks to a peaceful end of slavery at some time, as being wrong. These are the views they entertain in regard to it as I understand them; and all their sentiments—all their arguments and propositions are brought within this range. I have said and I repeat it here, that if there be a man amongst us who does not think that the institution of slavery is wrong in any one of the aspects of which I have spoken, he is misplaced and ought not to be with us. And if there be a man amongst us who is so impatient of it as a wrong as to disregard its actual presence among us and the difficulty of getting rid of it suddenly in a satisfactory way, and to disregard the constitutional obligations thrown about it, that man is misplaced if he is on our platform. We disclaim sympathy with him in practical action. He is not placed properly with us.

On this subject of treating it as a wrong, and limiting its spread, let me say a word. Has anything ever threatened the existence of this Union save and except this very institution of Slavery? What is it that we hold most dear amongst us? Our own liberty and prosperity. What has ever threatened our liberty and prosperity save and except this institution of Slavery? If this is true, how do you propose to improve the condition of things by enlarging Slavery—by spreading it out and making it bigger? You may have a wen or a cancer upon your person and not be able to cut it out lest you bleed to death; but surely it is no way to cure it, to engraft it and spread it over your whole body. That is no proper way of treating what you regard a wrong. You see this peaceful way of dealing with it as a wrong—restricting the spread of it, and not allowing it to go into new countries where it has not already existed. That is the peaceful way, the old-fashioned way, the way in which the fathers themselves set us the example . . .

[Judge Douglas] says he "don't care whether [slavery] is voted up or voted down" in the Territories. I do not care myself in dealing with that expression, whether it is intended to be expressive of his individual sentiments on the subject, or only of the national policy he desires to have established. It is alike valuable for my purpose. Any man can say that who does not see anything wrong in slavery, but no man can logically say it who does see a wrong in it; because no man can logically say he don't care whether a wrong is voted up or voted down. He may say he don't care whether an indifferent thing is voted up or down, but he must logically have a choice between a right thing and a wrong thing. He contends that whatever community wants slaves has a right to have them. So they have if it is not a wrong. But if it is a wrong, he cannot say people have a right to do wrong. He says that upon the score of equality, slaves should be allowed to go in a new Territory, like other property. This is strictly logical if there is no difference between it and other property. If it and other property are equal, his argument is entirely logical. But if you insist that one is wrong and the other right, there is no use to institute a comparison between right and wrong. You may turn over everything in the Democratic policy from beginning to end, whether in the shape it takes on the statute book, in the shape in the Dred Scott decision, in the shape it takes in conversation or the shape it takes in short maxim-like arguments—it everywhere carefully excludes the idea that there is anything wrong in it.

That is the real issue. That is the issue that will continue in this country when these poor tongues of Judge Douglas and myself shall be silent. It is the eternal struggle between these two principles—right and wrong—throughout the world. They are the two principles that have stood face to face from the beginning of time; and will ever continue to struggle. The one is the common right of humanity and the other the divine right of kings. It is the same principle in whatever shape it develops itself. It is the same spirit that says, "You work and toil and earn bread, and I'll eat it." No matter in what shape it comes, whether from the mouth of a king who seeks to bestride the people of his own nation and live by the fruit of their labor, or from one race of men as an apology for enslaving another race, it is the same tyrannical principle.

Source: *Political Debates Between Lincoln and Douglas* (Cleveland: Burrows Bros. Co., 1897).

WILLIAM SEWARD'S ON THE IRREPRESSIBLE CONFLICT SPEECH
OCTOBER 25, 1858

Selections from Seward's speech, delivered in Rochester, New York, in which he took Lincoln's "house divided" metaphor to a new "revolutionary" level.

Our country is a theatre, which exhibits, in full operation, two radically different political systems; the one resting on the basis of servile or slave labor, the other on voluntary labor of freemen . . .

The slave system is one of constant danger, distrust, suspicion, and watchfulness. It debases those whose toil alone can produce wealth and resources for defense, to the lowest degree of which human nature is capable, to guard against mutiny and insurrection, and thus wastes energies which otherwise might be employed in national development and aggrandizement. The free-labor system educates all alike, and by opening all the fields of industrial employment and all the departments of authority, to the unchecked and equal rivalry of all classes of men, at once secures universal contentment, and brings into

the highest possible activity all the physical, moral, and social energies of the whole state. In states where the slave system prevails, the
masters, directly or indirectly, secure all political power, and constitute a ruling aristocracy. In states where the free-labor system prevails,
universal suffrage necessarily obtains, and the state inevitably
becomes, sooner or later, a republic or democracy.

Russia yet maintains slavery, and is a despotism. Most of the other
European states have abolished slavery, and adopted the system of free
labor. It was the antagonistic political tendencies of the two systems
which the first Napoleon was contemplating when he predicted that
Europe would ultimately be either all Cossack or all republican.
Never did human sagacity utter a more pregnant truth. The two systems are at once perceived to be incongruous. But they are more than
incongruous—they are incompatible. They never have permanently
existed together in one country, and they never can. It would be easy
to demonstrate this impossibility, from the irreconcilable contrast
between their great principles and characteristics. But the experience
of mankind has conclusively established it. Slavery, as I have inti-
mated, existed in every state in Europe. Free labor has supplanted it
everywhere except in Russia and Turkey. State necessities developed
in modern times are now obliging even those two nations to encourage and employ free labor; and already, despotic as they are, we find
them engaged in abolishing slavery. In the United States, slavery
came into collision with free labor at the close of the last century,
and fell before it in New England, New York, New Jersey, and Pennsylvania, but triumphed over it effectually, and excluded it for a
period yet undetermined, from Virginia, the Carolinas, and Georgia.
Indeed, so incompatible are the two systems, that every new State
which is organized within our ever-extending domain makes its first
political act a choice of the one and the exclusion of the other, even
at the cost of civil war, if necessary. The slave States, without law, at
the last national election, successfully forbade, within their own limits, even the casting of votes for a candidate for President of the
United States supposed to be favorable to the establishment of the
free-labor system in new States.

Hitherto, the two systems have existed in different States, but side
by side within the American Union. This has happened because the
Union is a confederation of States. But in another aspect the United
States constitute only one nation. Increase of population, which is
filling the States out to their very borders, together with a new and

extended network of railroads and other avenues, and an internal commerce which daily becomes more intimate, is rapidly bringing the States into a higher and more perfect social unity or consolidation. Thus, these antagonistic systems are continually coming into closer contact, and collision results.

Shall I tell you what this collision means? They who think that it is accidental, unnecessary, the work of interested or fanatical agitators, and therefor ephemeral, mistake the case altogether. It is an irrepressible conflict between opposing and enduring forces, and it means that the United States must and will, sooner or later, become either entirely a slaveholding nation, or entirely a free-labor nation. Either the cotton and rice fields of South Carolina and the sugar plantations of Louisiana will ultimately be tilled by free labor, and Charleston and New Orleans become marts of legitimate merchandise alone, or else the rye-fields and wheat-fields of Massachusetts and New York must again be surrendered by their farmers to slave culture and to the production of slaves, and Boston and New York becomes once more markets for trade in the bodies and souls of men. It is the failure to apprehend this great truth that induces so many unsuccessful attempts at final compromises between the slave and free States, and it is the existence of this great fact that renders all such pretended compromises, when made, vain and ephemeral. Startling as this saying may appear to you, fellow-citizens, it is by no means an original or even a modern one. Our forefathers knew it to be true, and unanimously acted upon it when they framed the constitution of the United States. They regarded the existence of the servile system in so many of the States with sorrow and shame, which they openly confessed, and they looked upon the collision between them, which was then just revealing itself, and which we are now accustomed to deplore, with favor and hope. They knew that one or the other system must exclusively prevail . . .

I know, and you know, that a revolution has begun. I know, and all the world knows, that revolutions never go backward. Twenty senators and a hundred representatives proclaim boldly in Congress today sentiments and opinions and principles of freedom which hardly so many men, even in this free State, dared to utter in their own homes twenty years ago. While the government of the United States, under the conduct of the Democratic party, has been all that time surrendering one plain and castle after another to slavery, the people of the United States have been no less steadily and perseveringly gathering together the forces with which to recover back again all the fields and all the castles which have been lost, and to confound and over-throw, by one decisive blow, the betrayers of the constitution and freedom forever.

Source: "The Irrepressible Conflict: A speech by William H. Seward, delivered at Rochester, Monday, Oct. 25, 1858," *New York Tribune* pamphlet, 1860. http:/archive.org/stream/irrepressiblecon00insewa# page/n0/mode/2up

POLITICAL PLATFORMS
PRESIDENTIAL ELECTION, 1860
Republican Party

Although less fiery than its 1856 predecessor, the 1860 Republican plat-form, which carried Abraham Lincoln to the White House, remained uncompromising in its opposition to slavery's extension.

Resolved . . .

1. That the history of the nation, during the last four years, has fully established the propriety and necessity of the organization and perpetuation of the Republican party, and that the causes which called it into existence are permanent in their nature, and now, more than ever before, demand its peaceful and constitutional triumph.

2. That the maintenance of the principles promulgated in the Declaration of Independence and embodied in the Federal Constitution, "That all men are created equal; that they are endowed by their Creator with certain inalienable rights; that among these are life, liberty and the pursuit of happiness; that to secure these rights, governments are instituted among men, deriving their just powers from the consent of the governed," is essential to the preservation of our Republican institutions; and that the Federal Constitution, the Rights of the States, and the Union of the States must and shall be preserved.

3. That to the union of the States this nation owes its unprec-edented increase in population, its surprising development of material resources, its rapid augmentation of wealth, its happiness at home and its honor abroad; and we hold in abhorrence all schemes for disunion, come from whatever source they may. And we congratulate the coun-try that no Republican member of Congress has uttered or

countenanced the threats of disunion so often made by Democratic members, without rebuke and with applause from their political associates; and we denounce those threats of disunion, in case of a popular overthrow of their ascendancy, as denying the vital principles of a free government, and as an avowal of contemplated treason, which it is the imperative duty of an indignant people sternly to rebuke and forever silence.

4. That the maintenance inviolate of the rights of the states, and especially the right of each State to order and control its own domestic institutions according to its own judgment exclusively, is essential to that balance of powers on which the perfection and endurance of our political fabric depends; and we denounce the lawless invasion by armed force of the soil of any State or territory, no matter under what pretext, as among the gravest of crimes.

5. That the present Democratic administration has far exceeded our worst apprehensions, in its measureless subserviency to the exactions of a sectional interest, as especially evinced in its desperate exertions to force the infamous Lecompton Constitution upon the protesting people of Kansas; in construing the personal relations between master and servant to involve an unqualified property in persons; in its attempted enforcement everywhere, on land and sea, through the intervention of Congress and of the Federal Courts of the extreme pretensions of a purely local interest; and in its general and unvarying abuse of the power entrusted to it by a confiding people . . .

7. That the new dogma that the Constitution, of its own force, carries slavery into any or all of the Territories of the United States, is a dangerous political heresy, at variance with the explicit provisions of that instrument itself, with contemporaneous exposition, and with legislative and judicial precedent; is revolutionary in its tendency, and subversive of the peace and harmony of the country.

8. That the normal condition of all the territory of the United States is that of freedom: That, as our Republican fathers, when they had abolished slavery in all our national territory, ordained that "no persons should be deprived of life, liberty or property without due process of law," it becomes our duty, by legislation, whenever such legislation is necessary, to maintain this provision of the Constitution against all attempts to violate it; and we deny the authority of Congress, of a territorial legislature, or of any individuals, to give legal existence to slavery in any Territory of the United States.

9. That we brand the recent reopening of the African slave trade, under the cover of our national flag, aided by perversions of judicial power, as a crime against humanity and a burning shame to our country and age; and we call upon Congress to take prompt and efficient measures for the total and final suppression of that execrable traffic ...

11. That Kansas should, of right, be immediately admitted as a State under the Constitution recently formed and adopted by her people, and accepted by the House of Representatives ...

16. That a railroad to the Pacific Ocean is imperatively demanded by the interests of the whole country; that the Federal Government ought to render immediate and efficient aid in its construction; and that, as preliminary thereto, a daily overland mail should be promptly established.

17. Finally, having thus set forth our distinctive principles and views, we invite the co-operation of all citizens, however differing on other questions, who substantially agree with us in their affirmance and support.

Source: Edward Stanwood, *A History of Presidential Elections* (Boston: Houghton, Mifflin, 1896), 228–31.

Democratic Platform

The split within the Democratic Party in the 1860 presidential campaign was barely noticeable in the two factions' platforms. Both embraced the Cincinnati platform of 1856—curtailing federal power, condemnation of a national bank and federally financed internal improvements, frugality in governmental spending—and both embraced the extension of slavery.

Douglas Faction

... Inasmuch as difference of opinion exists in the Democratic party as to the nature and extent of the powers of a Territorial Legislature, and as to the powers and duties of Congress, under the Constitution of the United States, over the institution of slavery within the Territories,

> *Resolved*, That the Democratic party will abide by the decision of the Supreme Court of the United States upon these questions of Constitutional Law ...

Resolved, that the Democratic party are in favor of the acquisition of the Island of Cuba on such terms as shall be honorable to ourselves and just to Spain.

Resolved, that the enactments of the State Legislatures to defeat the faithful execution of the Fugitive Slave Law, are hostile in character, subversive of the Constitution, and revolutionary in their effects.

Resolved, That it is in accordance with the interpretation of the Cincinnati platform, that during the existence of the Territorial Governments the measure of restriction, whatever it may be, imposed by the Federal Constitution on the power of the Territorial Legislature over the subject of the domestic relations, as the same has been, or shall be hereafter determined by the Supreme Court of the United States, should be respected by all good citizens, and enforced with promptness and fidelity by every branch of the general government.

Source: Edward Stanwood, *A History of Presidential Elections* (Boston: Houghton, Mifflin, 1896), 219, 223.

Breckinridge Faction

Resolved, That the platform adopted by the Democratic party at Cincinnati be affirmed, with the following explanatory resolutions:

1. That the Government of a Territory organized by an act of Congress is provisional and temporary, and during its existence all citizens of the United States have an equal right to settle with their property in the Territory, without their rights, either of person or property, being destroyed or impaired by Congressional or Territorial legislation.

2. That it is the duty of the Federal Government, in all its departments, to protect, when necessary, the rights of persons and property in the Territories, and wherever else its constitutional authority extends.

3. That when the settlers in a Territory, having an adequate population, form a State Constitution, the right of sovereignty commences, and being consummated by admission into the Union, they stand on an equal footing with the people of other States, and the State thus organized ought to be admitted into the Federal Union, whether its Constitution prohibits or recognizes the institution of slavery.

Resolved, That the Democratic party are in favor of the acquisition of the Island of Cuba, on such terms as shall be honorable to ourselves and just to Spain, at the earliest practical moment.

Resolved, That the enactments of State Legislatures to defeat the faithful execution of the Fugitive Slave Law are hostile in character, subversive of the Constitution, and revolutionary in their effect . . .

Source: Edward Stanwood, *A History of Presidential Elections* (Boston: Houghton, Mifflin, 1896), 224.

Constitutional Union Party Platform

The minimalist platform of the party had only one aim: to hold the Union together.

. . . Resolved, that it is both the part of patriotism and of duty to recognize no political principle other than THE CONSTITUTION OF THE COUNTRY, THE UNION OF THE STATES, AND THE ENFORCEMENT OF THE LAWS, and that, as representatives of the Constitutional Union men of the country, in National Convention assembled, we hereby pledge ourselves to maintain, protect, and defend, separately and unitedly, these great principles of public liberty and national safety, against all enemies, at home and abroad; believing that thereby peace may once more be restored to the country; the rights of the People and of the States re-established, and the Government again placed in that condition of justice, fraternity and equality, which, under the example and Constitution of our fathers, has solemnly bound every citizen of the United States to maintain a more perfect union, establish justice, insure domestic tranquility, provide for the common defense, promote the general welfare, and secure the blessings of liberty to ourselves and our posterity.

Source: Edward Stanwood, *A History of Presidential Elections* (Boston: Houghton, Mifflin, 1896), 225–26.

LINCOLN'S FIRST INAUGURAL ADDRESS
MARCH 4, 1861

In his first inaugural address, Lincoln walked the fine line of reasserting Republican condemnation of slavery while trying to reassure the South that he would not interfere with slavery where it already existed.

Apprehension seems to exist among the people of the Southern States, that by the accession of a Republican Administration, their property, and their peace, and personal security, are to be endangered. There has never been any reasonable cause for such apprehension. Indeed, the most ample evidence to the contrary has all the while existed, and been open to their inspection. It is found in nearly all the published speeches of him who now addresses you . . .

I hold, that in contemplation of universal law, and of the Constitution, the Union of these States is perpetual. Perpetuity is implied, if not expressed, in the fundamental law of all national governments. It is safe to assert that no government proper, ever had a provision in its organic law for its own termination. Continue to execute all the express provisions of our national Constitution, and the Union will endure forever—it being impossible to destroy it, except by some action not provided for in the instrument itself.

Again, if the United States be not a government proper, but an association of States in the nature of contract merely, can it, as a contract, be peaceably unmade, by less than all the parties who made it? One party to a contract may violate it—break it, so to speak; but does it not require all to lawfully rescind it? . . .

It follows from these views that no State, upon its own mere motion, can lawfully get out of the Union,—that *resolves* and *ordinances* to that effect are legally void; and that acts of violence within any State or States, against the authority of the United States, are insurrectionary or revolutionary, according to circumstances.

I therefore consider that, in view of the Constitution and the laws, the Union is unbroken; and, to the extent of my ability, I shall take care, as the Constitution itself expressly enjoins upon me, that the laws of the Union be faithfully executed in all the States. Doing this I deem to be only a simple duty on my part; and I shall perform it, so far as practicable, unless my rightful masters, the American people, shall withhold the requisite means, or, in some authoritative manner, direct the contrary. I trust this will not be regarded as a menace, but only as the declared purpose of the Union that it *will* constitutionally defend, and maintain itself.

In doing this there needs to be no bloodshed or violence; and there shall be none, unless it be forced upon the national authority . . .

Plainly, the central idea of secession, is the essence of anarchy. A majority, held in restraint by constitutional checks, and limitations, and always changing easily, with deliberate changes of popular opinions and sentiments, is the only true sovereign of a free people. Whoever rejects it, does, of necessity, fly to anarchy or to despotism. Unanimity is impossible; the rule of a minority, as a permanent arrangement, is wholly inadmissible; so that, rejecting the majority principle, anarchy, or despotism in some form, is all that is left ...

Physically speaking, we [the North and the South] cannot separate. We cannot remove our respective sections from each other, nor build an impassable wall between them. A husband and wife may be divorced, and go out of the presence, and beyond the reach of each other; but the different parts of our country cannot do this. They cannot but remain face to face; and intercourse, either amicable or hostile, must continue between them. Is it possible then to make that intercourse more advantageous, or more satisfactory, *after* separation than *before*? Can aliens make treaties easier than friends can make laws? ...

My countrymen, one and all, think calmly and *well*, upon this whole subject. Nothing valuable can be lost by taking time ...

In *your* hands, my dissatisfied fellow countrymen, and not in *mine*, is the momentous issue of civil war. The government will not assail *you*. You can have no conflict, without being yourselves the aggressors. *You* have no oath registered in Heaven to destroy the government, while *I* shall have the most solemn one to "preserve, protect and defend" it.

I am loth to close. We are not enemies, but friends. We must not be enemies. Though passion may have strained, it must not break our bonds of affection. The mystic chords of memory, stretching from every battlefield, and patriot grave, to every living heart and hearthstone, all over this broad land, will yet swell the chorus of the Union, when again touched, as surely they will be, by the better angels of our nature.

Source: *Inaugural Addresses of the Presidents of the United States* (Washington, D.C.: U.S. Government Printing Office, 1989).

ANNOTATED BIBLIOGRAPHY

Anbinder, Tyler. *Nativism and Slavery: The Northern Know Nothings and the Politics of the 1850s.* New York: Oxford University Press, 1992. Argues that the northern Know-Nothing opposition to slavery was more pronounced than traditionally thought.

Baker, Jean H. *Affairs of Party: The Political Culture of Northern Democrats in the Mid-Nineteenth Century.* Stanford, CA: Stanford University Press, 1983. A helpful study of the political party in the years leading up to the Civil War.

Baker, Jean H. *James Buchanan.* New York: Henry Holt and Company, 2004. A political biography of the 15th president whom the author judges as having "failed miserably" while in office.

Bartlett, Ruhl Jacob. *John C. Frémont and the Republican Party.* Columbus, OH: Contributions in History and Political Studies, Number 13, 1930. The only book-length study of Frémont's presidential campaign of 1856.

Basler, Roy P. *The Collected Works of Abraham Lincoln.* New Brunswick, NJ: Rutgers University Press, 1953–1955. 8 volumes + index. The standard edition of Lincoln's writings.

Birkner, Michael J., ed. *James Buchanan and the Political Crisis of the 1850s.* Selinsgrove, PA: Susquehanna University Press, 1996. Collection of essays, the most relevant of which are Michael Holt's on the 1856 election, Mark Summers's on Buchanan and the press, and Peter Knupfer's on the 1860 election.

Bordewich, Fergus M. *America's Great Debate: Henry Clay, Stephen A. Douglas, and the Compromise That Saved the Union.* New York: Simon & Schuster, 2012. Narrative history of the 1850 Compromise.

Boritt, Gabor S. *Lincoln and the Economics of the American Dream*. Urbana and Chicago: University of Illinois Press, 1994. Helpful background on Lincoln's Whig-inspired political economy of protective tariffs and internal improvements.

Catton, Bruce. *The Coming Storm*. Garden City, NY: Doubleday, 1961. Vol. 1 of *The Centennial History of the Civil War*. The first two chapters cover events from the Democrat National Convention in Charleston, April 1860, to Lincoln's election a year and a half later.

Chaffin, Tom. *Pathfinder: John Charles Frémont and the Course of American Empire*. New York: Hill and Wang, 2002. Comprehensive biography of the first Republican presidential candidate. The 1856 campaign is examined in Chapter 25.

Crandall, Andrew Wallace. *The Early History of the Republican Party, 1854–1856*. Gloucester, MA: Peter Smith, 1960. Provides an especially good overview of the political background to the 1856 presidential election.

Davis, David Brion. *The Slave Power Conspiracy and the Paranoid Style*. Baton Rouge: Louisiana State University Press, 1982. Argues that northern charges of Slave Power conspiracies and southern countercharges of abolitionist ones were fueled by political paranoia.

Donald, David Herbert. *Charles Sumner and the Coming of the Civil War*. Alfred A. Knopf, 1960. Definitive biography of the antislavery Massachusetts senator up to the beginning of Lincoln's administration. A companion volume, *Charles Sumner and the Rights of Man* (1970) concludes the biography.

Donald, David Herbert. *Lincoln*. New York: Simon & Schuster, 1995. Comprehensive biography by one of the great Lincoln scholars of our time. The first 11 chapters discuss Lincoln's life up to his inauguration.

Earle, Jonathan H. *Jacksonian Antislavery and the Politics of Free Soil, 1824–1854*. Chapel Hill: University of North Carolina Press, 2004. Argues that the Free Soil movement's emphasis on egalitarianism and land reform benefited the cause of emancipation more than is traditionally recognized.

Egerton, Douglas R. *Year of Meteors: Stephen Douglas, Abraham Lincoln, and the Election That Brought on the Civil War*. New York: Bloomsbury Press, 2010. A social and political history especially strong on Southern fire-eaters' plans to split the Democrat convention, throw the election to the Republicans, and use the outcome as a pretext for secession.

Eisenhower, John S. D. *Zachary Taylor*. New York: Henry Holt and Company, 2008. Political biography of the southern-born president who opposed Clay's 1850 Compromise but wanted to admit California as a free state.

Engs, Robert F., and Randall M. Miller, eds. *The Birth of the Grand Old Party: The Republicans' First Generation*. Philadelphia: University of Pennsylvania Press, 2002. The first two essays on the ideology (Eric Foner) and mobilization (Michael F. Holt) of the early Republican Party are especially relevant, as is a profusely illustrated essay written by the editors on "The Genesis and Growth of the Republican Party."

Etcheson, Nicole. *Bleeding Kansas: Contested Liberty in the Civil War Era*. Lawrence: University Press of Kansas, 2004. Argues that the conflict in Kansas Territory was more about white political self-determination than slavery. The subtitle is misleading, since Etcheson's book deals almost exclusively with the pre-Civil War era.

Fehrenbacher, Don E., ed. *Abraham Lincoln: A Documentary Portrait through His Speeches and Writings*. Stanford, CA: Stanford University Press, 1964. A convenient chronological and abridged compendium of primary works. Easier for beginners to navigate than the Basler standard edition of Lincoln's collected works.

Fehrenbacher, Don E. *Prelude to Greatness: Lincoln in the 1850s*. Stanford, CA: Stanford University Press, 1962. A political history ranging from Lincoln's joining the fledgling Illinois Republican Party to his 1860 election to the White House.

Finkelman, Paul, ed. *Dred Scott v. Sandford: A Brief History with Documents*. Boston: Bedford/St. Martin's, 1997. Selections from the Court's decision and contemporary responses, prefaced by an instructive overview of the background and consequences of the case.

Finkelman, Paul, ed. *Millard Fillmore*. New York: Henry Holt and Company, 2011. A harshly critical political biography of the Whig president whose doughface policies exacerbated sectional tensions and damaged his own party.

Foner, Eric. *The Fiery Trial: Abraham Lincoln and American Slavery*. New York: W. W. Norton, 2010. Pulitzer Prize–winning history of Lincoln's—and the antebellum nation's—views on slavery.

Foner, Eric. *Free Soil, Free Labor, Free Men: The Ideology of the Republican Party Before the Civil War*. New York: Oxford University Press, 1995. Indispensable examination of the principles that shaped the Republican Party, stressing especially free labor.

Foner, Eric, ed. *Our Lincoln: New Perspectives on Lincoln and His World*. New York: W. W. Norton, 2008. A collection of essays on Lincoln, three of which shed particularly helpful light on pre-Civil War politics: Sean Wilentz on Lincoln and Jacksonian democracy, James Oakes on Lincoln and race, and Eric Foner on Lincoln and colonization.

Foner, Eric, and Olivia Mahoney. *A House Divided: America in the Age of Lincoln*. Chicago and New York: Chicago Historical Society and W. W. Norton, 1990. The first four chapters offer a well-researched and lavishly illustrated introductory history of the three decades leading up to Lincoln's election to the presidency.

Forbes, Robert Pierce. *The Missouri Compromise and Its Aftermath: Slavery and the Meaning of America*. Chapel Hill: University of North Carolina Press, 2007. An exhaustive history of the first great sectional crisis in the United States.

Gienapp, William E. *Abraham Lincoln and Civil War America: A Biography*. New York: Oxford University Press, 2002. A concise biography of Lincoln. Although focusing on his role as president, 80 pages of the book explore Lincoln's pre-presidential years.

Gienapp, William E. *The Origins of the Republican Party, 1852–1856*. New York: Oxford University Press, 1987. The definitive political history of the Republican Party's formative years.

Goodrich, Thomas. *War to the Knife: Bleeding Kansas, 1854–1861*. Lincoln: University of Nebraska Press, 2004. A history of the slavery conflict in Kansas Territory.

Green, Michael S. *Lincoln and the Election of 1860*. Carbondale and Edwardsville: Southern Illinois University Press, 2011. A concise history of Lincoln's campaign for the White House.

Guelzo, Allen C. *Fateful Lightning: A New History of the Civil War and Reconstruction*. New York: Oxford University Press, 2012. The first three chapters culminate in Lincoln's election to the presidency.

Guelzo, Allen C. *Lincoln: A Very Short Introduction*. New York: Oxford University Press, 2009. A convenient primer on Lincoln's life and times arranged in terms of a number of principles—for example, equality, advancement, rule of law, and liberty—valued and exemplified by Lincoln.

Guelzo, Allen C. *Lincoln and Douglas: The Debates That Defined America*. New York: Simon & Schuster, 2008. A narrative history of the debates; particularly good in analyzing the philosophical stakes of the debates.

Hamilton, Holman. *Prologue to Conflict: The Crisis and Compromise of 1850*. Lexington: University Press of Kentucky, 1964. Good introduction to the congressional struggle over Henry Clay's proposed settlement of the Mexican cession crisis.

Heidler, David S., and Jeanne T. Heidler. *Henry Clay: The Essential American*. New York: Random House, 2011. Biography of Lincoln's beau ideal of a statesman. Chapters 15 and 16 examine Clay's negotiations for his final great compromise of 1850.

Hesseltine, William B., ed. *Three Against Lincoln: Murat Halstead Reports the Caucuses of 1860*. Baton Rouge: Louisiana State University Press, 1960. Halstead was a Cincinnati journalist who covered the political conventions in the 1860 presidential election year. This invaluable volume reproduces his newspaper accounts.

Hoffer, Williamjames Hull. *The Caning of Charles Sumner: Honor, Idealism, and the Origins of the Civil War*. Baltimore: The Johns Hopkins University Press, 2010. A narrative of the events leading up to and the fallout from Preston Brooks's 1856 beating of Charles Sumner on the Senate floor.

Hofstadter, Richard. *The American Political Tradition and the Men Who Made It*. New York: Vintage, 1976. Chapter 5 explores Lincoln's Whiggish/Republican emphasis on the self-made entrepreneur.

Holt, Michael F. *The Fate of Their Country: Politicians, Slavery Extension, and the Coming of the Civil War*. New York: Hill and Wang, 2004. Political history that argues that sectional disagreements were partly the consequence of political parties creating adversaries to strengthen their own members' loyalty and resolve.

Holt, Michael F. *Franklin Pierce*. New York: Henry Holt and Company, 2010. A political biography of the president who signed the Kansas-Nebraska bill into law.

Holt, Michael F. *The Political Crisis of the 1850s*. New York: W. W. Norton, 1978. Political history of the rise of sectionalism and the breakdown of the Second Party System.

Holt, Michael F. *The Rise and Fall of the American Whig Party: Jacksonian Politics and the Onset of the Civil War*. New York: Oxford University Press, 1999. An unrivaled history of the Whig Party.

Holzer, Harold, ed. *The Lincoln-Douglas Debates: The First Complete, Unexpurgated Text*. New York: Fordham University Press, 2004. A careful editing of the debate transcripts that examines both Republican and Democratic newspaper accounts. Gives a much better feel for the debates than the cleaned-up transcript in Volume 3 of Basler's *Lincoln's Collected Works*.

Holzer, Harold. *Lincoln, President-Elect: Abraham Lincoln and the Great Secession Winter, 1860–1861*. New York: Simon & Schuster, 2008. Exhaustive treatment of the first few months after Lincoln's election. Part One covers the time period up to his inauguration.

Howe, Daniel Walker. *The Political Culture of the American Whigs*. Chicago: Chicago University Press, 1979. Useful background on the party of Henry Clay, to which Lincoln was loyal most of his adult life. Chapter 11 explicitly examines Lincoln's move from the Whigs to the Republicans.

Jaffa, Harry V. *A New Birth of Freedom: Abraham Lincoln and the Coming of the Civil War*. Lanham, MD: Rowman & Littlefield, 2000. A masterful survey of the political and intellectual debates about slavery on the eve of the Civil War. Chapter 7 offers an especially insightful discussion of John C. Calhoun's views on states' rights.

Jaffa, Harry V. *Crisis of the House Divided: An Interpretation of the Issues in the Lincoln-Douglas Debates*, 50th anniversary ed. Chicago: University of Chicago Press, 2009. An analysis of the political issues around which the debates revolved. Especially good at presenting Douglas's position.

Johannsen, Robert W. *Stephen A. Douglas*. New York: Oxford University Press, 1973. A biography of the "Little Giant."

Lehrman, Lewis E. *Lincoln at Peoria: The Turning Point*. Mechanicsburg, PA: Stackpole, 2008. Exhaustive treatment of the political context of Lincoln's first great speech.

Lence, Ross E., ed. *Union and Liberty: The Political Philosophy of John C. Calhoun*. Indianapolis, IN: Liberty Fund, 1992. An anthology of the major writings of the South Carolinian who advocated state sovereignty.

Levine, Bruce. *Half Slave and Half Free: The Roots of Civil War*, rev. ed. New York: Hill and Wang, 2005. A history of the sectional tensions leading up to the

Civil War, with alternating chapters on North and South. Handicapped by absence of citations for quoted passages.

Luthin, Reinhard H. *The First Lincoln Campaign*. Gloucester, MA: Peter Smith, 1964. Detailed history of the 1860 presidential election. Although a useful resource, superceded in some respects by Egerton's *Year of Meteors*.

May, Robert E. *Manifest Destiny's Underworld: Filibustering in Antebellum America*. Chapel Hill: University of North Carolina Press, 2002. Comprehensive history of filibustering efforts to extend slavery into Latin America and the Caribbean.

McPherson, James M. *Abraham Lincoln and the Second American Revolution*. New York: Oxford University Press, 1991. A collection of essays, the first two of which explore how both opponents and defenders of slavery viewed secession as a "second American revolution" for independence.

McPherson, James M. *Battle Cry of Freedom: The Civil War Era*. New York: Oxford University Press, 1988. The single best history of the era, from the Mexican War to the end of the Civil War. Chapters 1–7 focus on the lead-up to Lincoln's presidency.

Merk, Frederick. *Slavery and the Annexation of Texas*. New York: Alfred A. Knopf, 1972. Focuses on President Tyler's 1844 campaign to annex Texas and the national debate it stirred up.

Meyer, Marvin. *The Jacksonian Persuasion*. Stanford, CA: Stanford University Press, 1957. An insightful analysis of the Jacksonian foundations of the Democratic Party in mid-19th-century America.

Morris, Roy, Jr. *The Long Pursuit: Abraham Lincoln's Thirty-Year Struggle with Stephen Douglas for the Heart and Soul of America*. New York: HarperCollins, 2008. An excellent account of the parallel careers of Lincoln and Douglas.

Nevins, Allan. *The Emergence of Lincoln*. 2 vols. New York: Scribner, 1950. Covers the years 1857 to 1861. Especially good on the doughface Buchanan administration.

Nevins, Allan. *Ordeal of the Union*. 8 vols. New York: Scribner's, 1947–1971. Volumes 1–4 are detailed resources for the events culminating in the Civil War.

Oakes, Stephen B. *With Malice Toward None: A Life of Abraham Lincoln*. New York: Harper & Row, 1977. A classic biography of the 16th president. The first six chapters explore Lincoln's life and times up to his inauguration.

Oates, James. *The Radical and the Republican: Frederick Douglass, Abraham Lincoln, and the Triumph of Antislavery Politics.* New York: W. W. Norton, 2007. A parallel biography whose first three chapters deal with the decades leading up to Lincoln's election to the presidency. Especially good at exploring his changing views on slavery.

Peterson, Merrill D. *The Great Triumvirate: Webster, Clay, and Calhoun.* New York: Oxford University Press, 1987. A joint biography of the three leading American statesmen of their time and their roles in the crises leading up to the Civil War.

Potter, David. *The Impending Crisis, 1848–1861.* New York: Harper Perennial, 2011. A classic study of the series of antebellum sectional crises about slavery expansion in the two decades prior to the Civil War. Concludes with attack on Fort Sumter.

Quist, John W., and Michael J. Birkner, eds. *James Buchanan and the Coming of the Civil War.* Gainesville: University Press of Florida, 2013. Essays that explore and reassess Buchanan's performance as president.

Remini, Robert V. *At the Edge of the Precipice: Henry Clay and the Compromise That Saved the Union.* New York: Basic Books, 2010. A detailed account of the 1850 Compromise, with an opening chapter that explores the history of political compromises up to 1849.

Reynolds, David S. *John Brown, Abolitionist: The Man Who Killed Slavery, Sparked the Civil War, and Seeded Civil Rights.* New York: Random House, 2006. A sympathetic—perhaps overly so—study of Brown's virulent dislike of slavery, his life and execution, and his posthumous influence.

Richards, Leonard L. *The Slave Power: The Free North and Southern Domination, 1780–1860.* Baton Rouge: Louisiana State University Press, 2000. Argues that the Slave Power was real, although not conspiratorial as Lincoln and others charged.

Scripps, John Locke, and Abraham Lincoln. *Vote Lincoln! The Presidential Campaign Biography.* Edited by David Bradford. Sacramento, CA: Boston Hill Press, 2010. A generously annotated edition of Lincoln's 1860 campaign biography.

Sewell, Richard H. *A House Divided: Sectionalism and Civil War, 1848–1865.* Baltimore: The Johns Hopkins University Press, 1988. Argues that slavery was the primary cause of sectional dissent and eventual secession and war.

Sewell, Richard H. *Ballots for Freedom: Antislavery Politics in the United States, 1837–1860.* New York: W. W. Norton, 1980. A history of the political struggle against slavery from the formation of the Liberty Party to Lincoln's election.

Silbey, Joel H. *Storm Over Texas: The Annexation Controversy and the Road to Civil War.* New York: Oxford University Press, 2005. Argues that political sectionalism, although always present in the antebellum years, became virulent in the congressional battle over Texas.

Stampp, Kenneth M. *America in 1857: A Nation on the Brink.* New York: Oxford University Press, 1990. Masterful cultural and political history of the year in which the Lecompton scandal and the *Dred Scott* decision split the Democrats and polarized the nation.

Striner, Richard. *Father Abraham: Lincoln's Relentless Struggle to End Slavery.* New York: Oxford University Press, 2006. First three chapters deal with Lincoln's attitude to slavery in the pre-presidential years.

Taylor, John M. *William Henry Seward: Lincoln's Right Hand.* Washington, D.C.: Brassey's, 1991. Biography of the early Republican powerbroker and one-time Lincoln rival for the presidency.

van Deusen, Glyndon G. *Horace Greeley: Nineteenth-Century Crusader.* New York: Hill and Wang, 1964. A biography of the Republican journalist, reformer, and editor of the *New York Tribune.*

Varon, Elizabeth. *Disunion! The Coming of the American Civil War, 1789–1859.* Chapel Hill: University of North Carolina Press, 2008. Parts II and III explore the sectional crises of the 1840s and 1850s.

Walther, Eric H. *The Shattering of the Union: America in the 1850s.* Lanham, MD: SR Books, 2004. A rich social history of the decade leading up to the Civil War.

Walther, Eric H. *William Lowndes Yancey: The Coming of the Civil War.* Chapel Hill: University of North Carolina Press, 2006. Biography of the fire-eater who schemed the split of the Democrats in 1860.

Waugh, John C. *On the Brink of Civil War: The Compromise of 1850 and How It Changed the Course of American History.* Wilmington, DE: SR Books, 2003. Narrative history of the compromise proposed by Henry Clay and championed by Stephen Douglas.

Wilentz, Sean. *The Rise of American Democracy, Jefferson to Lincoln.* New York: W. W. Norton, 2005. Magisterial political history of American democracy up to the Civil War. Section III, "Slavery and the Crisis of American Democracy," is especially relevant.

Winders, Richard Bruce. *Crisis in the Southwest: The United States, Mexico, and the Struggle over Texas.* Lanham, MD: SR Books, 2004. Chapters 5 and 6 explore the political debate about the Mexican War and the sectional one about admission of Texas as a slave state.

INDEX

About the Author

KERRY WALTERS is the William Bittinger Professor of Philosophy and Professor of Peace and Justice Studies at Gettysburg College (PA), near the site of the historic Civil War battle. Walters is the author or editor of 30 books, including *The Underground Railroad* (ABC-CLIO), *Benjamin Franklin and His Gods*, *Revolutionary Deists: Early America's Rational Deists*, and critical editions of Thomas Paine's *The Age of Reason* and John Locke's *A Letter Concerning Toleration*.